I0793956

Finding HOPE during Times of Personal Trial

Finding HOPE during Times of Personal Trial

Marlene Bateman Sullivan
Joshua M. Sullivan, LCSW

CFI
An imprint of Cedar Fort, Inc.
Springville, Utah

Paperback ISBN 13: 978-1-4621-4711-3
eBook ISBN 13: 978-1-4621-4778-6

Published by CFI, an imprint of Cedar Fort, Inc.
2373 W. 700 S., Suite 100, Springville, UT 84663
Distributed by Cedar Fort, Inc., www.cedarfort.com

Library of Congress Cataloging Number: 2024930464

Cover design by Shawnda Craig

Edited by Liz Kazandzhy

Printed in the United States of America

10 9 8 7 6 5 4 3 2 1

Printed on acid-free paper

To Aby

Contents

Foreword

Finding Hope during Times of Personal Trial is not an official Church publication and does not represent the official doctrine or position of The Church of Jesus Christ of Latter-day Saints. The authors alone are responsible for the content and any limitations. The doctrine of the Church is declared only by the Lord's anointed prophets, seers, and revelators, whom we sustain wholeheartedly. We have done our best to make sure the content of this book is in harmony with the teachings of the scriptures, Church leaders, and Church doctrine. If there are doctrinal defects, they are due to our own shortcomings. We hope and pray that as you read, you will find hope from the love, mercy, and benevolence of Heavenly Father and Jesus Christ, who watch over us tenderly and whose sole aim is to help us during mortality so we can progress and be happy.

Note: One challenge of coauthoring a book is how to refer to each of us when relating a personal experience. We decided to refer to ourselves by name prior to sharing a personal story.

Acknowledgments

The authors would like to thank those who reviewed this manuscript: Jennie Stephens, Melanie Trottier, Michelle Jennings, Monica Miles, and an extra special thank-you to John Wells.

Introduction

While everyone's personal challenges are different, the dial on the wheel of adversity eventually points to each of us. Some trials may be minor and others heart-wrenchingly intense, but through them all, we can have hope. Because of Jesus Christ's atoning sacrifice on our behalf, we know that better days—full of light and happiness—can be ours. Life often has difficult twists and turns, and *Finding Hope during Times of Personal Trial* provides inspiration, hope, and practical suggestions for navigating the trials of mortality. While there is no quick fix for the challenges of living in the latter days, this book provides hope and help for those dealing with adversity through inspiring stories, quotes by Church leaders, therapeutic help, and powerful scriptures.

We do not claim to know all the answers, but within these pages are helpful gospel topics that will help us stay close to God and receive His divine power during these tumultuous times. The gospel of Jesus Christ offers hope, which acts as an anchor for the soul and allows us to press forward in faith. While tribulations are painful, they are not intended to make us miserable but rather to encourage us to develop the divine qualities we need in order to return to Heavenly Father's presence. Difficult moments can be prime opportunities for our optimal growth. When viewed from an eternal perspective, such hardships can be the stepping stones that lead us back to our heavenly home.

It's safe to say that we are seeing challenges never before faced in the history of the world. We live in a time of fear and commotion, which has been long prophesied and is now coming to pass as the forces of evil battle against the saints of God (see Doctrine and Covenants 88:91). "As the showdown between good and evil approaches with its accompanying trials and tribulations," President Ezra Taft Benson declared, "Satan is increasingly striving to overcome the Saints with despair, discouragement, despondency, and depression. Yet, of all people, we as Latter-day Saints should be the most optimistic and the least pessimistic. For while we know that 'peace shall be taken from the earth, and the devil shall have power over his own dominion,' we are also assured that 'the Lord shall have power over his saints, and shall reign in their midst' (Doctrine and Covenants 1:36)."[1]

Even though the future is uncertain as the world careens from one crisis to another, we have cause to hope. In the premortal world, we shouted for joy (see Job 38:7) when God announced His great plan of salvation to create a world where we could work to acquire celestial traits that would prepare us for the eternities (See Alma 12:24; 34:32). God told us He would send His Son, Jesus Christ, to earth to teach us and to atone for our sins. We were told the Holy Ghost would be our constant companion to comfort and support us through times of need. Certainly, we were assured that during our sojourn on earth, Heavenly Father would offer divine assistance by giving us His word through the holy scriptures, providing prophets to guide us, and giving us the gift of personal revelation.

Life wasn't meant to be easy, but we can have hope as we trust God, knowing that we are given challenges to learn how to rise above them, temptations to prove ourselves, struggles to develop spiritual strength, and pain so that we may learn patience. Despite personal trials, we can have peace as we patiently allow them to purify our souls and mold us into true sons and daughters of God.

1. Ezra Taft Benson, "Do Not Despair," *Ensign*, Nov. 1986, 65.

1

A Perfect Brightness of Hope

"Wherefore, ye must press forward with a steadfastness in Christ, having a perfect brightness of hope, and a love of God and of all men. Wherefore, if ye shall press forward, feasting upon the word of Christ, and endure to the end, behold, thus saith the Father: Ye shall have eternal life."

—2 Nephi 31:20

What is Hope?

Hope is a concept we deal with nearly every day. We hope for continued employment, that surgery will remove *all* of the cancer, that our spouse will gain a testimony of the gospel, or that our teenager will overcome their drug addiction. True hope is firm and unwavering. It is not flimsy, nor is it insubstantial. Hope is believing, trusting, and *knowing* that God will answer our prayers. Elder Neal A. Maxwell said, "Real hope is much more than wishful musing. It stiffens, not slackens, the spiritual spine. . . . Hope is realistic anticipation which takes the form of a determination—not only to survive adversity but, moreover, to 'endure . . . well' to the end."[2] Hope gives us the ability to persevere through adversity.

2. Neal A. Maxwell, "Hope through the Atonement of Jesus Christ," *Ensign*, Nov. 1998, 62.

Hope plays a significant role in helping us cope with the spectrum of life's difficulties. Hope is a positive emotion, allowing us to have a general expectation of positive outcomes in the future. When we exercise hope, we can look forward with a degree of confidence because it acts as a calming influence in our lives. Like many other positive emotions, hope enhances not only our spiritual selves but also our physical, mental, and social well-being.

True hope springs from a belief in Christ and is ever present at funerals, easing the sorrow that comes from being separated from our loved ones and replacing it with the joy of looking forward to a glorious reunion. It is because of hope for eternal life, and faith in Christ and the Resurrection, that we can look at death without terror (see Alma 27:28). Hope is not knowledge but rather an inward abiding trust that God will fulfill His promise of eternal life (see Doctrine and Covenants 59:23).

The Gospel Offers Hope

As spiritual beings, we came to live in a mortal world. While every generation is subject to unique trials, some are common to all, such as sickness, death, family discord, natural disasters, economic downturns, and political upheaval. In our day, we face worldwide trials, such as wars, fear of nuclear conflicts, global warming, and a worldwide pandemic when COVID-19 brought countries and global economies to their knees. And yet we continue to have hope, which is one of our doctrinal beliefs, as stated in the thirteenth article of faith: "We follow the admonition of Paul—We believe all things, we hope all things, we have endured many things, and hope to be able to endure all things."

When burdened by hardship, we can always find hope in the gospel. Heavenly Father can help us escape the darkness of despair and illuminate our path when we struggle, such as when we go through a bitter divorce, are left paralyzed from an automobile accident, long for children but are unable to conceive, or suffer the effects of a tornado destroying our home. Personal trials can wrench our souls. Perhaps we'd hoped to find a companion and marry but are not given that opportunity, or maybe we're struggling to break the bonds of addiction. Others hope their chronic physical or mental challenges will cease, or at least be reduced to a manageable level. In all of our personal challenges, we may struggle to hold on to the knotted—and possibly frayed—end of our rope of hope. Let us not be like the ancient Israelites who cried out, "Our bones are dried, and our hope is lost" (Ezekiel 37:11), for if we should lose our hope, we will have lost one of our most sustaining possessions.

Sometimes we wonder how to purge our pain when experiencing personal trials. Most often, hope comes when we turn to the Savior, knowing He will help us. We may not know if the blessings we seek will come sooner or later, but one thing we *can* be sure of is that eventually, blessings *will* come.

There will be times when our problems seem to multiply out of control. But even when we find ourselves knee-deep in trials, we can hold fast to hope, knowing that the Lord, who always fulfills His word, promised, "He that endureth in faith and doeth my will, the same shall overcome" (Doctrine and Covenants 63:20).

The hymn "The Lord Is My Shepherd" offers great hope and comfort:

> Thru the valley and shadow of death though I stray,
> Since thou art my Guardian, no evil I fear.
> Thy rod shall defend me, thy staff be my stay.
> No harm can befall with my Comforter near.[3]

In every generation, disciples of Christ have been invited to center their hope steadfastly on Christ. President Howard W. Hunter taught:

> For Latter-day Saints this is a time of great hope and excitement—one of the greatest eras . . . in any dispensation. . . . We need to have faith and hope, two of the greatest fundamental virtues of any discipleship of Christ. We must continue to exercise confidence in God. . . . He will bless us as a people. . . . He will bless us as individuals. . . .
>
> I promise you . . . in the name of the Lord whose servant I am that God will always protect and care for his people. . . . With the gospel of Jesus Christ, you have every hope and promise and reassurance. The Lord has power over his Saints and will always prepare

3. "The Lord Is My Shepherd," *Hymns*, no. 108.

> places of peace, defense, and safety for his people. When we have faith in God we can hope for a better world—for us personally and for all mankind.[4]

If we have hope, we don't have to give up. Ever.

Hope Emanates from Our Savior

The Apostle Paul called the Lord Jesus Christ "our hope" (1 Timothy 1:1). And indeed, hope does radiate from the Savior and transcends this mortal sphere as we look forward to a more excellent world. The prophet Mormon said, "Behold I say unto you that ye shall have hope through the atonement of Christ and the power of his resurrection, to be raised unto life eternal, and this because of your faith in him" (Moroni 7:41). Real hope is not associated with anything temporary or transient but rather in Christ who is immortal and eternal!

Hope is a principle of promise, and to receive its blessings, we must be proactive and make hope an integral part of our lives. We display hope each time we choose to live by the commandments and to repent when we have sinned. The great Nephite leader Moroni continued to have hope even after having witnessed the horrifying destruction of his people. He wrote, "And I also remember that thou [the Lord] hast said that thou hast prepared a house for man, yea, even among the mansions of thy Father, in which man might have a more excellent hope; wherefore man must hope, or he cannot receive an inheritance in the place which thou hast prepared" (Ether 12:32).

Surely our highest hope is to receive our own inheritance when we return to the heavenly realms above. Because of Christ's loving sacrifice for all mankind, He can, if we prove faithful, seal us up as His and bring about our everlasting salvation. Elder Steven E. Snow said, "Our hope in the Atonement empowers us with eternal perspective. Such perspective allows us to look beyond the here and now on into the promise of the eternities. We don't have to be trapped in the narrow

4. Howard W. Hunter, "Hope: An Anchor to the Souls of Men" (Brigham Young University devotional, Feb. 7, 1993), 3–5, speeches.byu.edu.

confines of society's fickle expectations. We are free to look forward to celestial glory, sealed to our family and loved ones."[5]

Having Hope Requires Patience

Patience is the medium that tethers us to hope and sustains us when clouds of darkness descend. With hope, we can "have patience, and bear . . . [our] afflictions" (Alma 34:41). Paul explained that "tribulation worketh patience; and patience, experience; and experience, hope" (Romans 5:3–4). For emotional health and spiritual stamina, we need to look forward with hope, having the patient assurance that doing so will enable us to endure our personal afflictions. Hope allows us to put one foot in front of the other even when we doubt our ability to take another step.

While on earth, we are to press forward with hope in the Resurrection and of exaltation in the life to come. Hope allows us to patiently wait for promised blessings while taking daily action to ensure we keep the covenants we have made.

Hope allows us to peer through the glass even when the surface is dark and murky. Patience teaches that even in the midst of difficulties, there is reason to rejoice, while hope allows us to know that in time, deliverance *will* come. Even when swamped by suffering, we can rely on the light of hope to see our way through. The spiritual endowment of hope gives us the ability to see a wider perspective, feel an inner serenity, and be suffused with the warm peace that comes from the Holy Ghost, which "filleth [us] with hope and perfect love" (Moroni 8:26). The one great hope we all cling to is to know that one day, we will be able to kneel at the feet of Jesus Christ and have Him say, "Well done, good and faithful servant" (Matthew 25:23).

Hope Provides an Anchor to Our Souls

Although it may not appear so at first, the story of Adam and Eve is actually one of hope. When cast out of the Garden of Eden and into the lone and dreary world, our first parents left God's presence, which must have been devastating. Despite difficult circumstances, Adam and Eve clung to God's hopeful promise that He would send

5. Steven E. Snow, "Hope," *Ensign* or *Liahona*, May 2011, 54.

messengers to teach them. Although going into a mortal world was challenging, it did provide an opportunity for Adam and Eve to learn important lessons. As they faced opposition in their new world, Adam and Eve cultivated qualities they might not have otherwise obtained. While in mortality, they made mistakes, as we all do, and were taught to repent. Learning about the plan of salvation must have given them much hope. Like Adam and Eve, we are blessed to know about God's plan, for without it, earthly life would be a miasma of fear and uncertainty. Knowing who we are and where we came from brings hope and peace.

When engulfed with hardships, we must dig deep into our faith and hold on to hope, which provides an "anchor to our soul" (Hebrews 6:19) that permits us to remain steadfast. "Life presses all kinds of burdens on each of us, some light but others relentless and heavy," Elder L. Whitney Clayton said. "People struggle every day under burdens that tax their souls. . . . They can be emotionally or physically ponderous. They can be worrisome, oppressive, and exhausting. And they can continue for years. . . . Through it all, the Savior offers us sustaining strength and support, and in His own time and way, He offers deliverance."[6]

When we cultivate hope and fortify it with faith, the combination creates a force strong as steel, connecting us to Christ. Although hardships can cause us to drift in the tide of despair, our celestial connection will help us hold fast to hope. "Wherefore, whoso believeth in God might with surety hope for a better world, yea, even a place at the right hand of God, which hope cometh of faith, maketh an anchor to the souls of men, which would make them sure and steadfast" (Ether 12:4).

The Reciprocal Relationship between Hope, Faith, and Charity

In the scriptures, hope is often linked with faith and charity. Paul speaks of these three principles: "And now abideth faith, hope, charity, these three" (1 Corinthians 13:13). Moroni also connected these

6. L. Whitney Clayton. "That Your Burdens May be Light," *Ensign* or *Liahona*, Nov. 2009, 12, 14.

virtues: "Wherefore, there must be faith; and if there be faith, there must also be hope; and if there must be hope, there must also be charity. And except ye have charity ye can in nowise be saved in the kingdom of God" (Moroni 10:20–21).

Why are these three principles intrinsically connected? Because hope is essential to faith, faith is necessary to have hope, and both are central to charity. President Dieter F. Uchtdorf spoke of this reciprocal relationship, saying, "Hope is one leg of a three-legged stool, together with faith and charity. These three stabilize our lives regardless of the rough or uneven surfaces we might encounter at the time. The scriptures are clear and certain about the importance of hope. The Apostle Paul taught that the scriptures were written to the end that we 'might have hope' (Romans 15:4)."[7]

Faith, hope, and charity can be thought of as interlacing virtues, each one having a critical part to play in developing and defining our testimonies. These three virtues are not easily separated because each complements the others. The links between these three are undeniable, for the brighter our hope, the greater our faith; and the stronger our hope, the more we will abound in charity.

Another reason faith, hope, and charity are often spoken of interchangeably is because these three virtues are interactive and mutually reinforcing. An increase in one tends to result in an increase in the others. Hope, faith, and charity all relate to our Redeemer; as President Nelson explained, "*Faith* is rooted in Jesus Christ. *Hope* centers in his Atonement. *Charity* is manifest in the 'pure love of Christ' (Moroni 7:47). These three attributes are intertwined like strands in a cable and may not always be precisely distinguished. Together they become our tether to the celestial kingdom."[8]

Hope and faith are cardinal virtues. While faith can be seen as having its roots in the past—such as in Christ's death, Resurrection, and Atonement—hope is more often focused on the future—such as our hope that if we prove faithful, we will attain exaltation. Faith

7. Dieter F. Uchtdorf, "The Infinite Power of Hope," *Ensign* or *Liahona*, Nov. 2008, 21.

8. Russell M. Nelson, "A More Excellent Hope," *Ensign*, Feb. 1997, 61; emphasis in original.

provides a foundation for our belief in Heavenly Father and Jesus Christ, which is critical to strengthening us during mortality. Hope, in turn, constitutes "the assurance of things hoped for" (Joseph Smith Translation, Hebrews 11:1 [in Hebrews 11:1, footnote *b*]) and the proof of things "not seen" (Ether 12:6). Charity further strengthens our foundation, for as we develop charity, we become better disciples of Christ (see Moroni 7:44).

Press Forward in Hope

As we move through life, hope allows us to be serene without being naive, strong without being stubborn, and steadfast without being obstinate. Hope creates a heartening determination within ourselves that helps us not only *tolerate* our trials but *endure them well.* Hope does not mean we are blind to reality, but it gives us the capability—when faced with difficulties—to see positive aspects and potential benefits. When hardships are beyond our power to control, hope helps us accept our circumstances without being cast down. People with hope make a sincere attempt to find a "silver lining," even during dire situations.

Hope blesses our lives because it gives us an assurance of a brighter tomorrow. Elder Jeffrey R. Holland urges us to have hope, even in these days when many hearts are failing: "May we press forward with love in our hearts, walking in the 'brightness of hope' (2 Nephi 31:20) that lights the path of holy anticipation we have been on now for 200 years. I testify that the future is going to be as miracle-filled and bountifully blessed as the past has been. We have every reason to hope for blessings even greater than those we have already received because this is the work of Almighty God, this is the Church of continuing revelation, this is the gospel of Christ's unlimited grace and benevolence."[9]

Having a strong and abiding faith in Jesus Christ and His promises encourages us to hope for better things to come. For this reason, Mormon counseled his son Moroni, "Be faithful in Christ; . . . May Christ lift thee up, and may his . . . mercy and long-suffering, and

9. Jeffrey R. Holland, "A Perfect Brightness of Hope," *Ensign* or *Liahona*, May 2020, 83–84.

the hope of his glory and of eternal life, rest in your mind forever" (Moroni 9:25).

Hope acts as a steadying force in our lives and gives us peace and confidence by supplying us with the power to endure. As we cultivate hope, we draw nearer to Christ, who can then comfort us in our afflictions and help us stay on the path that leads to exaltation. Hope pierces the darkness of our current painful circumstances by allowing us to catch a glimpse of the inspiring light of tomorrow. "The things we hope *in* sustain us during our daily walk," states President Uchtdorf. "They uphold us through trials, temptations, and sorrow. Everyone has experienced discouragement and difficulty. Indeed, there are times when the darkness may seem unbearable. It is in these times that the divine principles of the restored gospel we hope *in* can uphold us and carry us until, once again, we walk in the light."[10]

Hope is a treasured gift that supports us when the world is bleak. While we may go through many harsh experiences, we can look to the future with hope in the atoning sacrifice of our Savior, knowing we will have every cause to rejoice when we have concluded our mission, for "eye hath not seen, nor ear heard, neither have entered into the heart of man, the things which God hath prepared for them that love him" (1 Corinthians 2:9).

---

10. Dieter F. Uchtdorf, "The Infinite Power of Hope," 23; emphasis in original.

2
The Refiner's Fire

"Behold, the great day of the Lord is at hand; and who can abide the day of his coming, and who can stand when he appeareth? For he is like a refiner's fire, and like fuller's soap; and he shall sit as a refiner and . . . he shall purify the sons of Levi, and purge them as gold and silver. . . . Let us, therefore . . . as Latter-day Saints, offer unto the Lord an offering in righteousness."

—Doctrine and Covenants 128:24

The Refining Process of Mortality

While everyone's challenges are different, the dial on the wheel of sorrow eventually points to each one of us. Life comes with all kinds of tribulations that tax us spiritually, emotionally, and physically. Some challenges are light and temporary while others are heavy and continuous. The world has seen pandemics, violent conflicts, political upheaval, climate change, and natural disasters in the form of hurricanes, earthquakes, wildfires, tornadoes, drought, and floods. Besides these tribulations, we face challenges in our personal lives, with grief, loneliness, mental and physical illness, disabilities, relationship difficulties, and the responsibility of providing for our families. Our task is to remain firm and steadfast even when the heat is turned up in our private "furnace of affliction" (Isaiah 48:10).

Undergoing hardships is a refining process that purifies our spirits. The Lord tells us, "For, behold, I have refined thee, I have chosen thee in the furnace of affliction" (1 Nephi 20:10). Our souls are cleansed as we purge out those things in our lives that hold us back and develop divine qualities that fashion us into holier beings. While adversity is hard to bear, it can stretch our understanding, improve our character, and help us become more Christlike. The process of refining is not easy, but it's less arduous as we are faithful rather than fearful, realizing that our travails are a necessary part of helping us become true disciples of Christ.

We can take comfort in knowing that during this refining process, God stands by our side, strengthening us spiritually so we do not become overwhelmed and fall into despondency and despair. Heavenly Father's love for His children is boundless, and while the refining process may sometimes be painful and protracted, we never have to face it alone. As Elder D. Todd Christofferson reminds us, "With God, comfort replaces pain, peace replaces turmoil, and hope replaces sorrow. Remaining firm in the faith of Christ will bring His sustaining grace and support."[11]

It can be helpful for us to understand our mortal experiences in the context of Heavenly Father's great plan of salvation. God's divine plan for us has many names: the plan of happiness (see Alma 42:8), the plan of salvation (see Moses 6:62), the plan of redemption (see Jacob 6:8), and the plan of mercy (see Alma 42:15).

In the premortal world, we lived with heavenly parents as we grew and developed. When we progressed to the point where it was needful for us to gain a physical body, Heavenly Father presented us with the plan of salvation, explaining that He would create a new world where we could receive a body and have mortal experiences that would allow us to grow and become like our heavenly parents. President Spencer W. Kimball said, "We knew before we were born that we were coming to the earth for bodies and experience and that we would have joys and sorrows, ease and pain, comforts and hardships, health and sickness, successes and disappointments, and we knew also that after

11. D. Todd Christofferson, "Firm and Steadfast in the Faith of Christ," *Ensign* or *Liahona*, Nov. 2018, 32.

a period of life we would die. We accepted all these eventualities with a glad heart, eager to accept both the favorable and unfavorable. . . . We were willing to take life as it came."[12]

We witnessed Heavenly Father choosing Jesus Christ to be our Savior and knew that our Elder Brother would atone for our sins if we would repent. However, not everyone was happy about Heavenly Father's plan. Satan rebelled and convinced a third of Heavenly Father's children to follow him, and in so doing, they were cast out. It is Satan and his minions who create much of the opposition and suffering we experience on earth.

Knowing what occurred in the premortal world makes a great difference in how we view our current sufferings. We know this life is only temporary—a place where we can prepare ourselves to return to God and our *real* home. When we're plagued with earthly hardships, Satan tries hard to convince us God is imperfect, asleep, or uncaring, but we know that none of this is true. Armed with a knowledge of God's great plan, we understand that earthly challenges give us the opportunity to become more refined and spiritually perfected. We may experience much pain while in mortality, but we can trust Heavenly Father enough to know the suffering caused by the refiner's fire is meant to prepare us for exaltation and makes us worthy to become glorified beings and return to God's presence.

No One is Exempt from the Refiner's Fire

Sometimes people feel that if they are "righteous" enough, they won't face arduous trials, or that if hardships do come, they'll be able to pray their way out of it. But no one is exempt from the refiner's fire—not the rich and powerful, not the poor and lowly. Neither are the righteous spared. Adversity is not evidence of God's disfavor. We know this because many great and noble men and women have faced tremendous hardships.

Abinadi was a courageous prophet who single-handedly confronted the wicked King Noah and his priests. He rebuked them for their iniquity, pleaded for them to repent, and told them of the coming of Jesus Christ. Noah and his priests were offended at being told they

12. *Teachings of Presidents of the Church: Spencer W. Kimball* (2006), 20.

were wicked, and they ordered Abinadi to recall his words, telling him that if he refused, they would kill him. Abinadi stood by what God had told him to say and was burned to death.

God promised Abraham great lands of inheritance and innumerable posterity. Throughout his long life, Abraham trusted in God and waited patiently, year after year, for those promised blessings to be bestowed. However, Abraham didn't see them until he had grown old and had endured much sorrow and many hardships.

Another choice man of God was Joseph, yet he was betrayed by his own brothers and sold into slavery. Over time, Joseph rose to a position of power in the house of Potiphar, only to have his life come crashing down again when falsely accused by Potiphar's wife. Despite being imprisoned, Joseph endured his trials well. After deciphering the dreams of the Pharaoh's butler and baker, he eventually was brought before Pharaoh to interpret his dreams. This time, Joseph achieved and maintained a high position in Pharaoh's court, enabling him to save his father as well as the brothers who had sold him (see Genesis 37:39–41; 39–45).

Job was called "a perfect and upright" man (Job 1:1) but still faced a series of horrifying trials. While Job's friends assumed his suffering resulted from sin, the Lord felt otherwise, saying, "There is none like him in the earth, a perfect and an upright man" (Job 1:8). Job was a righteous man but had difficulty understanding why he had to endure so many afflictions and agonizing pain, crying out "Why?" sixteen times. And yet Job remained faithful. He realized afflictions that seem so devastating at the time are the ones that fortify and refine our character the most. "But he knoweth the way that I take: [when] he hath tried me, I shall come forth as gold" (Job 23:10).

The Prophet Joseph Smith was another exemplary man who faced extraordinary hardships. Not only did he face the loss of six of his children, but Joseph was tarred and feathered, betrayed by those he considered friends, and imprisoned multiple times. He endured hunger, cold, and extreme deprivations while languishing for five months in Liberty Jail. While there, he cried out in despair, "O God, where art thou?" (Doctrine and Covenants 121:1). The Lord taught Joseph principles of righteousness such as faith, patience, long-suffering, and hope (see Doctrine and Covenants 121:41–42). The Savior then comforted Joseph, saying, "My son, peace be unto thy soul; thine adversity and thine afflictions shall be for but a small moment. And then, if thou endure it well, God shall exalt thee on high; thou shalt triumph over all thy foes" (Doctrine and Covenants 121:7–8). Even after leaving Liberty Jail, Joseph continued to suffer numerous hardships, which ended only when evil men took his life.

Elder Orson F. Whitney summed up the purpose for our trials, saying, "There is [a] reason [for our hardships]. It is for our development, our purification, our growth, our education and advancement, that we buffet the fierce waves of sorrow and misfortune; and we shall be all the stronger and better when we have swum the flood and stand upon the farther shore. . . . We cannot suffer anything without receiving benefit from the experience."[13]

Everyone will be tested at times by the winds of adversity, but we can continue to trust God, who will use our trials to make us better people. President James E. Faust said, "Here then is a great truth. In the pain, the agony, and the heroic endeavors of life, we pass through a refiner's fire, and the insignificant and the unimportant in our lives can melt away like dross and make our faith bright, intact, and strong. . . . It is part of the purging toll exacted of some to become acquainted with God. In the agonies of life, we seem to listen better to the faint, godly whisperings of the Divine Shepherd."[14]

Life *Isn't* Fair

While on earth, there seems to be a never-ending supply of challenges. We may have long stretches when life goes smoothly, only to have adversity toss a grenade in our lap. We can question why others enjoy good health, great prosperity, and an astonishing life of ease while others face great adversity. At times, life can seem unfair when comparing those who are vastly wealthy and others who are homeless and don't know where their next meal is coming from. Why do some endure great physical trials with disease or disabilities and others struggle with mental illness? At times, we may feel like our pain is

13. Orson F. Whitney, "A Lesson from the Book of Job," *Improvement Era*, Nov. 1918, 6.

14. James E. Faust, "The Refiner's Fire," *Ensign,* May 1979, 53.

undeserved, that life has betrayed us, or that God has forgotten us. When life is grim, leaving us feeling heartbroken and alone and like the light at the end of the tunnel is a too-distant glimmer, we might cry out to God in confused pain.

Pondering on God's plan of salvation can help us understand that we are imperfect mortals living among other fallible people in a fallen world. Knowing about God's plan helps us realize that life was never *meant* to be fair—it's a time of testing. This world was created so we could learn, grow, make mistakes, repent, and grow some more. Our mistakes do not have to define us. Instead, they can refine us, giving us greater self-awareness. It is up to us to take whatever life doles out and use our hardships to become more like Christ. It is better for us to keep our chins up and our eyes focused on our goal of returning to our heavenly home, rather than looking down at the steep and rocky road we must traverse to get there.

When facing difficulties, we decide if we will grow from our sufferings or rail against them. Elder Richard G. Scott, who was no stranger to physical suffering, gives us this insight:

> When you face adversity, you can be led to ask many questions. Some serve a useful purpose; others do not. To ask, Why did this happen to me? Why do I have to suffer this? What have I done to deserve this? will lead you into blind alleys. It really does no good to ask questions that reflect opposition to the will of God. Rather, we can ask, What am I to do? What am I to learn from this experience? What am I to change? Whom am I to help? How can I remember my many blessings in times of trial?[15]

When our faith is challenged and we wonder why life is so hard, especially when we are doing our best to follow Jesus, we must remember that the Lord told us to expect troubles. Problems are part of God's plan and do not mean we have been abandoned; they are part of being one of those God calls His. Heavenly Father is more interested in our growth than He is in our comfort.

During times of trial, we must exercise patience as our faith is tested because, most often, the reason for our suffering is not revealed until *after* we have weathered the storm. The scriptures advise, "Dispute

15. Richard G. Scott, "Trust in the Lord," *Ensign*, Nov. 1995, 17.

not because ye see not, for ye receive no witness until after the trial of your faith" (Ether 12:6). We can let adversity break us or we can let it refine us. It may help to know that doing our best to endure the refiner's fire will accelerate our growth and help us become more like God.

Elder Christofferson taught, "In the midst of this refiner's fire, rather than get angry with God, get close to God. Call upon the Father in the name of the Son. Walk with Them in the Spirit, day by day. Allow Them over time to manifest Their fidelity to you. Come truly to know Them and truly to know yourself."[16]

Why Doesn't God Prevent Tragedies?

Every day on the news are tragic stories of murders, bombings, devastating natural disasters, terrible accidents, and atrocities in war-torn countries. With so many heartrending events, Satan finds it easy to stir up the hearts of many to cry out that there cannot be a God because He would not allow these horrible events to occur.

Although Heavenly Father is all-powerful and could prevent tragedies, He often does not because doing so would not be in our best long-term interest. As we learn more of God, we realize that His all-seeing eye knows the beginning from the end and that His wisdom far surpasses our puny understanding. While we do not know how much God *causes* to happen and how much He *permits* to happen, one thing we *do* know is that God knows and loves us more than we know and love ourselves.

At times, we may wonder if God is there for us personally. We have all heard stories of people who were miraculously cured after receiving a blessing. While we rejoice for them, we are also aware of others—perhaps someone in our own family—who received a blessing but was *not* cured. Why is this? Is it because their faith, or ours, was not strong enough? Why wasn't our loved one deserving of a miracle? Although we know Heavenly Father is truly a God of miracles, we can't know why God chooses to heal at certain times and not heal at other times. At those times, we must humbly acknowledge that we do not have the answers—but God does. We can also accept that God's

16. D. Todd Christofferson, "Our Relationship with God," *Liahona*, May 2022, 79.

ways are higher than ours (see Isaiah 55:9) and that our finite minds cannot completely understand the mind or will of God (see Romans 11:33–34).

Elder Holland responds to these types of questions with an appeal to trust in the Lord:

> Yes, God can provide miracles instantaneously, but sooner or later we learn that the times and seasons of our mortal journey are His and His alone to direct. . . . For every infirm man healed instantly as he waits to enter the Pool of Bethesda, someone else will spend 40 years in the desert waiting to enter the promised land. For every Nephi and Lehi divinely protected by an encircling flame of fire for their faith, we have an Abinadi burned at a stake of flaming fire for his. And we remember that the same Elijah who in an instant called down fire from heaven to bear witness against the priests of Baal is the same Elijah who endured a period when there was no rain for years and who, for a time, was fed only by the skimpy sustenance that could be carried in a raven's claw (see 1 Kings 17:1–7).[17]

Because God can see the beginning from the end—a perspective we currently lack—He has wise reasons for allowing certain events to transpire in our lives. To us, they are agonizing ordeals, but God perceives the vital lessons they can teach. Everything God does—or does not do—comes from the deep and abiding love He has for us. Our Heavenly Father wants us to become the person He knows we can become, and sometimes that means *not* preventing the accident and *not* healing the illness.

It also means God does *not* take personal agency away from those who deliberately choose to harm others. Every day, children are abused, woman are sold into sex trafficking rings, and murders are committed for gain. These intentional acts result in tremendous suffering, causing some to become angry at God for not stopping these evil actions. However, we know that God is and has always been committed to moral agency—a fundamental and necessary doctrine of the gospel. Agency is so essential to the plan of salvation that God allows every person to choose their own path, even when it hurts someone else.

17. Jeffrey R. Holland, "Waiting on the Lord," *Ensign* or *Liahona*, Nov. 2020, 116. See also 1 Kings 17:1–7.

And yet it is true that agency, when misused, can have terrible consequences on the innocent. When Alma and Amulek were in the city of Ammonihah, they taught and converted many to the gospel. The unrighteous leaders were so enraged at these conversions that they ordered that the "wives and children . . . [and] whosoever believed or had been taught to believe in the word of God . . . should be cast into the fire" (Alma 14:8). Even more devilish was bringing Alma and Amulek out of prison to witness the murders of those to whom they had taught the gospel.

Why were wicked leaders allowed their agency if they were going to use it to cause others to suffer so horribly? Part of the answer lies in Alma's reply to Amulek, who was so pained by the agony of those cast into the fire that he pleaded with Alma to use their priesthood power to stop the tortuous deaths. Alma replied, "The Spirit constraineth me that I must not stretch forth my hand; for behold the Lord receiveth them up unto himself in glory; and he doth suffer that they may do this thing, or that the people may do this thing unto them, according to the hardness of their hearts, that the judgments which he shall exercise upon them in his wrath may be just; and the blood of the innocent shall stand as a witness against them, yea, and cry mightily against them at the last day" (Alma 14:11).

God will not force us to obey His commandments; to do so would make growth impossible. In mortality, agency plays an important role in our time of testing. President Kimball said:

> If all the righteous were protected and the wicked destroyed, the whole program of the Father would be annulled. . . . No man would have to live by faith.
>
> If joy and peace and rewards were instantaneously given the doer of good, there could be no evil—all would do good but not because of the rightness of doing good. There would be no test of strength, no development of character, no growth of powers, no free agency, only satanic controls.
>
> Should all prayers be immediately answered according to our selfish desires and our limited understanding, then there would be little or no suffering, sorrow, disappointment, or even death, and if

these were not, there would also be no joy, success, resurrection, nor eternal life and godhood.[18]

Allowing His children to face hardships does *not* mean God doesn't care. And yet we know that God, who is perfect in love, is not indifferent to human suffering. God's love is true, and He loves us with a pure and complete love, but He will not deprive us of the lessons we can learn from adversity. To do so would subvert the plan of happiness. Our loving Father knows it would be unwise to shield us from all disappointments, sorrows, and suffering because they are the means of learning important lessons that will lead to our becoming more perfect and attaining eternal glory.

Even when we may not understand the "whys" behind our trials, we must continue to trust, knowing that at some future time, we will understand completely. It is quite possible that we may discover at that time that God prevented much more suffering than He allowed and lessened some horrific events from being much worse.

Opposition Allows Us to Progress

The scriptures teach there must be "an opposition in all things" (see 2 Nephi 2:11). In the premortal world, Satan provided opposition, and he continues to do so on earth. In the Garden of Eden, Satan encouraged Adam and Eve to partake of the forbidden fruit of the tree of life. Because we cannot remember the premortal world, Satan uses our tribulations to create doubt and cause us to turn away from God.

And yet opposition stimulates our growth. Opposition can be great or small, fleeting or continuous, but each is a teaching experience. President Dallin H. Oaks explained that life on earth "requires that we be subject to other mortal opposition, such as from the sins of others or from some defects of birth. Sometimes our needed growth is achieved better by suffering and adversity than by comfort and tranquility. And none of this mortal opposition could achieve its eternal purpose if divine intervention relieved us from all the adverse consequences of mortality."[19]

18. *Teachings of Presidents of the Church: Spencer W. Kimball* (2006), 15.

19. Dallin H. Oaks, "The Great Plan," *Ensign* or *Liahona*, May, 2020, 94.

Although some may think themselves weak because of the trials they face, the opposite is true. Opposition reaches out to test and try the souls of the strong, as evidenced by the tribulation that Nephi experienced. At the beginning of the Book of Mormon, Nephi states that he had "seen many afflictions in the course of [his] days" (1 Nephi 1:1) and then details many of those trials. For example, he was beaten by his brothers when they failed to obtain the brass plates from Laban. And when he broke his bow in the wilderness, his brothers were angered again when they were unable to obtain food.

When the Lord commanded Nephi to build a ship, his brothers mocked him and at first refused to help. Then, while crossing the ocean, when Nephi chastised Laman and Lemuel for making themselves merry and forgetting the Lord, they tied him up and treated him harshly (see 1 Nephi 18:9–15). Although grieved, Nephi declared, "Nevertheless, I did look unto my God, and I did praise him all the day long; and I did not murmur against the Lord because of mine afflictions" (1 Nephi 18:16).

Here then is a great lesson on how to respond to trials. Instead of complaining, we are to look to God and thank Him for our blessings. Every time Nephi turned to God in prayer, asking for help, he was delivered. Christ assures us that we will receive untold blessings if we prove faithful: "Behold the wounds which pierced my side, and also the prints of the nails in my hands and feet; be faithful, keep my commandments, and ye shall inherit the kingdom of heaven" (Doctrine and Covenants 6:37).

Opposition can be thought of as an incubator for faith because it encourages us to grow toward what our Heavenly Father would have us become. Opposition not only helps us learn important lessons; it also brings us to a deeper awareness of our Father's love and our dependence on Him. Sister Barbara Winder, former Relief Society General President, said, "If there were no sadness, we would not know joy; without bitterness, we would not recognize sweetness. We need opposition in order to progress. If all our prayers were answered to our satisfaction, there would never be any sickness, untimely deaths, unpleasant events, or poverty. But there would be no growth, either;

the purpose of our creation would be frustrated. It is in the furnace of trial and adversity that we forge celestial character and find true joy."[20]

At first glance, hardships appear to hinder our ability to achieve happiness. But opposition builds our strength, as evidenced by many natural laws. For example, if a person wants to build stronger muscles, resistance is required. If we want to train for a marathon, an opposing force is required to help us develop stronger muscles and more endurance. Opposition to our beliefs requires us to dig deeper into the scriptures and become more knowledgeable, which strengthens our faith.

Opposition can be a force for good if we use it to build our spiritual muscles. In mortality, we face opposition in many things, but those very trials are what help us refine our natures and grow toward perfection. When experiencing opposition, God wants us to be patient and submissive, "willing to submit to all things which the Lord seeth fit to inflict upon him, even as a child doth submit to his father" (Mosiah 3:19). Opposition is not meant to make us suffer for no discernible gain; it's meant to increase our ability to withstand Satan and amplify our determination to serve God and qualify for eternal blessings.

Challenges refine our spirits and lead us to reach heights we would not have been able to achieve otherwise. Peter spoke of this refining process, saying, "That the trial of your faith, being much more precious than of gold that perisheth, though it be tried with fire, might be found unto praise and honour and glory at the appearing of Jesus Christ" (1 Peter 1:7).

20. Barbara W. Winder, "No Joy without the Struggle," *Ensign*, June 1988, 73.

3
The School of Life

"For behold, this is my work and my glory—to bring to pass the immortality and eternal life of man."

—Moses 1:39

Mortality Prepares Us to Return to Our Father's Presence

Our earthly existence is a time for us to develop divine qualities and prepare ourselves in all things so we might prove worthy to return to our Heavenly Father's presence. Since this life is also a time of testing, we will experience difficulties and hardships. President Thomas S. Monson spoke of this, saying, "Life is a school of experience, a time of probation. We learn as we bear our afflictions and live through our heartaches."[21]

Although we may wonder at times why life is so hard, in the premortal world we were fully aware of the difficulties we would face, yet we still remained ecstatic at the thought of coming to earth. President Kimball reminds us, "We knew before we were born that we were coming to the earth for bodies and experience and that we would have joys and sorrows, ease and pain, comforts and hardships, health and sickness, successes and disappointments, and we knew also that after

21. Thomas S. Monson, "Look to God and Live," *Ensign,* May 1998, 52.

a period of life we would die. We accepted all these eventualities with a glad heart, eager to accept both the favorable and unfavorable. . . . We were willing to take life as it came."[22]

When Brigham Young was at Winter Quarters, he prayed to know how to lead the Saints west. The Lord responded, giving practical instructions on how to manage the move, and He also taught that during their journey, the Saints were to "promise to keep all the commandments and statues of the Lord" and to "walk in all the ordinances of the Lord" (Doctrine and Covenants 136:2, 4). The westward-bound Saints were assured that if they strove to keep their covenants and obey God, they would be blessed with power from on high to assist them in their journey (see Doctrine and Covenants 95:8), and they were promised that if they were obedient, "You shall be blessed in your flocks, and in your herds, and in your fields, and in your houses, and in your families" (Doctrine and Covenants 136:11). All of this was to remind the Saints that their conduct while *on* their journey was as important as reaching their destination. This revelation helped transform the Saints' westward trek from a difficult and miserable journey into a time of growth and learning.

This revelation is equally applicable to our journey through mortality. Although we may experience many difficult trials, we are encouraged to grow and develop. During our trek through life, we can strive to transform our hardships into opportunities to increase our spirituality. Just as the pioneers' westward journey tested, tried, and taught them, our mortal journey is meant to test, try, and teach us to focus on acquiring valuable spiritual qualities.

Heavenly Father's greatest desire is for us to become more perfect and acquire virtues that will enable us to return to Him. Mortal tribulations can accelerate our learning process. This life is a school that allows us to have hands-on experience as we deal with the ordeals of mortality. Elder Maxwell said, "Without our individual refining, therefore, life would become merely a pass-through, audited course—not a course for credit."[23] He sent Jesus Christ, His Beloved

22. *Teachings of Presidents of the Church*: Spencer W. Kimball (2006), 20–21.

23. Neal A. Maxwell, *If Thou Endure It Well* (Salt Lake City, UT: Bookcraft, 1996), 8.

Son, to come to earth and die for us so that we could repent and be cleansed from sin. Despite the abundance of trials we may face, Heavenly Father stands by us, giving us strength to triumph over our adversities. We need not resent our hardships when we understand that mortality is part of God's plan of salvation. Our time on earth is meant to test, try, and prove us to see if we will trust in Him, even when in the midst of suffering."[23]

Peter tells us not to be surprised at our trials, because they are a natural part of mortality. He even encourages us to rejoice in our sufferings, saying, "Beloved, think it not strange concerning the fiery trial which is to try you, as though some strange thing happened unto you: But rejoice, inasmuch as ye are partakers of Christ's sufferings; that, when his glory shall be revealed, ye may be glad also with exceeding joy" (1 Peter 4:12–13).

Earthly Life: A School of Instruction

God created this magnificent planet for us to be exalted as we gain a physical body that will unite with our spirit. It is awe-inspiring to realize that all the glories of this earth were meticulously prepared as a schooling ground to enable us to reach our divine potential. It is good for us to remember that this earthly life is not the whole of our existence but merely a pinprick on the continuum of eternal life. In the premortal world, each of us made the choice to come to earth to gain a body and have experiences that would help us develop godly virtues. We were informed that mortality would be a time of testing to see if we would remain faithful even when faced with adversity, sorrow, and death—necessary components of earthly life.

Our sojourn on earth is intended to help us better learn how to obey the principles of the gospel when our physical body becomes intertwined with our spiritual body. Elder David A. Bednar said, "In the school of mortality, we experience tenderness, love, kindness, happiness, sorrow, disappointment, pain, and even the challenges of physical limitations in ways that prepare us for eternity."[24] The hymn "The Day Dawn Is Breaking" reminds us that our purpose on earth is

24. "We Believe in Being Chaste," David A. Bednar, *Ensign* or *Liahona*, May 2013, 41.

to learn of God: "Still let us be doing, our lessons reviewing, / Which God has revealed for our walk in his way."[25]

As intelligent beings in the premortal world, we were no doubt thoroughly instructed on what we could expect from mortality. We happily agreed to come, knowing that tremendous blessings would be ours if we proved faithful. This time of testing is more than a simple multiple-choice quiz, for Heavenly Father is not just interested in what we choose to do or not to do but in how our choices shape us into becoming a better person.

It should come as no surprise that we must experience hard things in life. Hard has always been part of the plan, and trials can be our greatest teachers. As Elder Maxwell taught, "We can expect no immunity from either trial or temptation because these are the common lot of mankind. Mortality without the dimension of temptation or trial would not be full proving; it would be a school with soft credits and no hard courses. These features of mortality were among the very condition we agreed to before we understood this mortal experience."[26] If we respond to our trials with faith in God, they can sanctify us to become more like Heavenly Father.

The Importance of the Veil

Before coming to earth, we were told that in mortality, we would be subject to all kinds of tribulations. It is likely we were also informed that in order for this life to be a true test, a veil would be put over our minds so we would not be able to remember our premortal existence. Despite that, we shouted with joy at the prospect of coming to mortality, knowing that the rewards far outweighed the risks.

Knowledge of our former habitation has been hidden for prudent reasons. The veil hides the purposes, principles, and vital information we were given prior to being born, making it necessary for us to walk by faith on earth. President Wilford Woodruff made this clear when he said, "There is a [veil] between man and eternal things . . . and this [veil is there] for a wise and proper purpose in the Lord our God, to

25. "The Day Dawn Is Breaking," *Hymns*, no. 52.

26. Neal A. Maxwell, *We Will Prove Them Herewith* (Salt Lake City, UT: Deseret Book, 1982), 45.

prove whether the children of men will abide in his law or not in the situation in which they are placed here."[27]

Because of the veil, none of us has any memory of Heavenly Father presenting His plan of happiness. This lack of memory can, for those who have not learned about our premortal life, limit their perspective and can cause some to view mortality as chaotic and unfair. President Boyd K. Packer compared a person's inability to remember the premortal world to a person walking into the middle of a three-act play and trying to make sense of it all. He said, "The course of our mortal life, from birth to death . . . might be likened to a grand three-act play. Act 1 is entitled 'Premortal Life.' The scriptures describe it as our first estate. Act 2, from birth to the time of resurrection, is the 'Second Estate.' And act 3 is called 'Life After Death' or 'Eternal Life.'"[28]

President Packer continues:

> In mortality, we are like actors who enter a theater just as the curtain goes up on the second act. We have missed act 1 . . . As part of the eternal plan, the memory of our premortal life, act 1, is covered with a veil. Since we enter mortality at the beginning of act 2 with no recollection of act 1, it is little wonder that it is difficult to understand what is going on. . . .
>
> Remember this! The line "And they all lived happily ever after" is never written into the second act. That line belongs in the third act, when the mysteries are solved and everything is put right.[29]

In time, the veil will be removed from our mind. At that time, we will fully understand the promises, blessings, and clarification that will come in the third act, when we will rejoice in the resolution and fulfillment of Heavenly Father's great plan of salvation.

Life Is a Test

Heavenly Father provided this earth as a proving ground that allows us to learn how to fortify ourselves against evil. Life is a school of

---

27. Wilford Woodruff, in *Journal of Discourses,* 7:71.

28. Boyd K. Packer, "The Play and the Plan" (Church Educational System fireside for young adults, May 7, 1995), 2.

29. Boyd K. Packer, "The Play and the Plan," 2.

instruction, and since our time here is short, God allows us to accelerate our learning by overcoming earthly trials.

There is wisdom in God giving us trials, for they test our strength and teach us many valuable lessons, such as patience, long-suffering, obedience, and faith. While on earth, each of us encounters a unique set of tests, and we will be graded on how well we obeyed God despite those difficulties. Elder Maxwell said that while on earth, we cannot expect these trials to be painless: "Since we are here to be thus proved, how can that occur except we are tested? If we are here to learn to choose wisely, how can that occur except there be alternatives? If our soul is to be stretched, how can that happen without growing pains? How can personal development really occur amid routine unless we have authentic challenges to practice on?"[30]

One of our principal tests is to demonstrate our ability to obey God no matter what tribulations befall us. God said, "And we will prove them herewith, to see if they will do all things whatsoever the Lord their God shall command them" (Abraham 3:25). During our time of testing, we are encouraged to press forward faithfully and be obedient to God even though we are no longer in His presence. While in this school of life, we will face challenges that stretch our souls but which can also propel us forward, helping us gain knowledge and build our faith. God wants us to develop into the kind of person He knows we can become.

While on earth, we have the chance to show Heavenly Father that our minds are focused firmly on Him. Part of our test involves trusting Heavenly Father to provide for our needs, comfort us in our sorrows, and guide us during our earthly existence. As we increase in faith, we can receive divine help by living worthily. "For he will give unto the faithful line upon line, precept upon precept; and I will try you and prove you herewith. Therefore, be not afraid . . . that I will prove you in all things" (Doctrine and Covenants 98:12, 14).

Some Causes of Afflictions

Everyone who lives on earth faces pains, trials, and afflictions. Adversity is often a natural product of living in a mortal world. Other

30. Neal A. Maxwell, *We Will Prove Them Herewith*, 14.

trials come as a result of our own sins or from the misconduct of others. Some have the mistaken notion that having hardships means God is angry with them. Other people conclude that God is either unaware of or unconcerned with what happens to us. However, much of the suffering that occurs in our world comes not from God's indifference toward humans but from humans' indifference toward God. Heavenly Father, who is perfect in love, is not unsympathetic to human suffering. We are His spirit children and He loves us deeply.

Let's look at some reasons why we may experience afflictions during mortality.

Adversity Can Come as a Result of Transgression

Some challenges arise from disobedience to God's laws. Health problems can result from smoking and substance abuse. Incarceration may result from crime. Addiction to pornography, gambling, or drugs can lead to a number of significant problems. When we sin, we cause the Spirit of God to withdraw in part from us (see Isaiah 59:2). President Faust said, "Unfortunately, some of our greatest tribulations are the result of our own foolishness and weakness and occur because of our own carelessness or transgression. Central to solving these problems is the great need to get back on the right track and, if necessary, engage in each of the steps for full and complete repentance. Through this great principle, many things can be made fully right and all things better."[31]

Suffering Because of Another Person's Abuse of Agency

Many earthly hardships result from the improper use of agency by others. God gave His children their agency, which is essential for individual spiritual growth, and will not take it away, even when it is used to hurt others. Abuse, addictions, sin, incorrect traditions, repression, and crime cause genuine suffering and make home anything but a heaven on earth for innocent family members. Neglect and a lack of love and compassion also causes grief. Some trials come when we are persecuted "for righteousness' sake" (Matthew 5:10; 1 Peter 3:14). President Joseph F. Smith said there has never been a people who were

31. James E. Faust, "The Refiner's Fire," *Ensign,* May 1979, 54.

guided by revelation, or united of the Lord as His people, who were not persecuted and hated by the wicked and corrupt.[32]

Accidents Come from Living in a Mortal World

Much suffering comes from living in an imperfect and mortal world. In the latter days, we have seen an increasing number of natural disasters such as hurricanes, tornadoes, tsunamis, mudslides, wildfires, flooding, earthquakes, and so on.

In this mortal world, we also face problems from accidents. While driving on the interstate, a car tire blows and causes the vehicle to careen off the freeway. A pipelayer, working deep in a trench, is buried when one of the earthen walls unexpectedly collapses. While flying a private plane, a malfunction causes the pilot to lose control and the plane to crash. A boulder, loosened by a recent rain, crashes down the mountainside onto a bus. These are but a few of the hardships that come from living in a fallen and imperfect world.

In addition, much suffering is caused by the infirmities of our mortal bodies. Viral and bacterial diseases attack physical bodies; genetic abnormalities or harmful chemicals cause disabilities; and harmful toxins in the air, water, and ground are taken into our bodies, causing irreparable damage. Organs can fail to perform their proper function, and as we age, our bodies can fall prey to various defects. Regardless of the source of our trials, we can learn from them and grow spiritually as we refine our spirits and develop divine characteristics.

Let Us Not Suffer in Vain

The tragedy of suffering comes not from the pain—it comes when suffering ends up being pointless because we fail to learn the lessons it might have taught. Some allow tribulations to make their lives bitter, but how much better it is to gain something of worth.

Anne Morrow Lindbergh, wife of the pioneer aviator Charles Lindbergh, went through much suffering when their twenty-month-old son was kidnapped and murdered. She cautioned those who thought pain automatically produced an increase in virtue. Lindbergh said, "I do not believe that sheer suffering teaches. If suffering alone

32. See Joseph F. Smith, *Gospel Doctrine*, 5th ed. (1939), 46.

taught, all the world would be wise, since everyone suffers. To suffering must be added mourning, understanding, patience, love, openness, and the willingness to remain vulnerable."[33]

Hardships can be for our benefit, provided we look inward to discern what they can teach rather than refusing to absorb what they could have taught. Earthly challenges can be difficult, sometimes unbearably so, but we can always learn from them if we choose. As we do the work required to absorb our lessons, we fortify our connection to God.

The Apostle Paul was an unusually humble disciple. Paul prayed to have a personal trial removed, which he referred to as "a thorn in the flesh" (2 Corinthians 12:7). It must have been a grievous trial for Paul to refer to it in such a manner. And yet when the Lord replied simply that His grace was sufficient, Paul got the message. Instead of feeling grieved that the Lord would not remove his affliction, Paul responded with great energy and faith and declared, "Most gladly therefore will I glory in my infirmities that the power of Christ may rest upon me" (2 Corinthians 12:9). We learn a great lesson from Paul's reaction. Once Paul understood that his "thorn in the flesh" could bring him closer to Christ, he lost all interest in having his affliction removed. Instead, he preferred to rejoice in his suffering and stay closer to God.

Just as suffering by itself does not *teach*, time alone does not *heal* unless we allow our experiences to work a change in our hearts. Elder Maxwell observed, "By itself, of course, the passage of time does not bring an automatic advance. Yet, like the prodigal son, we often need the 'process of time' in order to come to our spiritual senses. (Luke 15:17.) The touching reunion of Jacob and Esau in the desert, so many years after their sibling rivalry, is a classic example. Generosity can replace animosity. Reflection can bring perception."[34]

We would never grow if we had a life free from all difficulties, but we can take advantage of them and use them to purify our souls. It does no good to put our heads in the sand and simply wait for the

---

33. Anne Morrow Lindbergh, quoted in Neal A. Maxwell, "Enduring Well," *Ensign,* Apr. 1997, 7–8. Also found in "Lindbergh Nightmare," *Time,* Feb. 5, 1973, 35.

34. Neal A. Maxwell, "Endure It Well," *Ensign*, May 1990, 34.

storm to pass. Instead, we can allow adversity to mold us into becoming more patient, compassionate, and understanding. As we allow our trials to refine our character, we ensure that our suffering is not in vain. While we may not reach the high pinnacle as Paul who gloried in his trials, we *can* work to learn something of value from them.

We Will Never Be Tested above Our Ability to Endure

During our mortal testing period, God will allow us to be tested—sometimes to the very core—but He will never allow us to be tempted beyond our ability to withstand. Even when we have faith, it can be difficult to hold on, and there may be times when we feel that our trials are more than we can bear. However, Elder Maxwell assures us:

> The thermostat on the furnace of affliction will not have been set too high for us—though clearly, we may think so at the time. Our God is a refining God who has been tempering soul-steel for a very long time. He knows when the right edge has been put upon our excellence and also when there is more in us than we have yet given. One day we will praise God for taking us near to our limits—as He did His Only Begotten in Gethsemane and Calvary.[35]

In times of trial, Alma counsels, "Humble yourselves before the Lord, and call on his holy name, and watch and pray continually, that ye may not be tempted above that which ye can bear" (Alma 13:28). In His mercy, our Father in Heaven, who knows us individually, will not give us more than we are able to endure. "There hath no temptation taken you but such as is common to man: but God is faithful, who will not suffer you to be tempted above that ye are able; but will with the temptation also make a way to escape, that ye may be able to bear it" (1 Corinthians 10:13).

35. Neal A. Maxwell, *All These Things Shall Give Thee Experience* (Salt Lake City, UT: Deseret Book, 1980), 46.

God Put Us on Earth to Triumph

Heavenly Father and Jesus love us deeply and are continually watching over us. They know us personally and understand the difficulties we face. Heavenly Father sent us to earth to triumph over every obstacle we encounter. It is His desire that we achieve the lofty goal of exaltation. In the premortal world, we were eager to prove we could prevail against Satan and the tribulations of earthly life, yet we may not have fully comprehended the suffering we would face. It is one thing to be told we would feel pain, but without a physical body, pain would surely have only been an abstract concept. Now that we're on earth, we better comprehend that overcoming earthly opposition serves a wise purpose in grinding away our imperfections. Instead of resenting our painful circumstances or railing against them, we can be grateful for Heavenly Father's plan of happiness, which allows us to progress and become more like Him.

God did not place anyone on earth to fail. In the premortal realm, Heavenly Father knew we were ready to face the ordeals of mortality. He was confident in our ability to succeed against Satan's opposition and life's travails. When the Saints were struggling in the early days of the Church, the Lord offered the following comfort: "And they that have been scattered shall be gathered. And all they who have mourned shall be comforted. And all they who have given their lives for my name shall be crowned. Therefore, let your hearts be comforted concerning Zion; for all flesh is in mine hands; be still and know that I am God" (Doctrine and Covenants 101:12–16).

To have strength to rise above our personal problems, we must cultivate a sustained faith in God. When adversity brings us to our knees, we can commune with God while there and receive power, comfort, and guidance. When struggling to hold on, it helps to think back over our life to the times God has blessed us to weather other storms, which gives us confidence to trust the Lord to deliver us yet again.

Painful experiences can turn us toward Christ, who can comfort us in ways no one else can. In the Book of Mormon, when the prophet Mormon mourned the destruction of his people, he cried out, "How could ye have rejected that Jesus, who stood with open arms to receive you!" (Mormon 6:17). With this statement, Mormon portrays a powerful image of the Savior standing with His arms open wide to clasp us in His embrace. In our day, Jesus is still standing with His arms outstretched, imploring us to come to Him. Christ's pure love will never fail.

Not now. Not ever.

While attending the school of life, we can know of a surety that God loves us. And as we rely on our Redeemer, He will bless us with His mighty strength and power so we can triumph over our hardships and overcome the world. Elder Maxwell assures us, "At times His best pupils experience the most rigorous and continuous courses. Eventually, each who proves to be a man or woman of Christ will thereby become a distinguished alumnus of life's school of affliction, graduating with honors."[36]

---

36. Neal A. Maxwell, *Lord, Increase Our Faith* (Salt Lake City, UT: Bookcraft, 1994), 50.

4

Trials Spiritually Purify Us

"My people must be tried in all things, that they may be prepared to receive the glory that I have for them, even the glory of Zion; and he that will not bear chastisement is not worthy of my kingdom."

—Doctrine and Covenants 136:31

Mortality Is a Proving Ground

Some trials are tough, others downright brutal. If given the choice, we would do almost anything to avoid them. However, mortality is a proving ground—a time of testing that brings problems so we can learn and grow. This earth was created for God's children to undergo a refining process to help prepare us for exaltation. Adversity, if handled well, can be a silver lining in our dark clouds and help us develop more godly attributes. In the Book of Mormon, Lehi comforted his son Jacob by telling him that God would consecrate all of his afflictions for his gain (see 2 Nephi 2:1–2). That knowledge helps us know that while life is not easy, our difficulties will prepare us to return to the kingdom of God.

Most often, we think of problems as stop signs when they are actually more like "caution" signs, warning us to pay attention, to draw closer to God, and, on occasion, to make important course changes. Although trials are never pleasant, they can nudge us to take inventory of our life and allow us to change the trajectory of our path so it leads more directly to Heavenly Father.

Since our time in mortality is meant to strengthen our souls, Heavenly Father will often "try" us in areas where we are weak and have the most need of improvement. "And if men come unto me I will show unto them their weakness. . . . If they humble themselves before me, and have faith in me, then will I make weak things become strong unto them" (Ether 12:27).

Converting our weaknesses into strengths can be difficult and requires work since change does not come easily. Noted author and theologian C. S. Lewis once likened the refashioning of our souls to the remodeling of a house. He said:

> Imagine yourself as a living house. God comes in to rebuild that house. At first, perhaps, you can understand what He is doing. He is getting the drains right and stopping the leaks in the roof and so on: you knew that those jobs needed doing and so you are not surprised. But presently, He starts knocking the house about in a way that hurts abominably and does not seem to make sense. What on earth is He up to? The explanation is that He is building quite a different house from the one you thought of—throwing out a new wing here, putting on an extra floor there, running up towers, making courtyards. You thought you were going to be made into a decent little cottage: but He is building a palace.[37]

There Is Purpose in Pain

Trials are like the cod liver oil of yesteryear—good for you but hard to swallow. Although no one likes hardships, they can be beneficial if we use them as learning experiences. Adversity allows us to change from our natural, lowly selves into more perfect beings. "For the natural man is an enemy to God . . . unless he yields to the enticings of the Holy Spirit, and putteth off the natural man and becometh a saint" (Mosiah 3:19). By meekly accepting our trials, we allow God to mold us into becoming more like He is. Henry Ward Beecher said,

37. C. S. Lewis, *Mere Christianity* (New York: Macmillan, 1960), 174.

"Man is the iron, and God is the smith; and we are always either in the forge, or on the anvil. God is shaping us for higher things."[38]

Sometimes it may take effort to find compensatory blessings from pain, but they are there, even if they are not immediately discernible. Going through a divorce can give us compassion for a friend who, years later, struggles under similar circumstances. Experiencing the pain of a chronic illness can teach us to have more gratitude for our "good days" and other blessings God gives. When we lose a beloved family member, we can gain a greater love for our remaining family. If we take time to ponder on our trials and what we can learn from them, we will see that they bring blessings we might not have received in any other way. We may also learn that some things in life are beyond our control, which creates a humbler spirit within, making it easier to turn to God. Wise is the individual who allows their difficulties to deepen their faith, draw closer to God, and shape themselves into a more perfect being.

It is also good to remember that problems don't need to be the *focus* of our lives. Sister Reyna I. Aburto of the Relief Society General Presidency said, "Your struggles do not define you, but they can refine you."[39]

Sam Jolley loved adventurous activities, and his first and greatest love was motocross. Sam started BMX biking when he was fourteen. After graduating from high school, he got a motorized dirt bike and continued entering competitions. On New Year's Day, Sam competed at the Delta Center in Salt Lake City. When he approached the triple-hill jump, Sam wanted to do something special, but then he realized he was going too fast and missed the jump. He recalled, "It put me over the handlebars headfirst so fast I just froze. I came down probably about thirty feet out of the air straight down on my head." Sam was rushed to the hospital with a broken neck, a serious head

38. Edna Dean Proctor, *Life Thoughts: Gathered from the Extemporaneous Discourses of Henry Ward Beecher* (London: Hamilton, Adams & Co., 1858), 35.

39. Reyna I. Aburto, "Thru Cloud and Sunshine, Lord, Abide with Me!," *Ensign* or *Liahona*, Nov. 2019, 59.

injury, collapsed lungs, and other injuries. Doctors put him into an induced coma for more than a month.

When Sam woke, he was a quadriplegic. He spent ten months in the hospital, struggling to learn life's most basic skills, and continued recovering the whole next year. Then, in 2004, he began working to regain his strength and learn new skills. Eventually, Sam regained his ability to drive with the help of a specially engineered truck. Since then, he has tried skiing, paragliding, and competed in bodybuilding competitions. Sam said, "What I've learned the most is the hard things in life are what strengthen you. They make you stronger, wiser. You really start to minimize smaller problems. You got through bigger problems, so you can get through this one. There's purpose in struggle, in pain. Things won't always be like this; this is just how they are today."[40]

Trials Help Us Acquire Divine Characteristics

Jesus asked us to strive to become more like Him and Heavenly Father: "Therefore I would that ye should be perfect even as I, or your Father who is in heaven is perfect" (3 Nephi 12:48). We work toward this lofty goal while experiencing the soul-stretching trials of mortality. God created this earth as a schooling ground, a place where we are allowed to have trials and develop virtues we might not have otherwise acquired. Hardships prepare us to become true sons and daughters of God (see Mosiah 27:24–27).

Challenges not only help us develop qualities we now lack, but they solidify progress we've already made. Elder Maxwell stated, "Built . . . into the seemingly ordinary experiences of life are abundant opportunities for us to acquire the eternal attributes, such as love, mercy, meekness, patience, submissiveness, and to develop and sharpen such skills as how to communicate, motivate, delegate, and manage our talents, time, and thoughts in accordance with eternal

---

40. Isaac Hale, "Pleasant Grove man stays active after paralyzing accident," *The Salt Lake Tribune*, Jan. 13, 2018, https://www.sltrib.com/pb/news/2018/01/13/pleasant-grove-man-stays-active-after-paralyzing-accident.

priorities. These attributes and skills are portable, are never obsolete; they will be much needed in the next world."[41]

Elder Orson F. Whitney said:

> Is not this God's purpose in causing his children to suffer? He wants them to become more like himself. God has suffered far more than man ever did or ever will, and is therefore the great source of sympathy and consolation. "Who are these arrayed in white, nearest to the throne of God?" asked John the Apostle, wrapt in his mighty vision. The answer was: "These are they who have come up through great tribulation, and washed their robes and made them white in the blood of the Lamb." There is always a blessing in sorrow.[42]

Lessons can be learned from our most trying circumstances. After torrential rains flooded a cave in northern Thailand, a group of twelve boys between the ages of eleven and sixteen, and their soccer coach, became trapped. In June and July of 2018, a massive rescue attempt ensued. After 18 days, British divers found the boys and their coach, and eventually all were rescued. When one of the boys, Mongkol Boonpiam, was asked what he had learned from this experience, he replied that it made him stronger, saying, "I have more patience, endurance, tolerance."[43]

An all-wise and all-knowing God allows trials to teach us specific lessons we need to learn. For this reason, we ought not to complain about life's problems but meekly allow them to shape us into the person God wants us to become. Because Heavenly Father knows us personally, He knows which circumstances will best help us overcome our personal weaknesses. Elder Maxwell offers further insight on this:

41. Neal A. Maxwell, *We Will Prove Them Herewith* (Salt Lake City, UT: Deseret Book, 1982), 11.

42. Orson F. Whitney, "A Lesson from the Book of Job," *Improvement Era,* Nov. 1918, 7.

43. Tassanee Vejpongsa and Kaweewit Kaewjinda, "Out of hospital, Thai boys share lessons learned in cave," *CTV News*, July 18, 2018, https://windsor.ctvnews.ca/out-of-hospital-thai-boys-share-lessons-learned-in-cave-1.4017925.

> Mortality presents us with numerous opportunities to become more Christlike: first, by coping successfully with those of life's challenges which are "common to man[kind]" (1 Corinthians 10:13). In addition, there are also our customized trials such as experiencing illness, aloneness, persecution, betrayal, irony, poverty, false witness, unreciprocated love, et cetera. If endured well now, "all these things" can be for our good and can "greatly enlarge the soul" (see Doctrine and Covenants 121:42), including an enlarged capacity for joy. Meek suffering often does the excavating necessary for that enlarging![44]

Elder Maxwell further stated, "If, indeed, the things allotted to each were divinely customized according to our ability and capacity, then for us to seek to wrench ourselves free of every schooling circumstance in mortality is to tear ourselves away from matched opportunities. It is to go against divine wisdom, wisdom in which we may once have concurred before we came here and to which we once gave assent."[45]

When adversity tears a hole in our spirit and we work to overcome it, we become strong in that area. This process can be likened to when a pair of pants is torn and then mended; the reinforced spot becomes stronger than any other place. If the pants were to sustain another tear, it would never be at the mended spot because that spot has become strong. Once we have become strengthened through adversity, our spirit is reinforced and becomes perfected so that no amount of adversity can cause it to be damaged in that same spot again.

As we face personal difficulties, Satan will tempt us to give up, but that is the moment when we must tighten our grip on the iron rod. Michelle Quist's fiancé called off their wedding six days before the big day. Devastated, Michelle lay in bed for three days, feeling like her world had ended. Her mother took care of canceling the wedding, but on New Year's Eve, Michelle sat alone in the apartment she had planned to share with her new husband. Despite that painful

44. Neal A. Maxwell, "Apply the Atoning Blood of Christ," *Ensign*, Nov. 1997, 22.

45. Neal A. Maxwell, *Things as They Really Are* (Salt Lake City, UT: Deseret Book, 1989), 31.

experience, Michelle realized an important truth: "Our trials are meant to strengthen us. And they do. Nobody plans to experience the heartaches and failures of life. Nobody expects their marriage to end in divorce, or their child to die, or their spouse to get sick. It just happens. . . . Trials are about rising above the pain and overcoming."[46]

Trials Purify Our Souls

Adversity provides us with opportunities to develop virtues that contribute to our eventual perfection. President Harold B. Lee said, "There is a refining process that comes through suffering . . . that we can't experience any other way than by suffering. We draw closer to [Jesus Christ,] who gave His life that man might be. We feel a kinship that we have never felt before. . . . But to the extent that we have suffered, somehow it seems to have the effect of drawing us closer to the divine, helps to purify our souls, and helps to purge out the things that are not pleasing in the sight of the Lord."[47]

Since God structured mortality to be a time of testing, we can expect a number of trials sprinkled into our lifetime. Adversity is to be the usual pattern, not some odd aberration. Understanding that trials are normal and can be opportunities for personal growth can relieve some of their sting. When leaving the Garden of Eden, Adam was told, "Cursed shall be the ground *for thy sake*" (Moses 4:23; emphasis added). Having to work hard each day can be a burden, but it is also a blessing and teaches many virtues, such as self-reliance and hard work.

Sometimes those moments when our hearts are the most sorrowful are when our souls are most open to the guidance of the Holy Ghost (see 3 Nephi 9:20). While teaching the Zoramites, Alma observed

---

46. Michelle Quist, "Michelle Quist: Our trials are meant to strengthen us. And they do," *The Salt Lake Tribune*, Nov. 22, 2017, https://www.sltrib.com/opinion/2017/11/23/michelle-quist-our-trials-are-meant-to-strengthen-us-and-they-do/.

47. Harold B. Lee, "Funeral services for Alfred W. Weseman," Church History Library, Salt Lake City, 7; spelling, punctuation, and capitalization standardized. Quoted in "Prisoner for Jesus Christ," Church History, accessed Nov. 10, 2023, https://history.churchofjesuschrist.org/content/prisoner-for-jesus-christ?lang=eng.

that their poverty and afflictions had humbled and prepared them to hear the word of God, which brought many marvelous blessings to them (see Alma 32:6, 13).

Still, trials are never easy. Prominent American rabbi and author Harold Kushner said that when his firstborn child, Aaron, was three, doctors discovered he had a rare terminal disease. Kushner writes:

> I am a more sensitive person, a more effective pastor, a more sympathetic counselor because of Aaron's life and death than I would ever have been without it. And I would give up all those gains in a second if I could have my son back. If I could choose, I would forgo all the spiritual growth and depth which has come my way because of our experience, and be what I was fifteen years ago, an average rabbi, an indifferent counselor, helping some people and unable to help others, and the father of a bright, happy boy. But I cannot choose.[48]

When he was eleven, President Uchtdorf and his family were refugees. They slept in one small room in a farmhouse near Frankfurt, Germany. Other children made fun of him because he had an accent, his family was poor, and they were refugees. President Uchtdorf recalled:

> Even though I still remember the hurt and despair, I can see now what I was unable to see then: this was a period of great personal growth. During this time, our family bonded together. I watched and learned from my parents. I admired their determination and optimism. From them I learned that adversity, when confronted with faith, courage, and tenacity, could be overcome. . . .
>
> While I would not be eager to relive those days of trial and trouble, I have little doubt that the lessons I learned were a necessary preparation for future opportunity. Now, many years later, I know this for a certainty; it is often in the trial of adversity that we learn those most critical lessons that form our character and shape our destiny.[49]

48. Harold Kushner, *Why Good Things Happen to Good People* (New York: Broadway Books, 2007), 121.

49. Dieter F. Uchtdorf, "Two Principles for Any Economy," *Ensign* or *Liahona,* Nov. 2009, 56, 58.

Whom God Loves He Chastens

Chasten is not a word we use often in today's world, but we find it occasionally in the scriptures. To chasten means to rebuke or reprimand. This is not something anyone enjoys, but it is a sanctifying method Heavenly Father uses to help us improve. "My son, despise not the chastening of the Lord; neither be weary of his correction: For whom the Lord loveth he correcteth; even as a father the son in whom he delighteth" (Proverbs 3:11–12). Chastening is God's way of reminding us that although He loves us, He wants us to do better.

Chastening has a purifying effect on our spirits. Elder Taniela B. Wakolo likened chastening to spiritual surgery. He said, "To those who need it and are willing to receive it, [chastening] can be life-saving. The Lord chastens whom He loves. The scriptures tell us so (see Hebrews 12:5–11; Helaman 12:3; Doctrine and Covenants 1:27; 95:1). That chastening, or spiritual surgery, will bring about needed change in our lives. We will realize, brothers and sisters, that it refines and purifies our inner vessels."[50]

We need not resent being chastened, for the changes God wants us to make are the things that will help us become more like Him. "For all those who will not endure chastening, but deny me, cannot be sanctified" (Doctrine and Covenants 101:5). President Brigham Young said, "When chastisements come, let them be what they may, let us always be willing and ready to kiss the rod, and reverence the hand that administers it, acknowledging the hand of God in all things"[51]

Chastening can also come from prophets, apostles, patriarchs, bishops, and other leaders. Such chastening is intended "for the perfecting of the saints, for the work of the ministry, for the edifying of the body of Christ" (Ephesians 4:12). We may feel the small but clear voice of chastisement when we study the scriptures, listen to speakers in church, read Church magazines, or listen to conference talks and are reminded of our imperfections, disobedience, or things we have neglected to do.

---

50. Taniela B. Wakolo, "God Loves His Children," *Ensign* or *Liahona*, May 2021, 96.

51. Brigham Young, in *Journal of Discourses*, 2:280.

President Wilford Woodruff said, "The chastisements we have had from time to time have been for our good, and are essential to learn wisdom, and carry us through a school of experience we never could have passed through without."[52] We can be grateful for chastening, knowing God uses it to guide us to a future we cannot now envision but which He knows is a better way.

When God Does Not Remove the Bitter Cup

There are many stalwart Saints who suffer great afflictions even though they have and are continuing to do their best to follow Christ. This may lead to confusion since we know that Heavenly Father hears every prayer and that He understands our needs, wants, and desires. Why then doesn't God remove the bitter cup? "It is quite useless for us mortals to try to do our own sums when it comes to suffering," declared Elder Maxwell. "We can't make it all add up because clearly we do not have all the numbers. Furthermore, none of us knows much about the algebra of affliction. The challenges that come are shaped to our needs and circumstances, sometimes in order to help our weaknesses become strengths.[53]

When we wonder why God doesn't answer our prayers, we could reflect on another question: Why did we come to earth? The answer, we all know, is that we came to earth to receive a body, be tested, and develop virtues that would allow us to become more like our Heavenly Father and return to His presence. When we heard God's plan in the premortal world, we shouted for joy (see Job 38:7) and agreed to submit ourselves to God's will, knowing that any mortal suffering would pale in comparison to the glorious blessings we could receive. We also knew that God would support us every step of the way. "The Lord knoweth all things from the beginning; wherefore, he prepareth a way to accomplish all his works among the children of men" (1 Nephi 9:6).

Alma and his people suffered greatly after being brought into bondage. When they prayed for release, the Lord declared that He would deliver them *in time.* Such an answer was probably different

52. Wilford Woodruff, in *Journal of Discourses*, 2:198.

53. Neal A. Maxwell, *Notwithstanding My Weakness* (Salt Lake City, UT: Deseret Book, 1981), 68.

than the one they were hoping for. However, they continued to trust the Lord. Because of their faithfulness, the Lord promised that while Alma and his people waited for deliverance, He would ease their burdens "that even you cannot feel them upon your backs . . . and this will I do that ye may . . . know of a surety that I, the Lord God, do visit my people in their afflictions" (Mosiah 24:14). The Lord strengthened them so much that "they did submit cheerfully and with patience to all the will of the Lord" (Mosiah 24:15). These same promises can come to us when we're heavily burdened. Isaiah states, "They that wait upon the Lord shall renew their strength; they shall mount up with wings as eagles; they shall run, and not be weary; and they shall walk, and not faint" (Isaiah 40:31).

Hope and peace are available to us through the gospel of Jesus Christ, even when we're suffering tremendous afflictions. Hyrum Shumway, a second lieutenant in the US Army, was severely injured and lost his eyesight after the D-Day invasion on June 6, 1944. Being blind ended his hope of becoming a medical doctor, but Hyrum chose to move on with his life. Since he wanted to marry at some point, Hyrum had to learn a job skill so he could support a family.

After spending three years in a rehabilitation hospital, Hyrum returned home to Lovell, Wyoming. Eventually, he found work in Baltimore, Maryland, as a rehab counselor and employment specialist for the blind. During his eight years there, Hyrum found more jobs for the blind than any other counselor in the United States. Feeling able to provide for a family, he proposed to his sweetheart, Sarah Bagley. Hyrum told her, "If you will read the mail, sort the socks, and drive the car, I can do the rest." Henry and Sarah were married in the Salt Lake Temple and, in time, had eight children.

In 1954 the Shumway family returned to Wyoming, and Hyrum was hired as the State Director of Education for the Deaf and Blind, a position he held for thirty-two years. Hyrum served seven years as a bishop then seventeen years as a stake patriarch. After retiring, he and his wife, Sarah, served in the London England South Mission.

Hyrum Shumway passed away in March 2011, leaving a great and enduring legacy of faith in the Lord.[54]

Although our lives, like Hyrum Shumway's, might be altered by severe adversity, we can still move forward. While we may never know in this life why we had to face such great hardships, we can trust God and know that in the next stage of our existence, we will have all of our questions answered. No mortal adversity can stop us from returning to God's presence if we move forward in faith.

We Have Miles to Go and Much to Learn

Some tribulations rock our lives so powerfully that we must pause and catch our breath. At such times, we often discover that things that once mattered so much are no longer important. Adversity often causes us to reevaluate our thoughts and actions. We may find that it is no longer necessary to hang on to an old grudge and instead decide to let things go. We might resolve to spend more time with our loved ones, read the scriptures more regularly, be less easily offended, or forego honking at someone who fails to wait their turn at a four-way traffic stop.

When in pain, we must cling to our courage and hold on to hope, knowing that God knows our heartache. "He is the very source of the light you seek," stated Elder Holland. "He does love you, and He knows your fears. He hears your prayers. He is your Heavenly Father, and surely He matches with His own the tears His children shed."[55]

While in mortality, we are not shielded from grief or pain. Everyone has times when the birds don't sing, the sun is slow to rise, and bells don't ring. How we react to trials correlates directly to how happy we are in life. The happiest people are those who, despite having their fair share of adversity, grow from it—becoming stronger, wiser, and more patient and allowing happiness into their lives. Wise is the person who understands that hard moments can be the time of

54. History received directly from Joseph Shumway, a descendant of Hyrum Smith Shumway; quoted in W. Christopher Waddell, "Turn to the Lord," *Ensign* or *Liahona*, Nov. 2017, 94–96.

55. Jeffrey R. Holland, "An High Priest of Good Things to Come," *Ensign*, Nov. 1999, 36.

greatest growth, and it is that growth which leads to joy in the next life. The Lord declared, "To him that overcometh will I grant to sit with me in my throne" (Revelation 3:21).

Bearing with adversity requires patience and faith in Jesus Christ. "Be still and know that I am God," the Lord told Joseph Smith (Doctrine and Covenants 101:16). When we suffer and God does not remove our trial, we can trust in Him and know that He is requiring something more from us—our growth. Endurance is made easier when we remain confident in Heavenly Father's plan and know that even pain can work for our best good—if not in this life, then in the next. The Savior told the Nephites, "Look unto me, and endure to the end, and ye shall live; for unto him that endureth to the end will I give eternal life" (3 Nephi 15:9).

We all have miles to go and much to learn before returning to God's presence. Because of that, we should not marvel when adversity seems to be our constant companion. Hardships may be as unavoidable as they are painful, yet they provide us with vital eternal lessons. Depending on our attitude, adversity can be either a stumbling block or a stepping stone. The choice is ours, and whatever decision we make determines our future. What happens to us does not matter—what we *become* because of the adversity we experience is what is significant because it proves our heart and allows us to have eternal happiness in the life to come.

5
Myriad Trials of Mortality

"Verily I say unto you my friends, fear not, let your hearts be comforted; yea, rejoice evermore, and in everything give thanks; Waiting patiently on the Lord, for your prayers have entered into the ears of the Lord of Sabaoth, and are recorded with this seal and testament—the Lord hath sworn and decreed that they shall be granted. Therefore, he giveth this promise unto you, with an immutable covenant that they shall be fulfilled; and all things wherewith you have been afflicted shall work together for your good, and to my name's glory, saith the Lord."

—Doctrine and Covenants 98:1–3

Fear Not, For God Is with Thee

In these latter days, all of us will experience myriad physical or mental trials. Whether our trials are small or more the size of a tsunami, we can turn to the Lord for help. "Cast thy burden upon the Lord, and he shall sustain thee; he shall never suffer the righteous to be moved" (Psalm 55:22).

In speaking about the many different challenges that can arise, Elder Holland said:

> I speak of the yearning of many who would like to be married and aren't or who are married and wish the relationship were a little more celestial. I speak of those who have to deal with the unwanted appearance of a serious medical condition—perhaps an incurable

> one—or who face a lifelong battle with a genetic defect that has no remedy. I speak of the continuing struggle with emotional and mental health challenges that weigh heavily on the souls of so many who suffer with them, and on the hearts of those who love and suffer with them. I speak of the poor, whom the Savior told us never to forget, and I speak of you waiting for the return of a child, no matter what the age, who has chosen a path different from the one you prayed he or she would take.[56]

Christ willingly took upon Himself our suffering as part of His Atonement, and in a miraculous manner we do not fully comprehend, He took upon Himself our pain and afflictions so that He would know how to help us according to our infirmities (see Alma 7:12). Because of this, we know that no matter what trial we face, Christ knows exactly *how* best to help us. How grateful we can be in our sufferings to know that our Savior understands precisely what we are going through and, because of that, can provide the strength for us to bear them.

Christ gives us these words of comfort: "Fear thou not; for I am with thee: . . . I will strengthen thee; yea, I will help thee" (Isaiah 41:10). Why does our Savior help us? Because He loves us. Jesus Christ and Heavenly Father love us with a pure, unconditional love and will help us bear our trials. When we endure them well, we will be blessed with healing and peace. We can take comfort in the words of the hymn that tells us, "Earth has no sorrow that heav'n cannot heal."[57]

Physical Trials

While on earth, people suffer from physical trials because of aging, disabilities, and illness. These disabilities in body or mind can make ordinary activities difficult, but we know that in the next life, our bodies and minds will be perfect. President Nelson said, "For reasons usually unknown, some people are born with physical limitations. . . . Nevertheless, the gift of a physical body is priceless . . . [and] a perfect body is not required to achieve a divine destiny. In fact, some of the sweetest spirits are housed in frail frames. . . . Eventually the time will

56. Jeffrey R. Holland, "Waiting on the Lord," *Ensign* or *Liahona*, Nov. 2020, 115.

57. "Come, Ye Disconsolate," *Hymns*, no. 115.

come when each 'spirit and . . . body shall be reunited again in . . . perfect form' (Alma 11:43)."[58]

When faced with a serious illness, you may feel alone and discouraged. After being diagnosed with cancer, Elder Anthony D. Perkins became acquainted with the pain of surgeries and the wretched effects of chemo and strong medications. Speaking from personal experience, Elder Perkins said:

> I testify that our Heavenly Father remembers His suffering Saints, loves you, and is intimately aware of you. Our Savior knows how you feel. "Surely he has borne our griefs, and carried our sorrows" (Isaiah 53:4). I know—as a daily recipient—that keeping covenants unlocks the power of Jesus Christ's atoning sacrifice to provide strength and even joy to you who suffer. For all who suffer, I pray, "May God grant unto you that your burdens may be light, through the joy of his Son" (Alma 33:23).[59]

Comfort can come in knowing that physical trials are temporary. In the next life, our bodies will be restored to a perfect state, and we will be freed from any disability and pain we now endure. The Book of Mormon teaches, "This restoration shall come to all, both old and young, both bond and free, both male and female, both the wicked and the righteous; and even there shall not so much as a hair of their heads be lost; but every thing shall be restored to its perfect frame" (Alma 11:44).

Personal and Family Problems

Another category of trials is personal and family troubles, which encompass a wide range of hardships. One of these is death. The pain of losing a loved one never really goes away, but in time, we can find ourselves progressing from a grief we can't handle to a loss we can manage. Relying on family and friends for support, seeing a therapist, and turning to God for comfort are positive actions that can help heal our grief. Although we grieve at the passing of a loved one, we

---

58. Russell M. Nelson, "We Are Children of God," *Ensign,* Nov. 1998, 85–86.

59. Anthony D. Perkins, "Remember Thy Suffering Saints, O Our God," *Liahona*, Nov. 2021, 105.

can imagine the great joy he or she feels when arriving in the spirit world and meeting joyfully with family and friends who have gone on before. The Prophet Joseph Smith, who experienced many personal losses, said, "My heart mourns for those who have been taken from us, but not without hope, for I shall see them again and be with them."[60]

Another of life's challenges is being single when you had hoped to marry and have a loving companion. However, all of God's blessings will be available to all who keep their covenants and remain faithful. Although the exact time when all will receive the blessings of exaltation are unknown, we know that eventually *they will come* (see Mosiah 2:41). Elder Gerrit W. Gong reminds us, "Our standing before the Lord and in His Church is not a matter of our marital status but of our becoming faithful and valiant disciples of Jesus Christ."[61]

Addiction covers a wide range of problems and can include being addicted to drugs, pornography, alcohol, tobacco, gambling, and other things. Repeated use of drugs, alcohol, and inhalants change how the brain functions, causing changes in behavior and personality, which limit the user's ability to make good choices. The onslaught of pornography and gambling in our day is not new and remains the cause of much grief. The challenge of addiction can feel overwhelming, embarrassing, or even insurmountable. But recovering from any type of addiction is possible through Christ (see Philippians 4:13). To find recovery meetings, visit the web page currently found at addictionrecovery.ChurchofJesusChrist.org.

Few things can cause more pain and frustration than being discriminated against because of the color of your skin or your culture. We are encouraged to remember that every person on earth is a divine child of heavenly parents and that all are equal in God's eyes. President Nelson said, "God does not love one race more than another. His doctrine on this matter is clear. He invites *all* to come unto Him, 'black and white, bond and free, male and female' (2 Nephi 26:33). I assure you that your standing before God is not determined by the color of your skin. Favor or disfavor with God is dependent

60. *Teachings of Presidents of the Church; Joseph Smith* (2007), 179.

61. Gerrit W. Gong, "Room in the Inn," *Liahona*, May 2021, 26.

upon your devotion to God and His commandments and not the color of your skin."[62]

Single parents have unique trials. Trust in God and ask Him to bless you in your efforts to raise your children. Stay close to the Savior and center your life by staying active in the Church. Reach out to family and friends for support. Allow those who are called to minister to you to help with household repairs, yard work, and other needs. Even though your circumstances are difficult, acknowledge the blessings that you have and make an effort to reach out and serve others who are in need.

Not being able to have children is a difficult trial, but those who face this challenge can be assured that the blessing of having children will come eventually, even if it does not occur in this life. Elder Neil L. Andersen offers these comforting words: "The unrealized dreams of life are difficult to understand if viewed only from the perspective of mortality. As the Lord's servant, I promise you that as you are faithful to Jesus Christ and your covenants, you will receive compensating blessings in this life and your righteous desires in the eternal time line of the Lord."[63]

Relationship problems are common. It happens to all married couples. Your relationship seems to be sailing along happily, then storm clouds suddenly descend and both partners seem to tie on boxing gloves and go ten rounds. Usually these unhappy times pass, but some couples can get entrenched in marital discord. To have a happy marriage, partners need to learn how to resolve conflicts so that each person feels understood and valued. Marriage counseling can be of great benefit. "If any of you are having difficulty in your marriage," President Thomas S. Monson counseled, "I urge you to do all that you can to make whatever repairs are necessary, that you might be as happy as you were when your marriage started out. We who are married in the house of the Lord do so for time and for all eternity, and then we must put forth the necessary effort to make it so."[64]

---

62. Russell M. Nelson, "Let God Prevail," *Ensign* or *Liahona*, Nov. 2020, 94.
63. Neil L. Andersen, "The Personal Journey of a Child of God," *Liahona*, May 2021, 47.
64. Thomas S. Monson, "Priesthood Power," *Ensign* or *Liahona*, May 2011, 69.

Broken covenants can break hearts. Discovery of infidelity typically causes both partners to be flung into crisis. Your life may feel uncertain, stressful, and full of pain. President Nelson said, "If you are married to a companion who has broken his or her covenants, your willingness to let God prevail in your life will allow your covenants with God to remain intact. The Savior will heal your broken heart. The heavens will open as you seek to know how to move forward. You do not need to wander or wonder."[65]

Divorce usually occurs because one partner has made the decision to end the relationship. But no matter who initiates the action, it's common to feel disoriented, anguished, and angry. Being single again can trigger anxiety and feelings of insecurity. At this time, it's essential to trust in the Lord and have faith in His power to bless you to heal from the pain. Be sure to take the time you need to grieve your loss. Writing in a journal can help you process your sadness. Ask for a priesthood blessing. Read the scriptures daily and pray for inspiration to guide you. Attend church and reach out to a friend to go to the temple with you. When in need of help, reach out to your ministering brothers or sisters. Stay close to family and friends. Counseling can be of great benefit. Above all, trust yourself and know that you are strong and capable.

Mental Health Challenges

Mental illness is a common health problem. According to the National Alliance of Mental Illness, or NAMI, mental illness affects approximately one in five adults in the United States every year.[66] Children are also at high risk. One in five students will develop a significant mental health problem during their school years, according to the Substance Abuse and Mental Health Services Administration. As a society, we are fortunate to have many effective treatments and medications.

Although education has enlightened many people, there is still a stigma attached to mental illness. Elder Holland said of this, "I wish

65. Russell M. Nelson, "Let God Prevail," 94.

66. See "Mental Health by the Numbers," National Alliance of Mental Illness, accessed Nov. 10, 2023, https://nami.org/mhstats.

to speak to those who suffer from some form of mental illness or emotional disorder, whether those afflictions be slight or severe, of brief duration or persistent over a lifetime. . . . These afflictions are some of the realities of mortal life, and there should be no more shame in acknowledging them than in acknowledging a battle with high blood pressure or the sudden appearance of a malignant tumor."[67]

Depression is one of the most common mental disorders in the United States. The National Institute of Mental Health shows that an estimated 21.0 million adults experienced a major depressive episode in 2020, which represents 8.4% of all US adults.[68] Depression can blind you to God's light and even make you wonder if there is light to be found anywhere. Sister Reyna I. Aburto spoke of depression and the importance of seeking treatment:

> It is normal to feel sad or worried once in a while. Sadness and anxiety are natural human emotions. However, if we are constantly sad and if our pain blocks our ability to feel the love of our Heavenly Father and His Son and the influence of the Holy Ghost, then we may be suffering from depression, anxiety, or another emotional condition. . . .
>
> Like any part of the body, the brain is subject to illness, trauma, and chemical imbalances. When our minds are suffering, it is appropriate to seek help from God, from those around us, and from medical and mental health professionals.[69]

Since depression is a serious mood disorder, seeking treatment at the earliest signs can help prevent it from worsening. There are a number of highly effective medications to treat depression's symptoms. Seeing a therapist or some other type of mental health professional is highly recommended. Some evidence-based approaches that are specific to the treatment of depression include cognitive behavioral

67. Jeffrey R. Holland, "Like a Broken Vessel," *Ensign* or *Liahona,* Nov. 2013, 40.

68. See "Major Depression," National Institute of Mental Health, accessed Nov. 10, 2023, https://www.nimh.nih.gov/health/statistics/major-depression.

69. Reyna I. Aburto, "Thru Cloud and Sunshine, Lord, Abide with Me!," *Ensign* or *Liahona,* Nov. 2019, 57.

therapy (CBT), interpersonal therapy (IPT), and problem-solving therapy.

Anxiety, or generalized anxiety disorder, is a group of mental illnesses that are characterized by feelings of worry, fear, and restlessness. Anxiety disorders affect 40 million adults in the US, or 18.1% of the population, every year.[70] Everyone feels anxious at times; however, people with an anxiety disorder often have intense or excessive anxiety over everyday situations. Medication is often effective in treating anxiety, especially when coupled with cognitive behavioral therapy, which involves learning how to lower anxiety when faced with upsetting situations.

Coping with Mental Illness

Mental health challenges, like physical health problems, are part of mortality, and we are urged to seek appropriate professional assistance. We can also pray for help, which opens the windows of heaven on our behalf. Educating yourself about your illness is important because information often precedes inspiration.

It takes strength and persistence to cope with mental illness, and sometimes those who are ill have difficulty feeling God's love. If this is true for you, Elder Erich W. Kopischke has some words of advice: "For all who are personally affected by mental illness, hold fast to your covenants, even if you might not feel God's love at this time. Do whatever lies in your power and then 'stand still . . . to see the salvation of God, and for his arm to be revealed' (Doctrine and Covenants 123:17)."[71]

There may be times when you feel weak or powerless against the battles you face, but the truth is that you are incredibly strong for living through them. When life feels out of control, remember you *do* have some control over your actions and feelings. Below are some practical ideas that may help. Choose a few that you feel are most suitable to your particular situation. Be sure to discuss them with your doctor and/or therapist.

---

70. See "Take the First Step - Understand the Facts," Anxiety & Depression Association of America, accessed Nov. 10, 2023, https://adaa.org/.

71. Erich W. Kopischke, "Addressing Mental Health," *Liahona*, Nov. 2021, 38.

Decide Ahead of Time How to Manage Your Symptoms

Living with mental illness is not easy. While you can't control that you *have* an illness, you can to some degree learn how to manage your symptoms. Stay aware of your emotions. Take note of when you're reaching your limits and need help. Plan ahead and develop a list of techniques that help you feel better emotionally and spiritually. If listening to calming music soothes you, have a playlist ready. If being in a quiet place helps, plan where you can go when needed. Decide who you can call if your symptoms worsen. Heavenly Father is an ever-present help, and you can always say a prayer in your heart and ask for help and strength. There is peace and power in reading scriptures, listening to conference talks, enjoying inspiring music, watching inspiring videos, or listening to uplifting podcasts.

Practice Positive Self-Talk

Some mental illnesses become worse if you allow negative thoughts to keep running through your mind. Self-talk—the words you choose to think—have a significant impact on your mood. Your self-talk greatly influences your feelings, thoughts, and behaviors, which is why it's vital to focus on positive thoughts and kick out the negative ones. While you may not have control over everything in your life, you do have a choice to kick out negative thoughts and think more constructive ones. Whenever a negative thought enters your mind, don't let it stay—replace it immediately with a more helpful, optimistic thought.

Be gentle and encouraging to yourself. Don't ever call yourself names or berate yourself. Never say anything to yourself that you would not say to a child or a friend. Talk to yourself the way you would imagine Christ would talk to you. Think of what loving, encouraging, and understanding words He might say.

To have more positive thoughts, you first need to become more aware of your thoughts. Then whenever a negative or unproductive thought pops up, change it to something more positive. Create a list of upbeat and encouraging thoughts and keep it handy.

Deep Breathing

When we feel stressed or anxious, we tend to take shallow breaths, which tends to increase our heart rate and blood pressure. On the other hand, taking slow, deep breaths can relieve tension and promote a feeling of calmness. According to the American Institute of Stress, twenty to thirty minutes of deep breathing a day can be effective in reducing anxiety and stress.[72] Deep breathing helps turn off the body's natural stress response and allows the tension in your muscles to relax, promoting an overall resiliency that can help you better withstand life's stressors.[73]

To relieve stress, breathe in deeply, imagining you are trying to fill a balloon in your abdomen. The increase in the amount of oxygen lowers your heart rate and blood pressure and produces a feeling of calmness. Close your eyes, and while imagining yourself in a beautiful, peaceful place, take deep abdominal breaths, exhaling slowly. Continue for five to ten minutes.

Therapy Is Invaluable

Most people with mental illness achieve great benefits from seeing a therapist. Sharing your thoughts and feelings with a trained professional plays an important part in how well you deal with your challenges. Seeing a therapist can help keep your brain healthy and mentally sharp, just as going to the gym and working out keeps your body physically fit and healthy. A therapist can teach you beneficial strategies to help you manage your illness.

Counseling also provides support when new challenges arise. Some people find it helpful to occasionally invite a spouse or loved one to a counseling session. To find a therapist, ask your bishop for recommendations. They may be able to offer Church-oriented counseling. You can also check with family and friends. Check out recommendations

---

72. See Daily Life, "Take a Deep Breath," The American Institute of Stress, Aug. 10, 2012, https://www.stress.org/take-a-deep-breath.

73. See Abria Blount, "Deep Breathing Helps Calm Anxiety," PsychCentral, last modified June 30, 2021, https://psychcentral.com/anxiety/why-deep-breathing-helps-calm-anxiety.

online to see if a therapist's specialties line up with your particular needs. Don't be discouraged if the first therapist you see isn't a good match. It can take time and require seeing a number of people before you meet a counselor you feel comfortable with.

Attend a Support Group for Your Particular Illness

Many people find it helpful to attend a support group in addition to seeing a counselor. There are many specialty support groups, and you can benefit greatly from attending a group for those who have the same mental illness. You can gain strength and find comfort in meeting and talking with people who have similar challenges and difficulties. Support groups create a warm sense of community and can decrease your feelings of loneliness and isolation. To find a support group, first check with your bishop, who may know of Church-supported groups. You can also ask your therapist, who should have a list of reputable support groups.

The Wounds of the Abused

Abuse is the mistreatment or neglect of a person in a way that causes physical, emotional, or sexual harm. Elder Patrick Kearnon of the Seventy said:

> There is no place for any kind of abuse—physical, sexual, emotional, or verbal—in any home, any country, or any culture. Nothing a wife, child, or husband might do or say makes them "deserve" to be beaten. No one, in any country or culture, is ever "asking for" aggression or violence from someone else in authority or by someone who is bigger and stronger.
>
> Those who abuse and who seek to hide their grievous sins may get away with it for a time. But the Lord, who sees all, knows the deeds and the thoughts and intents of the heart. He is a God of justice, and His divine justice will be served.[74]

Abuse comes in various forms, such as physical, emotional, or sexual. Physical abuse is the intentional use of force that can result in

74. Patrick Kearon, "He Is Risen with Healing in His Wings: We Can Be More Than Conquerors," *Liahona*, May 2022, 39.

injury. Emotional abuse is any kind of abuse that is emotional rather than physical in nature. In general, a relationship is labeled emotionally abusive when there is a consistent pattern of abusive words and bullying behaviors. Sexual abuse is defined as any nonconsensual interaction in which a person is used for the sexual gratification of another person. Victims of sexual abuse often feel confused, shamed, and unworthy.

The wounds of the abused often go unrecognized as they attempt to go on with their life as if nothing was wrong. However, if a person does not deal with their feelings and tries to ignore or deny the pain, those feelings are usually sent underground where they often fester. As in all mortal trials, there is hope in Christ, even when we may feel as though there is no way out of the personal trauma that has been inflicted by the cruel actions of others.

Sexual abuse has its own unique problems and challenges. Seeing a therapist is vital to help victims process the event, develop coping skills, and apply stress management strategies. Nanon Talley, an LDS Family Services counseling manager, said, "Many clients I have worked with who experienced sexual abuse in their childhood or youth are told to 'get over it,' 'leave it in the past,' or 'just forgive and forget.' These types of statements—especially when coming from close friends, family members, or church leaders—can lead the victim to increased secrecy and shame rather than healing and peace. Similar to a serious physical wound or infection, these emotional wounds do not just go away if ignored."[75]

Child sexual abuse, which is prevalent in our society, is highly destructive and causes deep emotional pain. President Gordon B. Hinckley said, "Now I wish to mention another form of abuse that has been much publicized in the media. Such abuse is not new. . . . It is a most despicable and tragic and terrible thing. . . . It is something that cannot be countenanced or tolerated. The Lord Himself said, 'But whoso shall offend one of these little ones which believe in me, it were better for him that a millstone were hanged about his neck, and

75. Nanon Talley, "A Bridge to Hope and Healing," *Ensign* or *Liahona*, Apr. 2017, 60.

that he were drowned in the depth of the sea' (Matthew 18:6). That is very strong language from the Prince of Peace, the Son of God."[76]

Residual Effects of Abuse

Abuse can leave a victim feeling traumatized and often changes the way they view themselves and others. Many victims feel unworthy, unloved, and unclean, even years afterwards. They struggle with low self-worth and find themselves constantly seeking approval from others, becoming passive, or putting up barriers to keep people at a distance. Victims often blame themselves, even though they are not at fault. Even if the perpetrator is not brought to justice, God will hold them accountable.

The impact of abuse often stays with the victim for years—sometimes for a lifetime. Survivors may feel less worthy or less valuable or less loved as a human being because of what someone else has done. Such thoughts come from Satan, who wants to make the victim feel miserable. Often these damaging thoughts prevent the abused from seeking help, leaving them to struggle alone with their lingering effects of shame and self-loathing.

It's a blessing to know that all who have been abused have already been rescued by the Savior, who has overcome all of the pain and suffering that has been inflicted. Jesus Christ gives us the power to not only survive the pain but to rise above the misery and anguish. Because of Christ, it is possible to replace the pain in your heart with peace.

Abuse often leaves its victims with the deeply-rooted inner belief—even if not outwardly expressed—that these horrific events were somehow the victim's fault and that they deserve to feel ashamed and guilty. Victims may think, "This was my fault—I could have stopped this," "God doesn't love me or else this wouldn't have happened," "I'm not worthy of being loved," or "I'm damaged and can never be whole."

It's important to cling to the truth and to know that the abuse was not your fault, despite what your abuser said to the contrary. If you have been a victim, your abuser is solely responsible. You are precious

76. Gordon B. Hinckley, "Personal Worthiness to Exercise the Priesthood," *Ensign*, May 2002, 54.

in God's sight, in a way you may not comprehend right now but which you *will* discover if you will trust in Him. "Since thou wast precious in my sight, thou hast been honourable, and I have loved thee: therefore will I give men for thee, and people for thy life" (Isaiah 43:4). As a precious child of God, you are not defined by the terrible things that were done to you. You are a glorious and magnificent child of God. He loves you with a perfect and infinite love. Trust in His ability to heal you fully and completely.

Elder Kearon further stated the following:

> You are not defined by these terrible things that have been done to you. You are, in glorious truth, defined by your eternally existing identity as a son or daughter of God and by your Creator's perfect, infinite love and invitation to whole and complete healing. . . .
>
> Though it may seem impossible, feel impossible, healing *can* come through the miracle of the redemptive might of the Atonement of Jesus Christ. . . .
>
> Our merciful Savior, victorious over darkness and depravity, has power to right *all* wrongs, a life-giving truth for those wronged by others. . . .
>
> From the depths of His atoning suffering, the Savior imparts hope you thought was lost forever, strength you believed you could never possess, and healing you couldn't imagine was possible. . . .
>
> With arms outstretched, the Savior offers the gift of healing to you. With courage, patience, and faithful focus on Him . . . you can let go of your pain and leave it at His feet. . . .
>
> Jesus specializes in the seemingly impossible. He came here to make the impossible possible, the irredeemable redeemable, to heal the unhealable, to right the unrightable, to promise the unpromisable. And He's really good at it. In fact, He's perfect at it.[77]

Abuse Makes It Difficult to Feel God's Love

One of the most devastating effects of abuse is an inability to feel God's love. Survivors may wonder why God didn't love them enough to prevent the abuse. The gospel of Jesus Christ teaches that a loving Father watches over all of us, but victims may be so wounded that

77. Patrick Kearon, "He Is Risen with Healing in His Wings," 39.

they are unable to feel God's love, even though they desperately want to. Abuse often causes such profound suffering that victims no longer feel worthy to even pray to God and so simply withdraw.

Satan, the prince of evil, plants many destructive ideas in the minds of the abused. He takes advantage of a person's darkest moments to alienate them from Heavenly Father, generate feelings of despair, and block them from feeling God's love. Just as a pack of lions in the wild seek out the wounded and weakest members of a herd of wildebeests, Satan is quick to double his efforts against those who have been injured by abuse. Satan's goal is to prevent those who are damaged by abuse from drawing close to God and being healed.

If you feel that God doesn't love you, understand that you are being manipulated by Satan. Jesus Christ deeply loves all people—*including you*! Read the scriptures and ponder the love and compassion Jesus Christ freely offers to *everyone*. Continue to pray and ask Heavenly Father for help to feel His love. God is aware of you, and even if you can't feel His love right now, trust that He *does* love you. President Monson said, "God's love is there for you whether or not you feel you deserve [it]. It is simply always there."[78] Although you may feel abandoned at being unable to feel His presence, the truth is that He has never left your side. God's love for all of His children is infinite, and you will be blessed with the power to move past your heartaches. You will not forever carry the burden of pain caused by the unrighteous actions of others.

Therapy for Survivors of Abuse

Therapy is a vital component of the healing process, and yet the shame associated with abuse often prevents individuals from seeking help. The devastating emotions felt at the time of abuse, if pushed aside or hidden deep, can last a lifetime unless steps are taken to recover. Healing comes through the mercy and power of God. Elder Scott assures, "Complete healing will come through your faith in Jesus Christ and His power and capacity, through His Atonement, to heal the scars of that which is unjust and undeserved. . . . He loves you. He gave His

78. Thomas S. Monson, "We Never Walk Alone," *Ensign* or *Liahona*, Nov. 2013, 124.

life that you may be free of needless burdens. He will help you do it. I know that He has the power to heal you."[79]

Therapy for abuse can be painful. Healing often entails being willing to temporarily hurt more in order to hurt less in the long term. But seeing a counselor validates your feelings. It can be powerfully healing to know someone finally understands how deeply the abuse has affected you. Elder Scott counseled:

> If you are currently being abused or have been in the past, find the courage to seek help. You may have been severely threatened or caused to fear so that you would not reveal the abuse. Have the courage to act now. Seek the support of someone you can trust. Your bishop or stake president can give you valuable counsel and help you with the civil authorities. Explain how you have been abused and identify who has done it. Ask for protection. Your action may help others avoid becoming innocent victims, with consequent suffering. Get help now. Do not fear—for fear is a tool Satan will use to keep you suffering. The Lord will help you, but you must reach out for that help.[80]

Healing from Abuse Is Possible through the Savior

Because of the deep pain that comes from abuse, it may seem impossible to feel whole, but healing *can* come through Jesus Christ. He has the power to right *all* wrongs and brought about the miracle of the Atonement, which offers light over darkness and allows victims to rise above their pain.

Continue to nurture your faith. As you seek assistance from a professional counselor and work to make yourself whole, your efforts—paired with Jesus Christ's infinite Atonement—will provide healing and bring peace back to your soul. While the consequences of abuse can greatly influence your life, they do not define you. All negative consequences of abuse can be healed through the power of Christ. Take comfort in His words: "I have heard thy prayer, I have seen thy

79. Richard G. Scott, "To Be Free of Heavy Burdens," *Ensign* or *Liahona,* Nov. 2002, 88.

80. Richard G. Scott, "To Heal the Shattering Consequences of Abuse," *Ensign* or *Liahona*, May 2008, 42.

tears: behold, I will heal thee" (2 Kings 20:5). We may never know why such hardships have befallen us, and yet we can trust in the Lord to heal us, even though, as President Faust taught, "some of the healing may take place in another world."[81]

If you will conscientiously study the Atonement and exercise your faith in Jesus Christ's power to heal, you will find relief. Elder Scott said, "The beginning of healing requires childlike faith in the unalterable fact that Father in Heaven loves you and has supplied a way to heal. His Beloved Son, Jesus Christ, laid down His life to provide that healing. But there is no magic solution, no simple balm to provide healing, nor is there an easy path to the complete remedy. The cure requires profound faith in Jesus Christ and in His infinite capacity to heal."[82]

Our Redeemer suffered "pains and afflictions and temptations of every kind" (Alma 7:11). His suffering was not only to redeem us from sin but to heal us when another person causes us to suffer. Healing can take much spiritual work and patience, but the power of Jesus Christ's Atonement can heal any pain, any wound, and any type of abuse. In the Book of Mormon, Jacob counseled his people, "Look unto God with firmness of mind, and pray unto him with exceeding faith, and he will console you in your afflictions" (Jacob 3:1).

Sister Carole M. Stephens, who served in the Relief Society General Presidency, said, "Healing may be a long process. It will require that you prayerfully seek guidance and appropriate help, including counseling with properly ordained priesthood holders. As you learn to communicate openly, set appropriate boundaries and perhaps seek professional counseling. Maintaining spiritual health throughout the process is vital!"[83]

In time—even if it feels impossible now—the healing power that comes from the Savior can allow you to forgive your abuser. The idea of forgiveness can be difficult for victims of abuse who may think that

---

81. James E. Faust, "Where Do I Make My Stand?," *Ensign* or *Liahona*, Nov. 2004, 21.

82. Richard G. Scott, "To Heal the Shattering Consequences of Abuse," 42.

83. Carole M. Stephens, "The Master Healer," *Ensign* or *Liahona,* Nov. 2016, 11.

forgiving the perpetrator is "letting them off the hook." But there is no need to fear that the abuser will not face any consequences for their actions if we forgive, for God is just. Trust in God's justice and leave such matters in His hands.

While forgiving is an important part of healing, it is one of the last steps. When you are beginning to heal, if the thought of forgiving causes great pain, it is an indication to put that step aside for a time until you are further along the healing journey. When you are able to forgive, you will feel blessed peace as you are relieved of the anger and pain that bound you. Our Savior will heal our hearts and enable us to forgive those who have hurt us.

When people are emotionally, physically, or sexually abused, they can become resigned to living in darkness. But binding yourself to the Savior through your covenants can heal the wounds caused by another person's unrighteous exercise of agency. Healing comes when those who are injured are empowered to take Christ's hand and walk with Him out of the darkness and into the light. Darkness will still exist, but you can choose not to dwell there.

Cast Your Burdens Upon the Lord

During mortality, we can all expect to face myriad hardships arising from physical and mental trials. At times, you may feel like no one understands the depth of your pain nor the intensity of your suffering, but there *is* someone who does: Jesus Christ. Elder Matthew S. Holland explained, "There is One who understands perfectly what you are experiencing, who is 'mightier than all the earth' (1 Nephi 4:1), and who is 'able to do exceeding abundantly above all that [you] ask or think' (Ephesians 3:20). The process will unfold in His way and on His schedule, but Christ stands ready *always* to heal every ounce and aspect of your agony."[84]

Jesus Christ grants us relief and comfort whenever we flounder. Our Savior is keenly aware of our physical, mental, and spiritual challenges and is ever merciful—ready to succor us in our hardships. He is supremely qualified to succor us because He personally experienced

84. Matthew S. Holland, "The Exquisite Gift of the Son," *Ensign* or *Liahona,* Nov. 2020, 46.

and took upon Himself *all* of our pain, sorrows, and infirmities (see Hebrews 2:18; 4:15; Doctrine and Covenants 62:1). The Resurrection includes the physical and mental restoration of our bodies so that not even a hair of our heads will be lost. Elder Gong said, "This promise gives hope to those who have lost limbs; those who have lost ability to see, hear, or walk; or those thought lost to relentless disease, mental illness, or other diminished capacity. He finds us. He makes us whole."[85]

The Prophet Joseph Smith knew of the importance of continuing on through difficulties—perhaps because he had so very many. One day, Joseph visited his cousin George A. Smith who was very ill. Joseph gave him some advice that George never forgot: "He [the Prophet] told me I should never get discouraged, whatever difficulties might surround me. If I were sunk into the lowest pit of Nova Scotia and all the Rocky Mountains piled on top of me, I ought not to be discouraged, but hang on, exercise faith, and keep up good courage, and I should come out on the top of the heap at last."[86]

Because of the Lord's atoning sacrifice, Jesus Christ understands perfectly the suffering that comes from physical challenges, personal problems, mental illness, and the wounds of abuse (see 2 Nephi 9:21). When injured by the thoughtless or selfish actions of others, we might feel that our hardships are unfair. But God is in control and will make sure all wrongs will be made right—if not in this world, then in the eternal world ahead. Because of His infinite understanding, Christ can bless us with the strength we need to handle our particular difficulties.

Elder Bednar explains:

> The Savior has suffered not just for our iniquities but also for the inequality, the unfairness, the pain, the anguish, and the emotional distresses that so frequently beset us.
>
> There is no physical pain, no anguish of soul, no suffering of spirit, no infirmity or weakness that you or I ever experience during our mortal journey that the Savior did not experience first. You and

85. Gerrit W. Gong, "Hosanna and Hallelujah—The Living Jesus Christ: The Heart of Restoration and Easter," *Ensign* or *Liahona*, May 2020, 54.

86. *Teachings of the Presidents of the Church: Joseph Smith* (2007), 235.

I in a moment of weakness may cry out, "No one understands. No one knows." No human being, perhaps, knows. But the Son of God perfectly knows and understands, for He felt and bore our burdens before we ever did. And because He paid the ultimate price and bore that burden, He has perfect empathy and can extend to us His arm of mercy in so many phases of our life. He can reach out, touch, succor—literally run to us—and strengthen us to be more than we could ever be and help us to do that which we could never do through relying upon only our own power.[87]

87. David A. Bednar, "Strength beyond Our Own," *New Era,* Mar. 2015, 5.

6

Help and Hope for Coping with Personal Challenges

"Many are the afflictions of the righteous: but the Lord delivereth him out of them all."

—Psalm 34:19

God Provides Help for Personal Challenges

We live in a time of unusual challenges, and if we are not firmly rooted in our faith in Jesus Christ, personal trials can lead to discouragement and despair. It is through the gospel of Christ that we can experience hope and happiness. If we can look beyond our woes to the far-reaching eternities that extend beyond this brief moment in mortality, we will rejoice in the incomparable blessings we can receive.

God created this earth to allow us to have challenges—a necessary part of our mortal schooling—but He is eager to lift us up and direct our steps. His sincere desire is for us to receive a fullness of joy in the eternities to come. To this end, God provides numerous avenues of help, such as the scriptures to teach and inspire us, personal revelation to guide us, prayer to communicate with us, prophets to guide us, and covenants that arm us with spiritual power. Following are various strategies and techniques that can help us manage life's difficulties.

Widening Our Perspective

If we stand in front of an immense boulder, nothing would be visible except the hard, rocky surface. But stepping back allows us a wider perspective and enables us to see the sky, trees, bushes, and grass around it. During times of adversity, it's natural to focus on the pain, but standing too close to our suffering limits our ability to see. Taking a few steps back allows us to notice other things in our life that can bring comfort and happiness. Our perspective can either imprison or free us. If we choose to focus solely on the negative impact trials have on our life, we will suffer. However, if we do our best to focus on other blessings we have in life, we can be happier.

To create a wider perspective, we can ponder on God's love and the many blessings He bestows upon us. As we work to see mortality from a more eternal perspective, problems that once loomed so large can be reduced to a more manageable size. Rather than seeing life as a series of painful experiences, we can understand that mortality is a short-term experience that leads to a long-term existence that will be more splendid than anything we could imagine. By widening our perspective, we can understand that our time on earth is a pinprick on our eternal timeline.

During the Passover, the Savior spent time with His disciples despite knowing He would soon face betrayal, unjust imprisonment, cruel torture, and agonizing pain. Christ held a wider perspective, which allowed Him to tell his followers, shortly before He willingly submitted to the greatest suffering that has or ever will take place, "Peace I leave with you, my peace I give unto you. . . . Let not your heart be troubled, neither let it be afraid" (John 14:27).

Why did our Savior, who had so much to fear in the coming hours and days, feel compelled to reassure His disciples? Possibly this came because Jesus could see the wider eternal perspective of what would soon transpire. He wanted to reassure His disciples, who at that time could *not* see the long-term ramifications of the events that would soon transpire.

Instead of focusing on the immense suffering He would soon experience, Jesus took a few steps back, which allowed Him to view the wider perspective, which extended from the premortal world into eternity. As we stay close to Christ, He can gently pull us back from our boulder of pain to see beyond our present circumstances into the glorious blessings that await us in eternity.

Listen to Uplifting Music

Music has great power to lift our spirits, energize us, comfort our wounded heart, and offer sorely needed peace. President Monson said, "Music can help you draw closer to your Heavenly Father. It can be used to educate, edify, inspire, and unite."[88] Listening to uplifting music can invite the Spirit into our lives and protect us from Satan. When Saul was troubled with an evil spirit, David played his harp, which caused the evil spirit to depart and brought Saul comfort (see 1 Samuel 16:23).

Music has power to crowd out discouraging thoughts and fill our minds with more encouraging ones. Hymns are especially effective at helping us draw closer to God. President Nelson said, "Worthy music is powerful. It has the power to make us humble, prayerful, and grateful. . . . Music has power to provide spiritual nourishment. It has healing power. It has the power to facilitate worship. . . . It provides power for us to express prayerful thoughts and bear testimony of sacred truths."[89]

Music plays an important role in our physical and emotional well-being. Science has shown that music affects the autonomic nervous system, which regulates brain function, blood pressure, and heart rate. It also has a great impact on the limbic system, which affects our feelings and emotions. Researchers at Stanford University found that listening to music could change brain functioning to the same degree as taking medication.[90] Because music provides a unique link to our emotions, it can be used as an effective stress management

---

88. Thomas S. Monson, "The Lighthouse of the Lord," *Ensign,* Nov. 1990, 98.
89. Russell M. Nelson, "The Power and Protection of Worthy Music," *Ensign*, Dec. 2009, 14–16.
90. See Vanessa Van Edwards, "The Benefits of Music: How the Science of Music Can Help You," Science of People, accessed Nov. 10, 2023, https://www.scienceofpeople.com/benefits-music/.

tool. In addition, listening to music can improve our overall mood, lessen anxiety, ease pain, and produce a feeling of relaxation.

Eat Healthy Foods

Eating healthily can help improve our mood and overall mental health. "Food can affect the mind," stated President Benson. "In general, the more food we eat in its natural state—without additives—and the less it is refined, the healthier it will be for us."[91] Although many people crave sugary or high-fat foods when stressed, those foods are the least likely to benefit our mental state. Research in nutritional psychiatry, which studies the relationship between diet and mental health, suggests that microbes in the stomach and intestines produce neurotransmitters like serotonin and dopamine, which regulate our mood and emotions. Studies have found that people who eat a lot of nutrient-dense foods, such as vegetables, fruits, fish, eggs, beans, and nuts, report less depression and more feelings of happiness.[92]

To help us be healthier and happier, the Lord gave us the Word of Wisdom, which states that every herb and fruit in the season are to be used with prudence, and that the flesh of beasts and fowls are to be used sparingly. This revelation also states, "All grain is ordained for the use of man . . . to be the staff of life" (Doctrine and Covenants 89:14). Those who adhere to the Word of Wisdom are promised that they "shall receive health in their navel and marrow to their bones; And shall find wisdom and great treasures of knowledge. . . . And shall run and not be weary, and shall walk and not faint" (Doctrine and Covenants 89:18–20).

Eating wholesome food allows our bodies and minds to function efficiently while lowering our risk for disease and increasing longevity. We don't have to make drastic alterations in our diet when choosing to eat more healthily; making small changes can add up. To start slowly, try cutting out one sugary food a day, adding one vegetable a day, or drinking an extra glass of water. Keep energy-boosting snacks

91. Ezra Taft Benson, "Do Not Despair," *Ensign*, Nov. 1986, 66.

92. See Anahad O'Conner, "How Food May Improve Your Mood," *The New York Times*, last modified Dec. 21, 2021, https://www.nytimes.com/2021/05/06/well/eat/mental-health-food.html.

on hand instead of fatty or high-calorie snacks. Here are some other tips on healthy eating:

- **Increase the number of vegetables and fruits you eat.** This is a great start since fruits and vegetables are packed with important nutrients such as antioxidants, vitamins, minerals, and fiber. Fill half of your plate with fruits and vegetables at every meal.
- **Choose whole grain foods.** Whenever possible, pick whole grain bread and crackers, brown or wild rice, quinoa, and oatmeal instead of over-processed or refined grains such as white bread and pasta. Whole grain foods have fiber, protein, and B vitamins.
- **Eat protein.** Some important sources of protein are legumes, nuts, seeds, tofu, fish, eggs, poultry, and lean red meats. Dairy products such as yogurt and cheese are also a good source of protein.
- **Limit highly processed food.** Processed foods lack nutrients and often contain added salt and sugar. Limit fast foods, hot dogs, chips, cookies, frozen pizza, deli meat, and white rice.
- **Avoid sugary drinks.** This includes soda, energy drinks, fruit drinks, and fruit juice. Drink water instead.

Set Limits on News and Social Media

With the world in turmoil, it's hard to keep events in perspective if too much time is spent on social media or watching the news. Many Americans report that watching the news causes stress and anxiety. Research by Graham Davey, a professor emeritus of psychology at Sussex University, also showed that TV news produced sadness and anxiety. While staying aware is helpful, too much news can spell trouble.[93] Because of the unreliability of certain news sources and social media sites, our mental health can be improved by setting limits on how we spend our time. While it's important to stay informed, some

93. See Markham Heid, "You Asked: Is It Bad for You to Read the News Constantly?," *Time*, last modified May 19, 2020, https://time.com/5125894/is-reading-news-bad-for-you/.

news sources are intentionally skewed to be sensational in order to grab viewers' attention and get higher ratings.

While social media can be entertaining and informative, it can also be addictive and take time that could be better spent elsewhere. For some, social media is an emotional roller coaster of comparison and perfection. There is a tendency to see fun and perfection in everyone else's lives but not our own, making us feel that we are losing out on all the fun others are having or, worse, that we are not good enough. There can also be contentious dialogue and extreme viewpoints, which can be upsetting. One study from Guilford Press Periodicals showed that limiting social media to thirty minutes a day led to a general increase in mental health and well-being.[94]

It's hard to stop turning to our phones whenever we have a free moment, but once again, it can be helpful to find other activities that are more fulfilling. "Limit news and social media to 10 to 20 minutes per day," advises internist Erika Schwartz. "Instead, turn on healing music, read a book, watch comedies and romantic movies, or watch a documentary. And maybe you just limit watching TV, phone, or tablets to two hours a day maximum. Watch how much better you'll feel."[95]

One of the authors of this book, Joshua Sullivan, makes the following comment:

> The age of over-information has made it so that we are exposed a hundred-fold to other people's troubles and misfortune. There is a mental weight we carry when we hear about other people's trials. Social media is not inherently bad, but it can be negative for those who carry the mental weight of hearing bad news or who have warped expectations of what reality is. People who are sensitive may find that social media is full of extremes in life—the extreme good and the extreme bad. Being exposed to this can dull

94. See "8 Signs You Need to Take a Break from Social Media," Cleveland Clinic, Nov. 5, 2020, https://health.clevelandclinic.org/signs-you-need-to-take-a-break-from-social-media/.

95. Carina Wolff, "Life Feel Hard To Handle? Here's What Mental Health Experts Recommend," mindbodygreen, July 30, 2020, https://www.mindbodygreen.com/articles/tips-for-dealing-with-life-and-getting-through-hard-times.

our sensitivity to those around us in our "real lives" who need our care and compassion.

Feast On the Word of God

One way to fill our souls with hope in a world full of challenges is to spend time reading the word of God daily. Drawing closer to God through daily scripture reading and reading other good books can ground and center us, providing a calming influence.

In a memorable general conference talk, Elder Peter M. Johnson of the Seventy counseled, "Read and study the Book of Mormon every day, every day, every day. . . . The Prophet Joseph Smith spoke truth when he declared, 'The Book of Mormon [is] the most correct of any book on earth . . . and a man [or a woman will] get nearer to God by abiding by its precepts, than by any other book.'"[96]

Learning more of God by reading the scriptures gives us a spiritual uplift. We also have the inspired manual, *Come, Follow Me*, which is a focused, clear, and inspired study guide. Reading the Church magazines gives timely counsel, inspiration, and comfort from Church leaders and others. Reading other good books can teach us and enlighten our minds. Finding time to read can be difficult for those with busy lives, but making this a priority will bring blessings. Remember, how long you spend matters less than the consistency with which you read every day. Some people enjoy listening to the scriptures, the *Liahona*, conference talks, and podcasts while taking a walk, doing household chores, or simply relaxing. Taking time to feast on the word of God can deepen your faith and increase your spirituality.

Sleep Is Vital

Getting enough sleep is essential to good health because it enhances learning, helps you focus, and aids you to make better decisions. At night, your mind needs time to unwind and process the day's events. Sleeping supports healthy brain function, which helps your brain to work properly. When stressed, your body needs additional sleep.

---

96. Peter M. Johnson, "Power to Overcome the Adversary," *Ensign* or *Liahona*, Nov. 2019, 111–112.

Not getting enough sleep can lead to difficulty controlling your emotions and coping with change, and it can reduce your ability to solve problems. Having sufficient sleep also plays an important role in physical health by boosting your immune system. Sleep deficiency increases the risk of obesity, can cause you to take longer to finish tasks, and increases the number of mistakes you make.[97]

Ensuring you get enough sleep at night helps your brain and body function at maximum efficiency during the day. It is not easy to get enough quality sleep, but the following suggestions can improve your sleep habits:

- Establish a sleep routine by going to bed and waking up at the same time *every* day. Don't stay up late or sleep in on weekends because that disrupts your body's sleep cycle.
- Develop a regular routine before going to bed. An hour before bedtime, turn off some lights to signal your body that it's nearing bedtime. Avoid strenuous exercise and bright artificial light, such as from a TV, computer screen, tablet, or phone because this causes the brain to believe it needs to stay awake.
- Avoid eating a large meal within a few hours of going to bed.
- Try to be physically active during the day.
- Keep your bedroom quiet, cool, and dark.
- Daytime naps can be beneficial, but keep them short, no longer than thirty minutes.
- Melatonin is a hormone your body naturally produces that plays an important role in regulating your sleep-wake cycle. Taking melatonin as a supplement one to two hours before bedtime can promote your ability to sleep.

Smile More

If you want to be happier, smile—even when you don't feel like it. Studies have shown that smiling, even if you're not feeling happy, can improve your mood. The physical act of smiling signals your brain

97. See "What Are Sleep Deprivation and Deficiency?," NIH: National Heart, Lung, and Blood Institute, accessed Nov. 10, 2023, https://www.nhlbi.nih.gov/health/sleep-deprivation.

that you *are* happy and stimulates good feelings. Smiling creates positive feelings, which will make you—and others around you—happier. Trying to smile more can even change the way you think and give you more energy. We often think of smiling as an involuntary response, but smiling can also be a conscious choice.

Whether your smile is genuine or not, it affects your body and mind in positive ways. How? Smiling triggers the release of neuropeptides such as dopamine, endorphins, and serotonin, which are sent to your brain and boost your mood. If you smile, even when you don't feel like it, you are influencing your brain to release natural chemicals that will make you feel happier.[98]

Smiling also boosts your immune system. When you smile, your body releases neurotransmitters, which make you feel more relaxed, and feeling calmer helps your immune system function better. In addition, smiling may also lower your blood pressure and temporarily reduce pain because of the natural chemicals that are released when you smile.[99]

Exercise Is Vital to Mental and Physical Health

Exercise is one of the best things you can do to be physically and mentally healthy. Everyone, no matter their age, ability, or size, can benefit from being physically active. The best part is you can choose the type of exercise that interests you and adjust the intensity of your activity to your personal level. When you exercise, various chemicals are released in your body that work to improve your mood, lower your stress level, and fight depression and anxiety. This occurs because physical activity causes your brain's hypothalamus and pituitary gland to discharge endorphins into your body, which create and promote general feelings of well-being.[100]

---

98. See Mark Stibich, "10 Big Benefits of Smiling: Choose to smile every day to boost mood and health," Verywell Mind, last modified Feb. 17, 2023, https://www.verywellmind.com/top-reasons-to-smile-every-day-2223755.

99. See Mark Stibich, "10 Big Benefits of Smiling."

100. See "Exercise: 7 benefits of regular physical activity," Mayo Clinic, Aug. 26, 2023, https://www.mayoclinic.org/healthy-lifestyle/fitness/in-depth/exercise/art-20048389.

Physical activity can also calm anxiety and improve brain health. Studies show that after a session of moderate to vigorous physical activity, short-term feelings of anxiety were reduced. The Center for Disease Control and Prevention (CDC) states, "Regular physical activity can help keep your thinking, learning, and judgment skills sharp as you age."[101] Exercise also lowers and can prevent many health conditions, such as high blood pressure, arthritis, various types of cancer, anxiety, type 2 diabetes, stroke, and depression. In addition, exercise can help you control your weight. Exercising also builds muscle strength, which helps the cardiovascular system work more efficiently. Exercise also helps you fall asleep faster and sleep better at night.

Become more physically active by engaging in activities you enjoy, such as playing racquetball, pickleball, or volleyball or going rock climbing. You might want to go hiking, bike riding, ice skating, or swimming with your family. You can take up jogging, take your dog for a walk, or work out at the gym. Yoga can quiet your mind while keeping your body limber.

Exercise is most beneficial if you work out three to five times a week for at least thirty minutes, but check with your doctor before starting any new exercise routine. Also, when setting personal goals, aim for consistency rather than endurance. Many people enjoy listening to audiobooks, podcasts, or music while exercising. Simple actions can help you become more physically fit. Try parking a distance away from the store, taking the stairs instead of the elevator, or ramping up your yard work and household chores.

Strive to Have a Positive Attitude

Part of being happy in today's world involves having a more optimistic attitude. The hymn "You Can Make the Pathway Bright" tells us we can be happy even in difficult circumstances: "You can live a happy life / In this world of toil and strife, / If there's sunshine in your heart."[102]

101. "Benefits of Physical Activity," CDC: Centers for Disease Control and Prevention, accessed Nov. 10, 2023, https://www.cdc.gov/physicalactivity/basics/pa-health/index.htm#brain-health.

102. "You Can Make the Pathway Bright," *Hymns*, no. 228.

Being more upbeat is an art we can cultivate with time. The first step is realizing that our emotions do not have to take a nosedive whenever we encounter problems. We can adopt a positive attitude irrespective of outside events. In other words, *what* happens to us is not as important as *how* we react. Everyone has the power to control their thoughts, actions, and reactions, but it does take mindfulness, work, and, most of all, practice. Often when we encounter an unhappy or stressful situation, we focus on how upset, angry, or miserable we feel, which does us no good at all. Instead, we must change the way we think.

One technique to creating a more positive attitude is to replace negative thoughts with positive ones. This is important because thoughts are powerful and frame our reality. For example, if you are driving to a doctor's appointment and get stuck in traffic, it's easy (and normal) to start stressing. Negative thoughts may pop up, like "This *always* happens to me" or "I'm going to be so late that the doctor won't be able to see me." Reframe those thoughts to more encouraging ones such as "This doesn't happen very often," "Things will work out," or "Even if I'm late, I'm sure the doctor will work me in." Consciously pushing aside upsetting thoughts and reframing them into something more positive will improve your mood and help you start to develop a more positive attitude.

Another technique when upset is to repeat a short positive statement, which is often called a mantra, replacing your gloomy thought with a happier one. Our brain is made in such a way that only one thought can be fully present at a time, and mantras work by changing our thoughts, which then improves our feelings. President Packer stated, "Did you know that every time you think a good thought, there is no room for a bad one? To know this is of significant worth. Our minds may switch from one thought to another very quickly; nevertheless, there is only a single circuit—only one thought is processed at a time. . . . It is important that we know this because then we can give priority to significant and important thoughts."[103]

103. Boyd K. Packer, *That All May Be Edified* (Salt Lake City, UT: Bookcraft, 1982), 35.

Mantras are an easy way to push out discouraging thoughts and instill positive ones. One common way Church leaders have recommended to crowd out and stop negative thoughts is to think of the words of your favorite hymn. It's normal to have to repeat your affirmation many times before it kicks in, so don't be discouraged—eventually the message will start to sink in. Be prepared ahead of time with helpful statements to repeat in your mind when negative thoughts arise. Following are some positive mantras. Change the wording if desired to make them your own.

- I will remain happy and calm.
- Heavenly Father loves me, and I can feel His comforting Spirit.
- I may not be able to control what happens, but I can control how I will react.
- God will bless me with comfort and peace.
- I am strong and resilient.
- I can overcome this and be happy.
- I will only have good thoughts because they create my future.
- I am strong and capable.
- God loves me and knows I am a good person.
- Heavenly Father knows what is happening and is here with me.
- Depart from me, Satan. I will have nothing to do with you.
- Go away, Satan. I will only follow Jesus Christ
- I am thankful for the many blessings I do have.
- I know God hears my prayers and that He will bless me.

Visualization and Relaxation

Visualization is a powerful cognitive process that allows you to picture, create, and bring about worthwhile objectives. It has been in existence since the beginning of time. The earth was created spiritually before it was formed physically. "For I, the Lord God, created all things, of which I have spoken, spiritually, before they were naturally upon the face of the earth" (Moses 3:5).

Using visualization can lower your stress level and give comfort in times of sorrow. One helpful visualization is to picture yourself in a beautiful room talking to Jesus Christ, who listens intently as you pour out your feelings. Picture Him asking you questions and offering loving and wise counsel.

Another visualization when having conflicts with another person is to picture yourself standing strong and remaining peaceful even when that person speaks harshly in anger or is unfairly critical.

If you are far from home and feel lonely, imagine yourself in a beautiful place surrounded by family and friends who show their love for you.

If you have recently lost your spouse, you might picture him or her returning to visit. Sit and talk with them, basking in their love.

In times of trouble, you might want to picture yourself going to a beautiful, brightly lit location where you feel peace and love and know that everything will be alright.

When you long for tranquility, the simplest visualization is to picture yourself in what some people call their "happy place." Think of a beautiful place that brings you peace. It might be an idyllic spot you visited on vacation, or sitting on a lovely beach watching the waves roll in. You might picture yourself hiking through a leafy green forest, relaxing on the grassy bank of a rippling stream, riding a horse along a picturesque trail, or standing high on a mountaintop looking over the sunny countryside. Feel the beauty of your surroundings and let peace fill your heart.

You can also use visualization to rid yourself of negative feelings. To do this, picture yourself putting whatever negative emotions you want to get rid of (hurt, anger, bitterness, hate, jealousy, etc.) into a burlap bag. Then see yourself digging a deep hole in the ground. Place the bag inside and cover it with dirt. Take a moment to pray and ask Heavenly Father to bless you to leave those negative feelings buried. Feel peace, serenity, and tranquility fill your mind and heart.

Relaxation is a physical process that can help reduce stress, anxiety, and sadness. Learn more about specific relaxation techniques online or try the following quick, easy-to-follow exercise.

First, relax your body. It helps to know how relaxed muscles feel, so first tighten and then relax various muscles in your body. Start by tightening your face, neck, and jaw muscles for 3–7 seconds, then consciously relax those muscles. Notice how much better it feels when your muscles are relaxed. Next, tense your arms. As you relax, notice the difference in the way it feels. Proceed with tightening then relaxing your hands, stomach, legs, and feet.

While tensing and relaxing, focus on your breathing. Take long, slow breaths and exhale slowly through your mouth. Think about how good and relaxing it is to relax your muscles.

Next, take a deep breath, and when you exhale, imagine you are blowing all of your sadness, anxiety, or hurt into a balloon. Take another breath or two and exhale until you have filled the balloon. As you blow out, feel the negative emotions moving out of your body and into the balloon.

When the balloon is full, picture yourself sealing it. Then release the balloon and watch it rise and go far, far away from you, carrying away your sadness, fear, or stress.

Seek Counseling

There are times in everyone's life when they feel overwhelmed. It may be sorrow at the death of a loved one, loss of a job, divorce, anxiety, addiction, mental illness, depression, relationship difficulties, anger issues, or a host of other problems. Nearly everyone can benefit from the skilled care of a trained therapist, who can teach coping techniques and assist in reprogramming the way you see yourself, others, and the world.

Some people hesitate to see a therapist for various reasons, but there are innumerable benefits. Elder Holland counseled:

> If things continue to be debilitating, seek the advice of reputable people with certified training, professional skills, and good values. Be honest with them about your history and your struggles. Prayerfully and responsibly consider the counsel they give and the solutions they prescribe. If you had appendicitis, God would expect you to seek a priesthood blessing *and* get the best medical care available. So too with emotional disorders. Our Father in Heaven expects us to use *all* of the marvelous gifts He has provided in this glorious dispensation.[104]

104. Jeffrey R. Holland, "Like a Broken Vessel," *Ensign* or *Liahona,* Nov. 2013, 41.

A few people view therapy the same way they do a fire alarm—to be used only in case of emergency. But therapy should never be reserved just for dark moments; it's for *preventing* dark moments. Counseling is for overall well-being. There is no need to wade through the swamp by yourself until you become well and truly stuck. Counseling can be a great source of strength and support for any kind of problem—a place where you learn important and necessary skills. A trained therapist can help you see your problems in a new light and teach ways of managing your difficulties.

Some people avoid counseling because they fear it will be too expensive. If this is a worry, first check with your insurance to see what they will cover. Some people turn to their parents for monetary assistance. Your bishop might be able to recommend highly-rated counselors who charge on a sliding scale. A less expensive alternative is group counseling, which can be extremely helpful. There are many groups tailored to specific needs, such as depression, abuse, divorce, and so on. Some focus on physical illnesses, such as diabetes, amputation, or breast cancer. Other groups provide support for divorced fathers, suicide survivors, battered women, those who have lost a spouse or a child, and so on.

Humor Helps

Humor can be one of your most valuable coping skills because it lightens burdens, connects you to others, and keeps you grounded. A good laugh can go a long way. One of the best benefits is that it cultivates and nurtures optimism. Although it is difficult to be lighthearted when facing serious problems, seeing the humor in them can lessen stress. Laughter shifts your perspective, allowing you to see things from a different angle, often in a more realistic and less threatening light. Laughter also boosts your mood because you can't feel anxious, angry, or sad when you're laughing. Kendra Cherry, an educational consultant, says, "Sometimes, simply recognizing the potential humor in a situation can lessen your stress and brighten your outlook. . . .

Learning to think positively is like strengthening a muscle; the more you use it, the stronger it will become."[105]

When you laugh, endorphins are released into your body, which naturally elevate your mood. A group of researchers, led by Lee Berk and Stanley Tan at Loma Linda University in California, found that two hormones—beta-endorphins, which alleviate depression, and human growth hormone (HGH), which helps boost immunity—increased by 27 percent and 87 percent respectively when volunteers expected to watch a humorous video. Simply *anticipating* they would laugh boosted the volunteers' health-protecting hormones and chemicals.[106]

Since the mind and body are fundamentally connected, it comes as no surprise that humor also has physical benefits. For one thing, humor protects the heart by decreasing a person's heart rate and blood pressure while improving the function of blood vessels. Dr. Mehmet Oz, a heart surgeon in New York City, explains, "When you push any engine, including your body, to its maximum, every once in a while, it slips a gear. The ways the body manifests that are irregular heartbeats, high blood pressure, and increased sensitivity to pain. When people use humor, the autonomic nervous system just tones down a bit to take it off high gear, and that allows the heart to relax."[107]

Humor also gives the immune system a boost by lowering stress hormones while increasing immune cells and infection-fighting antibodies. Biophysical studies show that laughter increases the movement of lymphatic fluid through your body, which cleanses your system and results in better immunity from all diseases. Lee Berk of the Loma Linda School of Medicine said, "For the most part, when you go and get medical treatment, a clinician is not necessarily going to tell you to take two aspirin and watch Laurel and Hardy, but the reality is that's

105. Kendra Cherry, "How to Think Positive," Verywell Mind, last modified Apr. 28, 2021, https://www.verywellmind.com/think-positive-2794771.

106. See "Anticipating A Laugh Reduces Our Stress Hormones, Study Shows," Science News, Apr. 10, 2008, https://www.sciencedaily.com/releases/2008/04/080407114617.htm.

107. Therese J. Borchard, "9 Ways Humor Heals," Huffpost, last modified Nov. 17, 2011, https://www.huffpost.com/entry/9-ways-humor-heals_b_165383.

where we are and it's more real than ever. There's a real science to this. And it's as real as taking a drug."[108]

Ask for Priesthood Blessings

Priesthood blessings are given through the authority of the priesthood. There are many different types of priesthood blessings, such as when a child is born, when receiving a church calling, patriarchal blessings, father's blessings, and blessings that are given for comfort, guidance, and spiritual strength.

Another type is a blessing of healing, which is to help a person overcome mental or physical illness or injury. These blessings are given by the laying on of hands by two men who hold the Melchizedek Priesthood. Typically, one man anoints the person with consecrated oil and the other seals the anointing and pronounces the blessing. However, one man can do it if no one else is available.

Those who receive a priesthood blessing for healing should have faith they can be healed if it is expedient in Christ. If the person receiving the blessing is not healed, loved ones must accept God's will and await the miracle of the Resurrection. While God honors priesthood blessings, those receiving them still need to seek and follow competent professional care for whatever physical or mental health challenges they face.

When a person needs guidance, comfort, or counsel, or is striving to overcome various types of adversity, they can ask for a priesthood blessing. President Oaks said, "Do not be hesitant to ask for a priesthood blessing when you are in need of spiritual power."[109]

It's Okay to Cry

Sometimes a person just needs to cry. There is no need to feel bad if you shed a few tears over your problems. Crying does not mean you're weak, and it doesn't mean you're having a pity party. It

108. Lee Berk, quoted in Sebastian Gendry, "Why Laughter Is Good for the Immune System, Opens Inner Cellular Pharmacy," Laughter Online University, accessed Nov. 10, 2023, https://www.laughteronlineuniversity.com/laughter-immune-system/.

109. Dallin H. Oaks, "Priesthood Blessings," *Ensign*, May 1987, 39.

means you need to let some of the stress and sadness out, and that's okay. Tears contain the mood-regulating chemical manganese, which soothes you when you're sad. Studies have shown that crying can help a person feel better. Why? Because emotional tears releases oxytocin and endorphins—chemicals that improve a person's mood and sense of well-being while decreasing emotional pain.[110]

"Crying activates the body in a healthy way," says Dr. Stephen Sideroff, a clinical psychologist at UCLA. "Letting down one's guard and one's defenses and [crying] is a very positive, healthy thing. The same thing happens when you watch a movie and it touches you and you cry. . . . That process of opening into yourself . . . it's like a lock and key." Sideroff adds that stress "tightens muscles and heightens tension, so when you cry you release some of that. [Crying also] activates the parasympathetic nervous system and restores the body to a state of balance."[111]

Be Slow to Anger

When our lives are harmed because of another person, pain results. This pain can turn into anger—like anger at an unfaithful spouse, a drunk driver whose carelessness left your teenager paralyzed, or the person who left the gate open to your apartment's pool, leading to your child's drowning. Such anger is understandable and can even feel good because it can dull the pain, which would otherwise be too relentless and overpowering as we muddle through the first days of shock and disbelief.

Satan knows how destructive anger can be and will feed our anger, insisting we have every right to be angry. He knows that anger acts as poison upon the soul and that it erodes a person from the inside out. Satan is fully aware that harboring anger ensures that someone else owns a piece of our soul.

110. See Leo Newhouse, "Is Crying Good for You?," Harvard Health Publishing, Mar. 1, 2021, https://www.health.harvard.edu/blog/is-crying-good-for-you-2021030122020.

111. Serusha Govender, "Is Crying Good for You?," WebMD, accessed Nov. 10, 2023, https://www.webmd.com/balance/features/is-crying-good-for-you.

Because anger is a powerful emotion and can be destructive, we are counseled to control and rise above it. "He that is slow to anger is better than the mighty; and he that ruleth his spirit than he that taketh a city" (Proverbs 16:32).

Anger can be damaging not only spiritually but also physically. When we become angry, two chemicals—cortisol and adrenaline—are released into our bodies, which weakens the immune system, causes muscles to tense, and accelerates heart rate. These chemicals can also damage the judgment area of neurons in the brain and override our better judgment, causing us to act in ways detrimental to our well-being.[112] It's not easy to overcome anger, especially when someone has damaged our life or the life of a loved one, but we must work hard to conquer our anger. It is vital to our happiness and peace to learn how to overcome anger. The following suggestions can help.

Ask God for Help

One of the most effective ways of managing anger is to ask God for strength to control it. Heavenly Father has the power to change and soften our hearts and will bless us with patience and understanding, which can minimize and even take away anger. Elder Gordon T. Watts said, "Prayer is a powerful weapon through which anger and contention can be 'done away.' Blessed are those who, when stirred to anger, engage in silent prayer, thus making themselves more receptive to the guidance of the Spirit."[113]

Do Something Physical

Anger produces a lot of energy, which stays inside the body for some time. These chemicals gradually dissipate, but it is helpful to get these troubling chemicals out of your body quickly. Use your extra energy to do something constructive: scrub the floor, clean the shower, exercise, weed the yard, or fix that broken gate. Even fifteen

---

112. See Melinda Ratini, "How Can Anger Hurt My Heart?," MedicineNet, accessed Nov. 10, 2023, https://www.medicinenet.com/how_can_anger_hurt_my_heart/article.htm.

113. Gordon T. Watts, "Slow to Anger," *Ensign,* Feb. 2003, 62.

to twenty minutes of being physically active will help clear your mind and reduce your anger.

Communicate

Anger can be lessened, and even removed, by remaining calm and talking with the person with whom we are angry and finding out more about the situation. Too often we refuse to talk with those we are angry with, which eliminates any chance of working things out. If possible, speak to the person face to face. *Always* avoid texting, emailing, or using social media, which contain no body language or voice inflections to help discern the other person's feelings and so can easily inflame emotions rather than soothe them. If meeting in person is not possible, use an app like Zoom or Facetime that will allow you to see each other. If that isn't possible, then call. Stay calm when talking. Do not attack, but explain how their words or actions made you feel. Then listen carefully and empathetically to their response.

Take an Anger Management Class

Anger is very prevalent in our complicated world, and many people benefit from taking anger management classes. The instructor helps class members gain a better understanding of their emotions, teaches how to handle anger in more productive ways, and helps people learn how to interact with others in a more positive way. You'll learn tips and techniques for avoiding anger and learn how to act when in volatile situations.

Hold Your Peace

When the Savior was arrested, He was mocked, spit upon, ridiculed, and slapped. When the high priest Caiaphas asked Jesus what He had to say about the "witnesses" who had spewed false and despicable accusations against him, the scriptures state, "Jesus held his peace" (Matthew 26:63). Instead of railing against the injustice of the proceedings, the physical abuse, and the false testimonies, Jesus did not censure or denounce those who disparaged Him. Instead, He remained calm and held His peace. We learn from this that we need not react angrily but can stay calm and avoid contention.

Do Not Vent Your Anger

It is commonly believed that venting your anger is a good way to "let off steam," but it usually has the opposite effect. After venting, a person most often finds themselves angrier than before. Venting makes a person feel justified in the way they feel, which increases anger. Venting is like lighting a match to a bonfire. Some older self-help books recommend pounding a pillow, screaming when alone, or throwing rocks at a tree as ways of releasing anger, but these actions can increase aggressive behavior and almost guarantee that you will feel worse.[114]

Controlling anger leads to greater personal happiness. President Hinckley counseled:

> I plead with you to control your tempers, to put a smile upon your faces, which will erase anger; speak out with words of love and peace, appreciation, and respect. If you will do this . . . your marriages and family relationships will be preserved. You will be much happier. You will do greater good. You will feel a sense of peace that will be wonderful. May the Lord bless you and inspire you to walk without anger, without bitterness of any kind, but to reach out to others with . . . appreciation and love.[115]

Forgiveness Is Essential

Forgiveness is the antidote to anger's poison, but it can be difficult to forgive when we have been hurt deeply. Feelings of bitterness and anger can overwhelm us, especially if we feel that our hurt was undeserved. To liberate us from pain and help us move forward, we must forgive. Fortunately, we do not have to do this on our own. When wounded by others, the Savior will help us forgive. Elder Ulisses Soares assures that we can receive help "by inviting our Savior to help us to replace our stony hearts with new hearts." He explains:

---

114. See Amy Morin, "11 Anger Management Strategies to Help You Calm Down," Verywell Mind, last modified Nov. 2, 2023, https://www.verywellmind.com/anger-management-strategies-4178870.

115. Gordon B. Hinckley, "Slow to Anger," *Ensign* or *Liahona,* Nov. 2007, 66.

> For this to happen, we need to come before the Lord with our weaknesses and implore His help and forgiveness, especially during the sacred moment when we partake of the sacrament each Sunday. May we choose to seek His help and take an important and difficult step by forgiving those who have hurt us so that our wounds may begin to heal. I promise you that in your doing so, your nights will be full of the relief that comes from a mind at peace with the Lord.[116]

When we forgive, we give up our perceived right to judge another person and turn it over to Jesus Christ, who will judge the world with mercy and justice. Our only job—and it is not an easy one—is to forgive and trust the Savior to do His job. Forgiveness can be more difficult when the offender does not apologize or even acknowledge the hurt they caused. President Kimball spoke of this: "Remember that we must forgive even if our offender did not repent and ask forgiveness. . . . Do we follow that commandment or do we sulk in our bitterness, waiting for our offender to learn of it and to kneel to us in remorse?"[117]

Marlene Bateman Sullivan, one of this book's authors, shares the following experience:

> Many years ago, someone did something cruel to me, which hurt me profoundly. Although this person knew I was devastated, they did not try to explain their behavior nor apologize. Pain gave way to anger, and soon my feelings hardened. I began to feel I had been treated so unjustly that I had a right to be angry. And yet I was miserable. One day, I was reading in Matthew where it talks about how the body can be full of darkness (see Matthew 6:22–23). I realized that even though this person had treated me harshly, *I* was the one stuck in darkness. I had to choose between staying in darkness or forgiving.
>
> Knowing I couldn't forgive without divine assistance, I prayed that Heavenly Father would help me let go of my anger. Days passed, and the pain and anger remained. I continued praying and studying the scriptures. Gradually, bits of inspiration came to me,

116. Ulisses Soares, "Take Up Our Cross," *Ensign* or *Liahona*, Nov. 2019, 115.
117. Spencer W. Kimball, in Conference Report, Oct. 1949, 132.

> chipping away at the bitterness. At times, I felt Satan stirring me up to anger, but in the coming days, I received a few more drops of inspiration. I was blessed to realize it was fruitless to hold on to my anger because I could not undo what had been done. I also came to understand I had no control over this person or their actions—I only had control over myself. Although it took what seemed to me an unreasonably long time to forgive, as I continued to pray, read the scriptures, and follow Christ, I was strengthened to finally forgive this person.

Without forgiveness, there can be no inner peace—only anger, hurt, and bitterness, which saps our life energy. As imperfect beings, we may not be able to stop waves of anger from crashing over us from time to time, but we can choose whether we will *remain* angry. When we forgive, we are refusing to be held hostage by negative feelings that come from those who have harmed us.

We must keep in mind that forgiving is not pardoning bad behavior; it is about letting our negative feelings go so that peace and happiness can be ours once more. Although we are to forgive those who hurt us, there are certain times, such as in cases of abuse, when we are justified in establishing boundaries to prevent further injury. In such situations, we must understand that forgiveness doesn't mean we condone the abuse. Neither do we allow perpetrators to further mistreat us or our loved ones. We can forgive but still maintain boundaries to protect ourselves and our loved ones.

As we forgive those who have injured us, our burdens will be lifted and our wounds cleansed so we can be healed, bringing peace to our soul. President Packer spoke of this:

> The first thing a doctor does with a wound is to clean it out. He gets rid of all foreign matter and drains off infection—however much it hurts.
>
> Once you do that spiritually, you will have a different perspective. . . .
>
> And that is my counsel to you. . . . You may not be able to control things out there with others, but you can control things here, inside of you. . . .

> You may need a transfusion of spiritual strength to be able to do this. Then just ask for it. We call that prayer. Prayer is powerful, spiritual medicine. . . .
>
> All of us carry excess baggage around from time to time, but the wisest ones among us don't carry it for very long. They get rid of it. . . .
>
> We call that forgiveness. It is powerful, spiritual medicine.[118]

Developing Our Divine Potential

All of us experience various challenges in life—some large and some small. Some may forever alter our lives, but we have the potential to grow from them. Those who have a beloved child leave for college, go on a mission, join the military, or depart for other new and exciting adventures have tender feelings and do all they can to ensure their child has a good experience while away from home. Parents hope their child will remember what they were taught and that they will choose the right, learn, grow, and be happy. And even though the child is no longer with them, parents will stay in close communication, talking and listening to them, offering advice, and doing anything they can to help.

When you and I left our heavenly home and came to earth, Heavenly Father had tender feelings at our departure. Because God loves us, He wants us to choose the right, learn important lessons, and be happy. He will do everything He can to help and stays in close contact with us, listening when we pray and giving us counsel. Most of all, Heavenly Father wants us to develop our divine potential, for that is one of the reasons He created this earth. He allows opposition so we can cultivate godly virtues. When beset with tribulation, God may not take away our hardships, but instead, He gives us strength to rise above them, patience to endure them, and wisdom to know how to get through them. God's love for us is never-ending, and as His children, we can be assured that our Father will do all He can to help us reach our potential and receive a fulness of joy.

We were put on earth to develop our divine potential, and our circumstances can mold us into becoming more like God. Our

118. Boyd K. Packer, "The Balm of Gilead," *Ensign,* Nov. 1977, 59–61.

progress may come so slowly and imperceptibly that we may not see our growth, but God does. The plan of happiness was developed to stretch, shape, and refine us, and if we absorb our lessons, we will emerge from mortality as a better person. Elder Andersen said, "Like the intense fire that transforms iron into steel, as we remain faithful during the fiery trial of our faith, we are spiritually refined and strengthened."[119] The opposition we face on earth provides opportunities for spiritual growth. As we become more holy and pure, we will be able to return home where Heavenly Father is waiting to enfold us in a loving embrace.

119. Neil L. Andersen, "Trial of Your Faith," *Ensign* or *Liahona*, Nov. 2012, 42.

7

Hope Originates in Christ, the Master Healer

"Truly my soul waiteth upon God: from him cometh my salvation. He only is my rock and my salvation; he is my defence: I shall not be greatly moved. . . . In God is my salvation and my glory: the rock of my strength, and my refuge, is in God. Trust in him at all times; ye people, pour out your heart before him: God is a refuge for us."

—Psalm 62:1–2, 7–8

Christ: The Master Healer

One of the purposes of the Atonement of Jesus Christ is to provide healing to those who are wounded. When we are shattered, our Savior can restore what we cannot repair. Christ can heal the wound we cannot mend and fix that which has been broken. Our Savior is an ever-present help in time of need, and as we yoke ourselves to Him, our burdens will be made light. Because Christ has the power to lift us up through any misery we experience, He can be called the Master Healer.

Christ's ministry was all about healing. While on earth, Christ blessed those who were physically, emotionally, or spiritually afflicted. "And I beheld multitudes of people who were sick, and who were afflicted with all manner of diseases. . . . And they were healed by the power of the Lamb of God" (1 Nephi 11:31). Hope comes in knowing that Christ will carry us through our afflictions (see Isaiah 53:4).

After His death and Resurrection, Jesus Christ appeared to the Nephites. When it was time for Him to go, the people yearned for Him to stay but dared not ask. Jesus discerned their thoughts, and showing great love and compassion, He asked, "Have ye any that are sick among you? Bring them hither. Have ye any that are lame, or blind, or halt, or maimed, or leprous, or that are withered, or that are deaf, or that are afflicted in any manner? Bring them hither and I will heal them" (3 Nephi 17:7). He caused the blind to see, the deaf to hear, and the palsied, withered, and maimed to be restored. He cleansed lepers and cast out unclean spirits (see Matthew 14:36; 15:28; Mark 6:56; 10:52; Luke 17:19; John 5:9). Jesus, the Master Healer, set no limits on His healing. He did not reserve healing for only the rich, those of a certain age, or those who had only physical ailments. He healed them *all.* Jesus "did heal them *every one* as they were brought forth unto him" (3 Nephi 17:9; emphasis added).

Myriad and great are the trials we suffer on earth. However, Christ stands ever ready to help, even when we're facing devastating trials that cut through to the heart—when facing an inoperable brain tumor, discovering that our spouse has been unfaithful, or being greeted by police officers who have come to tell us that our teenager has been struck and killed by a car. All of us suffer in diverse ways, but the ultimate source of relief is the same: Jesus Christ.

Although heartache and challenges have proliferated since the beginning of time, the current dispensation surely carries some of the most challenging conditions humanity has ever faced. There is daily unrest from political upheaval, social turmoil, and personal challenges. Much of the chaos of our day comes from Satan, who has a great hold upon the world and stirs up the hearts of men to cause much suffering. We live in frightening times, and to survive, we need the strength we can receive from God. President Nelson said, "There has never been a time in the history of the world when knowledge of our Savior is more personally vital and relevant to *every human soul.*"[120]

120. Russell M. Nelson, "Pure Truth, Pure Doctrine, and Pure Revelation," *Liahona*, Nov. 2021, 6; emphasis in original.

Heavenly Father knew we would face turbulent times, and to help us, He gives us direction through prophets, the scriptures, and personal revelation. He offers us the opportunity to make covenants that will bind us to Him and provide us with power to overcome the adversary. We can counsel with Him in daily prayer. God can aid us to withstand temptation and master our souls as we strive to become more obedient and worthy. We are not left to struggle on our own. Though we have challenges in life—sometimes extremely difficult ones—faith in God helps us move forward. President Nelson said that a belief in Deity can help people "rise from the ashes of our lives and become the men and women we were sent to earth to become. Financial stress, ill health, fractured relationships and dreams, personal loss, unfairness at the hands of conspiring men and women—each of these can fill our hearts with anxiety and fear. But it is my conviction that our Savior can strengthen and enable us to reach our highest highs and be able to cope with our lowest lows."[121]

We know from reading the scriptures that the world is not going to glide along calmly toward the Second Coming. There is an ever-increasing darkness that surrounds us, but that blackness only serves to make the light of Christ brighter and more precious. As the light of the world, Christ can bless us with His light and ease our burdens. As we strive to keep God's commandments, repent, and learn line upon line, we gather light into our souls. The Savior possesses the healing balm to salve every wound, right every wrong, correct every imperfection, repair every injury, and dispense every blessing in the next life that we did not receive on earth.

One of our daily tasks is to make a sincere effort to draw nearer to the Lord. And when life doesn't turn out the way we'd hoped, we can focus *upon* and trust *in* Jesus. Hope comes because of the loving kindness of Heavenly Father and the marvelous goodness of Jesus Christ and His infinite Atonement. Both of Them will strengthen us to endure whatever comes our way.

---

121. David Noyce, "President Russell Nelson says belief in God is 'pre-eminent force for good,' urges Latter-day Saints to boost faith at home," *The Salt Lake Tribune*, Feb. 10, 2019, https://www.sltrib.com/religion/2019/02/10/belief-god-is-pre-eminent/.

For This Cause Came Christ into the World

As the Savior knelt in the Garden of Gethsemane and felt the awful weight of the approaching Atonement, He acknowledged, "For *this cause* came I into the world" (John 18:37; emphasis added).

What was "this cause"? To break the bands of death and bring about the miracle of the Resurrection, to take our sins upon Himself and atone for them, and to learn from personal experience how we feel when suffering so He could succor us in our trials.

The Book of Mormon describes Jesus's Atonement as an "infinite atonement" (Alma 34:12). What we may not realize is that an infinite Atonement requires infinite suffering. While in the Garden of Gethsemane, Jesus did not merely kneel down; He "*fell* on the ground" (Mark 14:35; emphasis added). The pain was so unbearable that Jesus Christ—the Son of God—*collapsed* and bled at every pore (see Doctrine and Covenants 19:18). Because of the intensity of His suffering, Jesus became "sore amazed" and "very heavy" (Mark 14:33), words which in Greek mean "astonished and awestruck" and "depressed and dejected." King Benjamin declared that Jesus's anguish was "more than man can suffer" (Mosiah 3:7). Christ's physical and spiritual anguish produced such enormous pain that an angel was sent to strengthen Him (see Luke 22:43).

Christ said his suffering caused Him "to suffer both body and spirit—and would that I might not drink the bitter cup and shrink" (Doctrine and Covenants 19:18). However, Christ did not shrink—He fulfilled His mission. As we deal with our own lesser trials, we can follow Christ's example and pray for the strength to endure. Partaking of our bitter cup without becoming bitter is one way we can emulate Christ. In the hymn "Reverently and Meekly Now," the poignancy of Christ's sacrifice is portrayed:

> Think of me, thou ransomed one; Think what I for thee have done.
> With my blood that dripped like rain, Sweat in agony of pain,
> With my body on the tree, I have ransomed even thee.

And in the last verse, it says, "And be constant unto me / That thy Savior I may be."[122]

As we ponder on the words "That thy Savior I *may* be," we realize that Jesus is gently asking *permission* to be our Redeemer. In essence, He is tenderly inquiring if we will *permit* Him to be our Savior. It is striking to think that even in such weighty matters, Christ allows us our agency to choose if we *want* Him to be our Savior. Christ will not use coercion. He allows us to freely choose.

We need never wonder if Christ knows how we feel, for after suffering more in the flesh than we can possibly imagine, He knows perfectly the depth and breadth of our pain. The grim physical agonies Jesus Christ bore in Gethsemane allowed Him to take upon Himself all of our hurts, illnesses, injustices, and suffering in order to understand our pain and know best how to succor us. President Henry B. Eyring taught, "It will comfort us when we must wait in distress for the Savior's promised relief that He knows, from experience, how to heal and help us. . . . And faith in that power will give us patience as we pray and work and wait for help. He could have known how to succor us simply by revelation, but He *chose to learn by His own personal experience.*"[123]

Christ not only suffered for the things we do wrong but also for the painful things that happen *to* us—things over which we have no control. "And he shall go forth, suffering pains and afflictions and temptations of every kind; and this that the word might be fulfilled which saith he will take upon him the pains and the sicknesses of his people. . . . And he will take upon him their infirmities, that his bowels may be filled with mercy, according to the flesh, that he may know according to the flesh how to succor his people according to their infirmities" (Alma 7:11–12).

It's interesting to note that in the verses above, nowhere is the word *sin* mentioned. Instead, pay attention to the *other* factors Jesus took upon Him: pains, afflictions, temptations, sicknesses, and infirmities.

---

122. "Reverently and Meekly Now," *Hymns*, no. 185.

123. Henry B. Eyring, "Adversity," *Ensign* or *Liahona,* May 2009, 24; emphasis added.

All of this teaches us that the Atonement of Jesus Christ has the power to help us through *all* of our personal tragedies.

Jesus Christ, who has suffered more than anyone born on earth, also has the most compassion for us who suffer so much less. Despite the tremendous suffering He had just experienced in the garden, Christ reached out to others. When Peter smote off a soldier's ear, Christ tenderly restored the ear. Such an act of kindness! If we had experienced such torturous pain, it is doubtful we would notice someone's lesser wound (see Luke 22:50–51). Later, while suffering excruciating pain on the cross, Jesus Christ continued to think of others and made sure John would take his mother, Mary, into his house and care for her (see John 19:26–27). In another tender act, Christ spoke to one of the thieves who hung beside him and reassured him, "To day shalt thou be with me in paradise" (Luke 23:43).

Our Savior is not a silent observer. He knows in a very real and personal way the personal pangs we suffer. He alone can offer peace in times of adversity. Christ knows the depths of our trials and the intensity of our suffering. It was for this cause that Christ came into the world.

Not Only Does Christ *Know* Us—He Knows How to Help Us

An old African American spiritual song contains the moving and insightful line, "Nobody knows the troubles I've seen; nobody knows but Jesus."[124] How true that phrase is. In the Old Testament, Christ assured the Israelites who were in bondage that He knew of their afflictions: "And the Lord said, I have surely seen the affliction of my people which are in Egypt, and have heard their cry by reason of their taskmasters; for I know their sorrows" (Exodus 3:7).

Heavenly Father and Jesus Christ know each one of us personally—by name—and tailor Their aid to us in a highly individual manner. Elder Maxwell said, "I testify to you that God has known you individually . . . for a long, long time. He has loved you for a long, long time. He not only knows the names of all the stars (see Psalm

124. Quoted in Neal A. Maxwell, "Apply the Atoning Blood of Christ," *Ensign*, Nov. 1997, 23.

147:4; Isaiah 40:26); He knows your names and all your heartaches and your joys!"[125]

At age fourteen, Joseph Smith had to be one of the least conspicuous human beings on earth, and yet the God of heaven knew him and *called him by name* in the Sacred Grove.

When Enos went into the woods to pray, he recorded, "There came a voice unto me, saying: *Enos,* thy sins are forgiven thee, and thou shalt be blessed" (Enos 1:5; emphasis added).

When God spoke to Moses, He said, "I have a work for thee, *Moses,* my son" (Moses 1:6; emphasis added).

The Lord knew Jacob's name and changed it to Israel to more accurately reflect his mission on the earth: "Thy name is Jacob: thy name shall not be called any more Jacob, but Israel shall be thy name" (Genesis 35:10).

In latter-day revelation, the Lord spoke to Emma, saying, "Hearken unto the voice of the Lord your God, while I speak unto you, *Emma Smith,* my daughter" (Doctrine and Covenants 25:1; emphasis added). Elder Bednar said, "The most impactful thing I've learned is how real it is to say that the Lord knows us. He knows us by name. He knows us one by one."[126]

Elder Richard Norby was serving with his wife, Pam, as missionaries for The Church of Jesus Christ of Latter-day Saints, when he learned by personal experience how Christ can succor us individually when we're scourged by afflictions. Elder Norby was serving in the Paris France Mission when three terrorists detonated bombs at an airport in Brussels on March 22, 2016. One of the bombs went off near where Elder Norby and three young missionaries were standing. All received serious injuries. A fourth missionary, who had already gone through airport security, received minor injuries. Thirty-two people were killed, sixty-two people were critically injured, and an additional 270 people were injured.

Elder Norby already had a personal testimony that Heavenly Father loved him, and that testimony was strengthened because of

---

125. Neal A. Maxwell, "Remember How Merciful the Lord Hath Been," *Ensign* or *Liahona,* May 2004, 46.

126. David A. Bednar, "How We Follow Jesus Christ," *Liahona*, Mar. 2023.

this experience. After the bombing, Elder Norby said, "God knew who I was and where I was and what had happened and what I was feeling."

After the bombing, Elder Norby was rushed to the hospital with burns over half of his body, severe shrapnel wounds, and a severe injury to his leg. Because of his burns, doctors put him in a medically induced coma. After four weeks, Elder Norby flew home to Utah to continue his recovery. Three and a half years after the bombing, Elder Norby said, "We are all wounded in one way or another. It doesn't have to be in an airport. It can be in an accident, or disease, or senility. Whatever it might be, I want to give gratitude for everything that I have experienced. I want to give, give, give."[127]

Because Christ atoned for all of our hurts and all of our sins, He knows, in a way no one else can understand, exactly what we need in order to recover. When we doubt our ability to change ourselves and become better people, or to overcome our suffering, the Savior stands ready to help. He is there for us and helps us change and heal, no matter what our particular burden is—whether reeling from a daughter's suicide, experiencing painful personal trials because of bipolar disorder, or being left to raise several children after losing a spouse in a mass shooting.

In John 2:1–11, we read about the Savior turning water to wine. Christ did not just make wine-flavored water; He made wine so excellent that the governor of the feast praised the bridegroom for keeping the best wine until the end—the opposite of what was usually done. Changing water into wine is no easy task. Water has a simple molecular structure, but wine has a complex mixture of hundreds of chemical compounds. This miracle demonstrates Christ's ability to change ordinary things into something extraordinary and shows that the Savior

127. Sam Penrod, "Utah man finds healing after returning to site of Brussels terror bombings 3 years later," KSL, Nov. 4, 2019, https://www.ksl.com/article/46667505/utah-man-finds-healing-after-returning-to-site-of-brussels-terror-bombings-3-years-later. See also Faith Heaton Jolley, "4 LDS missionaries injured during explosion in Brussels airport," KSL, Mar. 22, 2016, https://www.ksl.com/article/38999050/4-lds-missionaries-injured-during-explosion-in-brussels-airport.

has the power to transform our suffering and trials—indeed, our very character—into something else entirely. When we feel overwhelmed, we can remember how Christ changed water into wine and how He promises to change our ashes for beauty (see Isaiah 61:3). Through His power, Christ can turn our mistakes and pain into growth, changing us from what we are into what He wants us to become—heirs of the kingdom of God.

The blessings of Christ's atoning sacrifice extend to all who accept Jesus Christ as their Savior. President Packer wrote, "For some reason, we think the Atonement of Christ applies *only* at the end of mortal life to redemption from the Fall, from spiritual death. It is much more than that. It is an ever-present power to call upon in everyday life. When we are racked or harrowed up . . . or burdened with grief, He can heal us. . . . The Atonement has practical, personal, everyday value; apply it in your life."[128]

As we exercise faith in Jesus Christ, we will be strengthened to overcome our trials. President Oaks said, "Some are born with physical or mental disabilities that cause personal suffering for them and struggles for those who love and care for them. For many, the infirmity of depression is painful or permanently disabling. . . . [The Savior] knows of our anguish, and He is there for us. . . . The healing and strengthening power of Jesus Christ and His Atonement is for all of us who will ask."[129]

His Grace Is Sufficient

What is the grace of God? It God's favor and kindness as He helps us do something we are not strong enough to do on our own. Grace is divine assistance given not necessarily because we deserve it but because of God's mercy. Grace can also be thought of as the unmerited assistance of God toward His children. There is a difference between who we are now and who God wants us to become, and sometimes, to help make up the difference, God blesses us with His grace, which

128. Boyd K. Packer, "Touch of the Master's Hand," *Ensign,* May 2001, 23–24; emphasis in original.

129. Dallin H. Oaks, "Strengthened by the Atonement of Jesus Christ," *Ensign* or *Liahona*, Nov. 2015, 63–64.

acts as a bridge between who we are and who we want to become. Grace takes us from where we are to where we need to be. Through grace, God mercifully takes our hand to help us take that extra-long step, which is too far for us to make by ourselves.

Being gracious is one of God's attributes (see Exodus 34:6). Everything God does shows His grace, including creating this earth, sending His beloved Son to earth on our behalf, and watching over us constantly. When we find ourselves falling short, God's grace makes up the difference. The wonderful thing about grace is that we don't have to be perfect to experience it. All we need to do is our best, which includes repenting when we sin and trying to do better. All God desires is for us to follow Him and move forward from grace to grace. Elder Maxwell said, "Grace is God's favor, help, or gift that comes to us according to our needs and our personal righteousness. So it is, when we feel inadequate, if we are humble and weak, that His grace is sufficient for us."[130]

Being partakers of God's grace does not grant us an absence of adversity, but it *does* mean God will bless us with strength to overcome. At times our problems may seem enormous, but Heavenly Father, who watches over us, knows when we need His grace and when we can be stretched just a little further. His grace brings us the necessary inner strength to endure, and He reassures us, "My grace is sufficient for thee" (2 Corinthians 12:9). While Satan constantly tries to make us fall short, God's grace gives us that extra little push—or sometimes a very large one—so we end up where we need to be. As we strive to overcome our personal challenges, Heavenly Father will, through His matchless power and grace, do for us what we are not capable of doing for ourselves.

As we press forward, God will help us. "But the God of all grace, who hath called us unto his eternal glory by Christ Jesus, after that ye have suffered a while, make you perfect, stablish, strengthen, settle you" (1 Peter 5:10). The lyrics of the hymn "Not Now but in the Coming Years," found in the Portuguese hymnal, teaches us that although we will experience trials, Jesus will sustain us:

---

130. Neal A. Maxwell, *We Will Prove Them Herewith* (Salt Lake City, UT: Deseret Book, 1982), 120.

If clouds instead of sun spread shadows o'er our heart,
If pain afflicts us, never mind; we will soon know who Thou art.
Jesus guides us with His hand, and He will tell us why;
If we listen to His voice, He will tell us by and by.
Confide in God unwaveringly, and let Him us sustain;
Sing His glory endlessly, for later He'll explain.[131]

To attain His saving grace, the prophet Moroni invites us to draw close to our Savior: "Yea, come unto Christ, and be perfected in him . . . and love God with all your might, mind and strength, then is his grace sufficient for you, that by his grace ye may be perfect in Christ" (Moroni 10:32).

In the New Testament we are told, "Let us therefore come boldly unto the throne of grace, that we may obtain mercy, and find grace to help in time of need" (Hebrews 4:16). To go *boldly* to the throne of grace does not mean we do so brashly but rather with confidence that He will help us. Because of what the Savior did for us long ago in a very private garden and on a very public hill in Jerusalem, we are blessed to receive the grace of God in our lives.

The Savior Is Our Refuge from the Storm

All of us go through turbulent storms. Even when skies are clear and life is sailing along smoothly, clouds can arise causing unexpected storms. To prepare against life's storms, we must strengthen ourselves spiritually.

When a physical storm threatens, the first thing to do is take precautions against possible damage. One of the authors, Marlene Bateman Sullivan, relates that one night, she and her husband saw an emergency weather report flash across the TV screen, warning of high winds, heavy rain, and possible flash floods. The report warned people to take shelter and stay away from windows in case trees were uprooted by the heavy rain and strong winds. Because of advance warning, Marlene and her husband had time to take precautions and protect their home and property.

131. "Not Now but in the Coming Years," translated from "Agora Não, mas Logo Mais," *Hymns* (Portuguese), no. 156.

Although there are times when we are beset by the storms of life, which are not announced ahead of time, we can still find shelter by staying close to God. Elder Ricardo P. Gimenez spoke of this, saying:

> I know that we are all children of God, that He loves us, and that we are not alone. I invite you to come and see that He can lighten your burdens and be the refuge you are seeking. Come and help others find the refuge that they so yearn for. Come and stay with us in this refuge, which will help you resist the storms of life. . . .
>
> As we face the storms of life, I know that if we make our best effort and rely upon Jesus Christ and His Atonement as our refuge, we will be blessed with the relief, comfort, strength, temperance, and peace that we are seeking, with certainty in our hearts that at the end of our time here on earth, we will hear the words of the Master: "Well done, thou good and faithful servant: . . . enter thou into the joy of thy lord" (Matthew 25:21).[132]

Because storms can cause much damage, we would be wise to make preparations *before* winds begin to blow. The best preparation is to strengthen our relationship with the Savior. In times of trouble, Jesus Christ is our protector—a buckler in times of danger. In the Bible, the Lord is occasionally referred to as a buckler, which is a small shield used to deflect an opponent's weapon in hand-to-hand combat. Since the word of the Lord "is a buckler to all those that trust in him" (Psalms 18:30), we can depend upon the Savior to shield us from danger.

Challenging times befall all of us, and followers of Christ are not exempt. However, we can take heart in Christ, who is "our refuge and strength, a very present help in [times of] trouble" (Psalm 46:1). One of the striking things about this scripture is the modifier *very*. When the scriptures state Christ is a *very* present help, it means Jesus is close by. The Lord is not far away—He is right beside us when we are in need. He doesn't leave us to fend for ourselves as storms swirl around us but remains nearby. Our Redeemer, who loves us and understands our troubles, will bless us according to our needs. Jesus Christ is truly our refuge from the storms of life.

---

132. Ricardo P. Gimenez, "Finding Refuge from the Storms of Life," *Ensign* or *Liahona*, May 2020, 103.

Be of Good Comfort—Thy Faith Can Make Thee Whole

The Apostle Paul tells us God is "the Father of mercies, and the God of all comfort" (2 Corinthians 1:3). The Greek translation for the word *comfort* used in this verse is *parakaleo,* which means "to call to one's side, speak to, in the way of exhortation, console or teach."

At the beginning of His ministry, Jesus told His followers that He had been sent "to heal the brokenhearted, to preach deliverance to the captives, and recovering of sight to the blind, to set at liberty them that are bruised" (Luke 4:18). Quite often, the people Christ healed had to demonstrate faith. Some, such as Naaman—a mighty man who suffered from leprosy—had to take action to be healed (see 2 Kings 5:1–27). Some people traveled long distances to find Jesus. Others simply placed themselves where He would walk past, then extended their hand to Him.

One of these healings occurred when Jesus was on His way to heal the daughter of Jairus. A woman who had suffered for twelve years with an issue of blood saw a crowd and heard people say that Jesus was coming. She'd heard of Jesus and pressed through the crowds with the idea that if she could reach out and touch the hem of the Savior's robe, she could be healed. This act showed her to be a woman of faith, making it likely she had prayed for God to heal her. Twelve years is a long time to suffer, and despite seeking help, she had only gotten worse. If anyone had a right to feel hopeless, it was this woman, yet she still had faith. In fact, she had so much faith that she didn't expect the Savior to heal her by what we might consider a proper blessing—by Jesus laying His hands on her head and pronouncing a blessing—but instead, she believed she could be healed *simply by touching His clothes* (see Mark 5:27–29).

The woman positioned herself on the road and waited. When Jesus walked by, she stretched her hand out to touch His garment. It's easy to see the symbolism of this gesture and understand that in stretching herself to the utmost, she was stretching herself spiritually to reach out to the Savior. When the woman touched His robe, she was instantly healed. The Lord knew that someone had touched Him, and after turning around, He saw her. In that huge crowd, not only did Jesus know who had touched Him, but He also knew *why*. Tenderly, Jesus told her, "Daughter, be of good comfort; thy faith hath made thee whole. And the woman was made whole from that hour" (Matthew 9:22).

We know that this woman was humble and unassuming because she did not show herself openly to Christ. She was meek and mild. Both attributes are required for the Lord to bless us. The Apostle James explained this, saying, "Humble yourselves in the sight of the Lord, and he shall lift you up" (James 4:10). This woman also had faith—so much that she believed she could be healed even without asking directly for a blessing. The scriptures repeatedly testify that if we ask in faith, we shall receive: "Whatsoever thing ye shall ask in faith, believing that ye shall receive in the name of Christ, ye shall receive it" (Enos 1:15).

Some paintings depicting this scripture story show the woman sitting on the ground, grimacing with the effort it took to stretch out to the Savior. It took much effort to reach out to Christ to access His power. Do *we* press through the crowds to reach Christ? Do we, in our suffering, stretch ourselves to the utmost to Jesus, believing He can heal our sorrows?

Just as this woman reached out to the Savior, Jesus extends His arm to us. No matter what pain we are experiencing, if we will reach out to Christ in faith, He will stretch out His powerful arm to us. By reaching out to our Savior, we will be blessed with healing and comfort (see Doctrine and Covenants 88:63). It doesn't matter what challenge we face, nor how immense our problem is or how long we have been afflicted—we can have hope. We may struggle with chronic illness, relationship problems, poverty, addiction, or any one of a hundred other trials, but when we have faith in Jesus Christ and stretch out not only our arms but our hearts, minds, and spirits, we can have the power and blessing of our Savior to heal our life.

Christ Is Our Good Samaritan

When tragedies overtake us and we are left alone, bruised, and wounded, we may feel like the traveler who was attacked while traveling from Jerusalem to Jericho. After robbers beat and left him half dead, others saw him but did not stop. However, when a Samaritan saw the injured man, he had compassion and rushed to give aid. He poured wine and oil on the traveler's wounds, then took him to an inn where he further cared for him. He promised the innkeeper to return and repay the traveler's debt (see Luke 10:30–37).

At times, all of us find ourselves traveling the dusty road to Jericho. As we journey from premortal life to earth, we find ourselves subject to sin and death. We may find ourselves assailed, wounded, and left alone. When we have taken a beating, and life hurts so much we can hardly breathe, Christ is our good Samaritan. When we lay wounded, He has compassion on us and binds up our spiritual wounds. He lifts us up and carries us to safety. Christ has paid the price for our sins.

Our Savior will always come to our aid. He cares for the individual, not just the large crowd. Christ spoke to the woman of Samaria at the well—an audience of one—offering her living water (see John 4:7–26). Jesus visited Paul who was lonely and discouraged, telling him to "be of good cheer" (Acts 23:11). When a thief cried out to Jesus as they suffered on their cruel crosses, Jesus reassured the man that he would soon be with Christ in the spirit world (see Luke 23:39–43).

As our good Samaritan, Jesus Christ tends to our bruised spirits and eases our pain. Elder Soares said, "As we draw nearer to Him, surrendering ourselves spiritually to His care, we will be able to take upon ourselves His yoke, which is easy, and His burden, which is light, thus finding promised comfort and rest. Furthermore, we will receive the strength we all need to overcome the hardships, weaknesses, and sorrows of life, which are exceedingly difficult to endure without His help and healing power."[133]

Christ Heals All Who Mourn

When in need of healing, we can turn to Christ, the Master Healer, and receive compassion, help, and healing. We all need the power of Him who is mighty to save. Elder Scott said, "I testify that the surest, most effective, and shortest path to healing comes through application of the teachings of Jesus Christ in your life. It begins with an understanding of and appreciation for the principles of moral

133. Ulisses Soares, "Jesus Christ: The Caregiver of Our Soul," *Liahona*, May 2021, 84.

agency and the Atonement of Jesus Christ. It leads to faith in Him and obedience to His commandments, and that brings healing. . . . Look up in faith to Jesus Christ. I know that the Master loves you and will heal you according to your faith in Him."[134]

Although life is difficult and at times our pain great, we can receive comfort through our Savior. Jesus Christ is aware of every facet of our lives. He knows our suffering and will bind up our wounds. In Isaiah, we read, "The Lord hath anointed me to preach good tidings unto the meek; he hath sent me to bind up the brokenhearted . . . to comfort all that mourn; To appoint unto them that mourn in Zion, to give unto them beauty for ashes, the oil of joy for mourning, the garment of praise for the spirit of heaviness; that they might be called trees of righteousness" (Isaiah 61:1–3).

Jesus offers peace through the Holy Ghost: "Peace I leave with you, my peace I give unto you: not as the world giveth, give I unto you. Let not your heart be troubled, neither let it be afraid" (John 14:27). Christ offers hope and comfort of better times to come as we endure our trials: "Blessed be God, even the Father of our Lord Jesus Christ, the Father of mercies, and the God of all comfort; Who comforteth us in all our tribulation" (2 Corinthians 1:3–4). With Christ as our good Samaritan, it is possible to overcome whatever adversity we face while traversing our dusty mortal roads. Our Savior will watch over us and heal us when we're wounded. He will give us "peace in this world, and eternal life in the world to come" (Doctrine and Covenants 59:23).

134. Richard G. Scott, "To Be Healed," *Ensign*, May 1994, 9.

8

Happy under Any Circumstance

"And it came to pass that there was no contention in the land, because of the love of God which did dwell in the hearts of the people. . . . And surely there could not be a happier people among all the people who had been created by the hand of God."

—4 Nephi 1:15-16

Happiness Comes through Heavenly Father and Jesus Christ

We come to earth as spiritual beings to live in a mortal world. Although every generation faces unique trials, some are achingly similar and part of the overall human experience, such as sickness, death, family discord, natural disasters, economic downturns, and war. Happiness can seem elusive, but if we turn to God, He can dispel fear and bring peace to our hearts, enabling us to be happy no matter our circumstances.

Hope and happiness come when we ponder the most breathtaking and magnificent act to transpire in the history of the world: the Atonement of Jesus Christ. Not only does Christ's Atonement pay for our sins—it saves us from death. We can also be happy when we realize God's plan of happiness can bring us joy on earth. Elder Scott said, "Your joy in life depends upon your trust in Heavenly Father and His Holy Son, your conviction that their plan of happiness truly can bring you joy. Pondering their doctrine will let you enjoy the beauties of this earth and enrich your relationships with others. It will lead you to the comforting, strengthening experiences that flow from prayer to Father in Heaven and the answers He gives in return."[135]

Happiness comes from knowing that Christ will help us rise above our mortal difficulties and bring peace to our wounded souls. "And the peace of God, which passeth all understanding, shall keep your hearts and minds through Christ Jesus" (Philippians 4:7). Despite our trials, we *can* find happiness on earth. "Saints can be happy under every circumstance," President Nelson taught. "The joy we feel has little to do with the circumstances of our lives and everything to do with the focus of our lives. When the focus of our lives is on God's plan of salvation . . . and Jesus Christ and His gospel, we can feel joy regardless of what is happening—or not happening—in our lives. Joy comes from and because of Him. He is the source of all joy."[136] Following are a few suggestions on how we can create more happiness in our lives.

Focus On the Savior

After teaching a great multitude, Jesus went off to pray while His disciples went to the seashore and set off in their boat (see Matthew 14:23). After some time, they found themselves caught in a ferocious storm. In the fourth watch of the night, Jesus saw their danger and took the most direct route to rescue them, striding across the waves (see Matthew 14:25). When the disciples saw a man walking on the water, they were stricken with terror, thinking that it was a phantom.

Christ called out, "It is I; be not afraid" (Matthew 14:27). When Peter recognized Jesus, he said courageously, "Bid me come unto thee on the water" (Matthew 14:28). Jesus bade him come, and Peter climbed out of the boat and walked on the water. However, Peter soon became distracted by the winds and the waves. When Peter took his focus off the Lord, he began to sink and called for help. Instantly, the Lord took hold of Peter and lifted him up. It's noteworthy to see that as long as Peter focused his attention on the Savior, he was able to

135. Richard G. Scott, "Finding Joy in Life," *Ensign*, May 1996, 24.

136. Russell M. Nelson, "Joy and Spiritual Survival," *Ensign* or *Liahona*, Nov. 2016, 82.

walk on the water. It was only when Peter turned his focus away from Jesus that he began to sink.

In our world, as the storms of our life increase both in frequency and intensity, we can be distracted and fearful. But the tempests cannot rob us of hope if we remain focused on God. As a certain hymn says, "When dark clouds of trouble hang o'er us / And threaten our peace to destroy, / There is hope smiling brightly before us, / And we know that deliverance is nigh."[137]

Savor the Scriptures

The scriptures contain the word of God and testify of His goodness, mercy, and intelligence. We have been counseled to study them *every day* to receive power to resist the adversary and meet life's challenges. Nephi counsels us to "feast" upon the words of Christ (see 2 Nephi 31:20). *Feast* is an interesting word; it goes far beyond simply "reading" the scriptures and suggests savoring and relishing them. By feasting upon the words of God, we will receive inspiration on how to deal with our problems. Thoughts will come to our mind, helping us know what to do. President Eyring said, "Going to the scriptures to learn what to do makes all the difference. . . . We will find answers in the scriptures. The Lord seemed to anticipate all of our problems and all of our needs, and He put help in the scriptures for us—if only we seek it."[138]

Reading the scriptures helps us to know God and His purposes, bringing us happiness. "Behold, canst thou read this without rejoicing and lifting up thy heart for gladness?" (Doctrine and Covenants 19:39). As we read, we see how God has dealt with His people and can better understand how He might deal with us. The scriptures testify of Christ, and as we ponder on His life and learn lessons originating from Nazareth, Capernaum, Jerusalem, and Galilee, we can have hope and happiness. "For whatsoever things were written aforetime were written for our learning, that we through patience and comfort of the scriptures might have hope" (Romans 15:4). The words of God

---

137. "We Thank Thee, O God, for a Prophet," *Hymns*, no. 19.

138. Henry B. Eyring, "A Discussion on Scripture Study," *Ensign*, July 2005, 24.

give us patience to endure our afflictions, strength to bear our grief, and confidence in meeting life's trials. Despite living in a world of chaos and uncertainty, we can be uplifted daily by taking time to read and ponder the scriptures, which will allow the Holy Ghost to impart wisdom and inspiration.

Stand Up to Satan

As the Savior's Second Coming draws ever closer, it is imperative that we stand up and fight against Satan if we are to prevail. Heavenly Father warned that evil would run rampant in the latter days because Satan would have great hold upon the hearts of men. Brigham Young said of our day, "It was revealed to me in the commencement of this Church, that the Church would spread, prosper, grow and extend, and that in proportion to the spread of the Gospel among the nations of the earth, so would the power of Satan rise."[139]

In the premortal world, Satan's plan was to "redeem all mankind" (Moses 4:1) so that no soul would be lost. While this sounds good on the surface, this plan would come at a cost, for Satan planned to take away our right to make our own decisions (see Moses 4:3). Satan's plan was in direct opposition to Heavenly Father's plan of happiness, which would give His children agency. God knew that for us to reach our divine potential, we had to be allowed to choose between good or evil and, while on earth, allowed to choose—of our own free will—to obey God.

Because Satan will never have a body, an eternal companion, or a family, he will never experience a fullness of joy. Because he is miserable, his sole desire is to make all of us miserable. Satan has gathered an enormous army—"a third part of the hosts of heaven" (Doctrine and Covenants 29:36)—to fight against us. Satan and his followers work diligently against anyone who believes in God. Helaman warns, "We are surrounded by demons, yea, we are encircled about by the angels of him who hath sought to destroy our souls" (Helaman 13:37). Satan is a master manipulator, and following are some of the techniques he uses against us.

139. Brigham Young, in *Journal of Discourses*, 13:280.

- Satan tries to convince us that our problems are a result of our own weaknesses and that we will never be "good enough" to make it back to God's presence. However, the truth is that Heavenly Father has given us the doctrine of repentance so we can change and rise above our weaknesses.
- Satan tells us that the reason we are suffering is because we are "bad" or "unworthy"—because God does not permit "good" and "righteous" people to suffer. However, the truth is that trials come to all, including good and righteous people. It matters not if you are virtuous and upright, or evil and immoral—every person on earth faces hardships.
- Satan focuses our attention on past sins. He tries to convince us that we will never be able to overcome our weaknesses and that we are past redemption. However, the truth is that God doesn't expect us to be perfect in this life, though He does want us to work toward that goal. God knew we would sin, which is why He provided a Savior. We can learn from our mistakes, repent, and change. No one is beyond redemption unless they stop trying.
- Satan tries to convince us that when we fall short and make mistakes, God is disappointed and turns away from us. However, the truth is that we are His children and He will *never* turn away. Heavenly Father's love is unconditional. However, unconditional love doesn't mean He doesn't expect us to progress and try a little harder to do a little better.
- If we have been deeply wounded, Satan tries to convince us that our afflictions came because God does not care about us. However, Heavenly Father knows us and has a deep and never-ending love for us. Although Satan will whisper that we are insignificant and unloved, the truth is that Heavenly Father loves us with a perfect and everlasting love. Everything He does is for our benefit.
- One of Satan's favorite lies is telling people there is no devil. If people do not believe he exists, Satan can get away with his evil schemes. In our day, Satan has convinced many that he doesn't exist. However, the truth is that Satan *does* exist. He

is real, works tirelessly against us, and has enormous power to hurt us.

There are hundreds of other lies Satan tells us, all customized as to what will influence and injure us the most. Satan tries to make us feel unequal to the demands of life, but we are stronger than we think and more capable than Satan wants us to believe. Satan has a unique ability to twist and corrupt all that is good. We must never underestimate Satan's power but pray for strength to rise above his deceits. President George Q. Cannon warned, "I have come to the conclusion that if our eyes were open to see the spirit world around us . . . we would not be so unguarded and careless . . . but we would be continually watchful and prayerful to our Heavenly Father for His Holy Spirit and His holy angels to be around about us to strengthen us to overcome every evil influence."[140]

The devil especially targets those who are on the pathway to exaltation. The scriptures teach that Satan "maketh war with the saints of God, and encompasseth them round about" (Doctrine and Covenants 76:29). The devil also aims his worst blows at those worn down by pain and suffering. When our defenses are stretched thin by adversity, Satan works extra hard to damage our faith.

In the Doctrine and Covenants, the Lord tells Oliver Cowdery, "There is none else save God that knowest thy thoughts and the intents of thy heart" (Doctrine and Covenants 6:16). This could be taken to mean Satan is not allowed access to our thoughts. While it is likely Satan is not able to know our thoughts, he can, because of his intelligence and knowledge, discover areas where we are vulnerable. We ought to be careful not to give up important information to Satan when we talk with others. Once he learns of our worries, fears, anger, and struggles, Satan will double his efforts and attack us in those specific areas.

Satan and his followers pay close attention to what we say and do, and if we reveal areas where we are the most weak, Satan will use that against us. Nevertheless, President Faust said that Satan "can have no power over us unless we permit it. . . . If we stand firm, he will retreat.

140. George Q. Cannon, quoted in Joseph G. Richardson, "Knowing the Tactics of Our Enemy," *Liahona*, Sept. 2021, 20.

The Apostle James gave us the same counsel: 'Submit yourselves therefore to God. Resist the devil, and he will flee from you' (James 4:7). He cannot know our thoughts unless we speak them."[141]

Although Satan and evil reign in our world, Heavenly Father stands ready to help. He has given us many tactics to thwart Satan. Some of them include keeping the commandments, repenting, attending church, going to the temple, studying the scriptures, and strengthening our faith. Satan may try to thwart Heavenly Father's plans, but God will prevail in the end.

Cleanse the Inner Vessel

Some trials come from our own sins and mistakes. In the Book of Mormon we read that "despair cometh because of iniquity" (Moroni 10:22). To be happier, we can examine our lives to see if we are in harmony with all of God's laws and make changes if we are not. Satan works hard to get us to sin, and sometimes we do, but when we repent, we avoid the misery he seeks to inflict upon us.

Repentance is turning away from sin and turning to God for forgiveness. Instead of making excuses for our behavior, we repent by acknowledging our sins, asking God for forgiveness, and making necessary changes in our lives. When we repent, our sins are washed away, bringing us happiness both now and in the eternities. "Though your sins be as scarlet, they shall be as white as snow" (Isaiah 1:18). Because Jesus Christ loves us, He is joyful when we accept His atoning sacrifice and are cleansed from sin (see Luke 15:4–7). When we repent, we are healed through our Savior's stripes. Without our Savior's sacrifice on our behalf, we would have no hope of lasting happiness.

Repentance should not be viewed as a punishment but as an opportunity to be forgiven and cleansed. Repenting with a contrite spirit helps us realign our will with God's and allows us to become increasingly pure and more fit for His kingdom. We will feel the peace of a clear conscience, which brings greater happiness. President Nelson said, "Nothing is more liberating, more ennobling, or more crucial to our individual progression than is a regular, daily focus on repentance. Repentance is not an event; it is a process. It is the key to happiness

141. James E. Faust, "The Great Imitator," *Ensign*, Nov. 1987, 35.

and peace of mind. When coupled with faith, repentance opens our access to the power of the Atonement of Jesus Christ."[142]

Repentance is powerful spiritual medicine for our souls. Everyone makes mistakes, and as we repent, we draw nearer to God, who in turn draws closer to us. Repentance is not easy because it entails changing ourselves—not an easy task. If we feel weak and doubt our ability to change, we can ask God for help. His grace will make up the difference between where we are and where we want to be. With a touch of humor, Elder Holland said, "God is our Father and is exceptionally good at forgiving and forgetting sins we have forsaken, perhaps because we give Him so much practice in doing so."[143]

When we repent, we freely confess and forsake our sins, and in return, God says He will remember them no more (see Doctrine and Covenants 58:42–43). While God may not in actuality *forget* them, He chooses, in His divine way, *not to remember them*. Likewise, we may not forget our old sins, but after repenting, we need to accept that God has forgiven us and refuse to continue scourging ourselves for them.

Repenting can be thought of as a recalibration: making a conscious effort to change, draw closer to the Lord, and be purified. Repentance is a sacred act, one where we assess our shortcomings, pray for forgiveness, take positive action to improve, and align ourselves more fully with Christ. God doesn't expect us to be flawless, but He does expect us to be relentless in our pursuit of perfection. Repenting can also be thought of as personally restoring ourselves. Repentance can be a joy because it invites the power of Jesus Christ into our life and cleanses us from iniquity. Great happiness comes when we rid ourselves of sin, are forgiven, and are "pained no more" (Mosiah 27:29).

Know What You Can Control and Accept What You Can't

When buffeted by trials, we may become discouraged, especially when they arise from events we have little or no control over, such as

142. Russell M. Nelson, "We Can Do Better and Be Better," *Ensign* or *Liahona*, May 2019, 67.

143. Jeffrey R. Holland, "The Greatest Possession," *Liahona*, Nov. 2021, 9.

losing a job after a company layoff, the destruction of a home in a hurricane, or the discovery of a cancerous tumor. While we may not have control over our tribulations, we do have control over our attitude.

One of the authors, Joshua Sullivan, shares the following:

> I've been a therapist in many sessions where someone is dealing with anxiety, depression, or other challenges. One routine skill that often comes up is knowing what you can control and what you can't.
>
> Once, I talked with a client who had a loved one who had been recently diagnosed with cancer. We talked about acceptance and being mindful of what we can control and what we can't control. Then, we discussed what cancer could do, and what it couldn't do. Cancer can end someone's life. But cancer cannot take away the love that person feels and receives from others. It cannot take away fond memories of what the person has shared with others. Cancer can make a person feel pain, nausea, fatigue, and so on. But cancer cannot break family and sealing bonds.
>
> In times of trial, it helps to look at what we have, not on what is being taken away from us. Like so many things in life, we have to focus on what we can control instead of the things we can't.

Ponder on Your Blessings

Adversity will never be a stranger to any of us, especially as the Lord's Second Coming draws nearer, but we can cultivate greater happiness by thinking of the blessings we *do* have rather than those we *do not*. The Greek philosopher Epictetus said, "He is a wise man who does not grieve for the things which he has not, but rejoices for those which he has."[144] Focusing on the blessings God has given us allows us to be happier, see the good in life, and avoid getting swamped in the mire of adversity.

Lehi suffered many travails after leaving Jerusalem, many of which were caused by his rebellious sons, Laman and Lemuel. Yet Lehi remained cognizant of the many gifts God had given him. Speaking

144. *The Discourses of Epictetus; with the Encheiridion and Fragments*, trans. George Long (1888), 429; quoted in Thomas S. Monson, "The Divine Gift of Gratitude," *Ensign* or *Liahona*, Nov. 2010, 88.

to his son Jacob, Lehi said, "Thou art my firstborn in the days of my tribulation in the wilderness. And behold, in thy childhood thou hast suffered afflictions and much sorrow, because of the rudeness of thy brethren. Nevertheless . . . thou knowest the greatness of God; and he shall consecrate thine afflictions for thy gain. Wherefore, thy soul shall be blessed" (2 Nephi 2:1–3). It is significant that Lehi focused on the comforting knowledge that God would consecrate his afflictions for good.

After preaching to the wicked people in Ammonihah, Alma was cast out and was "weighed down with sorrow . . . and anguish of soul" (Alma 8:14). An angel appeared and said, "Blessed art thou, Alma; therefore, lift up thy head and rejoice, . . . for thou hast been faithful in keeping the commandments of God" (Alma 8:15). At first, this message might seem unusual, but Alma took it as a comforting reminder that he would be richly blessed for doing all that God had asked him to do.

One great blessing that we all enjoy is knowing God loves us. God's love for us is the reason He developed the plan of happiness, which allows all of us to return to live with Him, where we can become "heirs of God, and joint-heirs with Christ" (Romans 8:17). God's plan ensures we will live forever, receive a fullness of joy (see 3 Nephi 28:10), and have the potential to "inherit thrones, kingdoms, principalities, and powers" (Doctrine and Covenants 132:19). Knowing that God offers us the blessing of a glorious celestial future can bring great happiness and help us endure the hardships we face on earth.

Cease Contending with Others

We live in a world full of strife, and each day it seems harder for people to resolve conflicts in a peaceful manner. In this day and age, people with divergent political opinions are angry and frustrated with those who do not hold their viewpoints. Contention has become so common that arguing and disputation is almost a normal way of life. However, contention is a choice, and as followers of Christ, we are charged to deal lovingly and peaceably with others. When we are filled with God's love, it becomes easy to stop contending with others. In 4 Nephi 1:15, we read, "And it came to pass that there was no contention in the land, *because of the love of God* which did dwell in the hearts of the people" (emphasis added).

We avoid contention because it violates everything the Savior stands for. Also, the Prince of Peace, Jesus Christ, has directly told us, "Cease to contend one with another; cease to speak evil one of another" (Doctrine and Covenants 136:23). If we are true disciples of Christ, we will control our emotions, be meek and peaceable, have love for one another, and treat everyone with respect. Although others may be argumentative, we do not have to retaliate in kind. While we cannot adjust the volume of contention in others, we can in ourselves.

Refusing to dispute with others does not mean we are abandoning our principles or beliefs—only that we choose not to argue and instead practice civility when expressing our personal beliefs. We do not attack those with whom we disagree, and we do not act scornfully toward people who hold different opinions. When we are filled with the love of God, we will have charity, which "suffereth long, and is kind; . . . seeketh not her own, is not easily provoked . . . beareth all things, believeth all things, hopeth all things, endureth all things" (1 Corinthians 13:4–5, 7).

When we become contentious, we give Satan power over us. In the Pearl of Great Price, we are told that when we contend with others, Satan laughs and the God of heaven weeps (see Moses 7:28, 33). And why would God weep? Because He has commanded us to love one another, and when we are contentious, our souls are filled with enmity instead of love. Those who follow Christ will not have the spirit of contention. Jesus plainly said, "He that hath the spirit of contention is not of me, but is of the devil, who is the father of contention, and he stirreth up the hearts of men to contend with anger, one with another. Behold, this is not my doctrine, to stir up the hearts of men with anger, one against another" (3 Nephi 11:29–30).

We would do well to follow Christ's example. When our Savior was betrayed, falsely accused, and beaten, how did He react? To some, He said not a word. To others, He stated the truth calmly and without anger. When we feel more love toward others and avoid contention, we demonstrate our willingness to be true disciples of the Lord and will feel more happiness in our own lives.

Pray Always

Never has there been a day and age when it has been more vital to recognize and receive the whisperings of the Spirit. When gripped by pain and uncertainty, we can pray and be guided by personal revelation to know what to do *in any circumstance.* The Lord has promised, "Pray always, and I will pour out my Spirit upon you, and great shall be your blessing" (Doctrine and Covenants 19:38).

Prayer is a blessed gift—one that allows us to commune with God and receive guidance and comfort. We are advised to counsel with the Lord continually. "Cry unto God for all thy support; yea, let all thy doings be unto the Lord," Alma said. "Counsel with the Lord in all thy doings, and he will direct thee for good; yea, when thou liest down at night lie down unto the Lord, that he may watch over you in your sleep; and when thou risest in the morning let thy heart be full of thanks unto God; and if ye do these things, ye shall be lifted up at the last day" (Alma 37:36–37).

In times of tribulation, we are encouraged to pray in faith for those things we need. However, we should keep in mind that God is infinitely wiser than we are and will answer our prayers in a way that is best for us, even if it's not what we prayed for. President Eyring spoke about his father praying when he was stricken with terminal cancer:

> When the pain became intense, we found him in the morning on his knees by the bed. He had been too weak to get back into bed. He told us he had been praying to ask his Heavenly Father why he had to suffer so much when he had always tried to be good. He said a kindly answer came: "God needs brave sons." And so he soldiered on to the end, trusting that God loved him, listened to him, and would lift him up. He was blessed to have known early and to never forget that a loving God is as close as a prayer.[145]

Quite often, our most earnest prayers arise from life's most difficult moments. It is a comfort to know that during such times, our loving Heavenly Father is always there to listen and to bless us with strength (see Alma 58:10). We should avoid asking for blessings

145. Henry B. Eyring, "Families and Prayer," *Ensign,* Sept. 2015, 4.

mindlessly, thinking God will answer our requests when we don't put any effort into gaining the things we desire. And we should not expect God to simply give us the answer (see Doctrine and Covenants 9:7–8). Heavenly Father is more likely to assist us if we have taken time to ponder, do research, and figure out possible solutions to our problem *before* praying.

Our prayers for guidance are only as effective as our efforts to listen to the still, small voice of the Holy Ghost. God is fully aware of what is happening in our lives and is always ready to answer our prayers. It is good to keep in mind that prayer works best when it's a two-way communication, not a monologue.

After praying, we are encouraged to take a few minutes to be still and listen for the quiet voice of inspiration. As we open our hearts and take time to listen, God will let us know His will concerning us. The more we pray to our Father in Heaven in Christ's name, the more we bring the Spirit of God into our lives and the more we will be blessed with strength beyond our own.

Happiness Comes by Keeping the Commandments

There are natural, divine laws that allow us to feel joy or misery. President Nelson talked about one of these laws, saying, "They're called commandments, but they are just as true as the law of life, the law of gravity. . . . If you want to be happy, keep the commandments."[146] When we stay in harmony with the statutes God has given us, we can achieve happiness and better prepare ourselves for the kingdom of heaven. As we live according to the principles of the gospel, we can enjoy a continual flow of blessings, have more control over our lives, and be blessed with increased faith. Nephi said, "And if it so be that the children of men keep the commandments of God, he doth nourish them, and strengthen them" (1 Nephi 17:3).

Keeping the commandments is one sure course that provides the happiness the Savior spoke of when He told His disciples, "These things I have spoken unto you, that in me ye might have peace. In the world ye shall have tribulation: but be of good cheer; I have overcome

146. Russell M. Nelson, in "Eternal Laws: From Scrabble to the Commandments" (video), *Church News*, Aug. 31, 2019, thechurchnews.com.

the world" (John 16:33). Obeying the commandments enables us to feel God's love more fully and brings quiet assurance that our course in life is pleasing to God. It also enhances our ability to deal with the challenges that come from living in mortality. As we hold to the iron rod, we will be blessed with the love of God, which is "most desirable above all things" (1 Nephi 11:22). Our souls will then be filled "with exceedingly great joy" (1 Nephi 8:12). Obedience also allows us to have confidence in God and in His willingness to listen to and answer our prayers. When we face ordeals, this confidence is beyond price because it gives us a firm foundation on which to stand.

Living in obedience to God's directives ensures that we are worthy to receive the comfort of the Holy Spirit, which brings happiness even during times of adversity. Mosiah told his people, "I would desire that ye should consider on the blessed and happy state of those that keep the commandments of God. For behold, they are blessed in all things, both temporal and spiritual; and if they hold out faithful to the end they are received into heaven, that thereby they may dwell with God in a state of never-ending happiness. O remember, remember that these things are true; for the Lord God hath spoken it" (Mosiah 2:41).

Live Up to Your Covenants

Making sacred covenants enables us to receive the power of godliness in our lives and prepares us to return to our heavenly home. As covenant people of God, we need the faith, endurance, happiness, and courage that only God can provide. As we worthily make sacred covenants, we link ourselves with God, unlocking God's power in our lives (see Doctrine and Covenants 84:20). President Nelson said, "Your commitment to follow the Savior by making covenants with Him and then keeping these covenants will open the door to every spiritual blessing and privilege available to men, women, and children everywhere."[147] When we humbly kneel at the altars of the temple and make covenants out of a sincere desire to obey, we become holier and more fit for the kingdom. Living in accordance with our covenants allows us to enjoy more happiness because they connect us more securely to the Savior.

147. Russell M. Nelson, "As We Go Forward Together," *Ensign*, Apr. 2018, 7.

We may have heard Church leaders counsel us to follow the covenant path. What is the covenant path? Simply put, it is making and keeping sacred covenants. Those covenants begin with baptism and confirmation. For young men, it means being ordained to the Aaronic Priesthood and then the Melchizedek Priesthood. The next step is to receive the temple endowment, and if we marry, be sealed in the temple. Faithfully following the covenant path prepares us to return to live with God.

The ordinances of the Lord's house provide us with vision along with a determination to improve so we can qualify to receive all that the Lord has promised we may receive through our faithfulness. Elder Christofferson said:

> Divine covenants make strong Christians. I urge each one to qualify for and receive all the priesthood ordinances you can and then faithfully keep the promises you have made by covenant. In times of distress, let your covenants be paramount and let your obedience be exact. Then you can ask in faith, nothing wavering, according to your need, and God will answer. He will sustain you as you work and watch. In His own time and way, He will stretch forth his hand to you, saying, "Here am I."[148]

Keeping our covenants can be a great source of spiritual strength. They also help us develop a clear, distinct course of direction for our lives. "Life will challenge you," said Elder Holland. "Difficulties will come. Heartbreaks will strike. Loved ones will die. So, wherever you are going, make your way to Jesus Christ first. Remember that His suffering and Resurrection make possible our victory over difficulty and death. Make your covenants with Him and keep them as you journey on."[149]

Great blessings are promised to those who keep their covenants. In a vision, Nephi wrote of our day, saying that he "beheld the power of the Lamb of God, that it descended upon the saints of the church

---

148. D. Todd Christofferson, "The Power of Covenants," *Ensign* or *Liahona*, May 2009, 22.

149. Jeffrey R. Holland, "Pursuing the Fulness of Christ," *Liahona*, Apr. 2021, 11.

of the Lamb, and upon the covenant people of the Lord, . . . and they were armed with righteousness and with the power of God in great glory" (1 Nephi 14:14). When we make and keep our covenants with God, we are armed with His divine power, blessed with glory, and earn the privilege of having angels round about us (see Doctrine and Covenants 109:22).

During times of trial, remaining faithful to our covenants allows us to feel the hand of the Lord lifting and strengthening us. By keeping ourselves worthy of our covenants, we are sanctified through the grace of Jesus Christ. This is where "the power of godliness is manifest" in our lives, giving us much-needed power and strength in these latter days (see Doctrine and Covenants 84:20).

Remember Who You Are

One of the most fundamental doctrines of the gospel is that we are children of God. We hear this so often that it may begin to seem ordinary, when actually it is one of the most extraordinary pieces of knowledge we could ever have. Many of us have sung the beloved primary song "I Am a Child of God,"[150] but do we truly understand our wonderful divine heritage as true sons and daughters of God? Happiness comes from fully comprehending who we really are: children of a divine Father and Mother. All of us have a divine origin, nature, and potential. While in the premortal world, we proved faithful in the first estate. We were valiant children of God then, and we can continue to prove our worthiness in this mortal estate. God loves us for who we are *and* for who we can become. Repentance is one of the first steps we make while on the journey back to our heavenly home.

In today's world, evil abounds, but we can be blessed with power when we live in accordance with our divine heritage. Knowing who we are changes how we think, what we feel, and what we do. As we come to truly understand that we are children of God, we develop an eternal perspective and can better see our way toward our goal of becoming more like our heavenly parents. Realizing our identity gives us a new perspective of mortality that extends far beyond our current limited understanding. When we face hardships, temptations, and

150. "I Am a Child of God," *Hymns*, no. 301.

trials, we can remind ourselves who we are and gain the confidence to know that Heavenly Father will support us through our challenges. By remembering who we are, we can trust that He who loves us will bless us to overcome every pain we face in mortality. We also know that those very trials are meant to prepare us to become more like our divine parents so that we can attain an eternal inheritance and enjoy the glories of a heavenly kingdom.

Reading the Book of Mormon helps us remember our relationship to our Elder Brother, Jesus Christ. Elder Peter M. Johnson said, "The Book of Mormon contains the words of Christ and helps us remember who we are."[151] Truly, we can be happy under any circumstance by knowing of our divine relationship to Jesus Christ and our Heavenly Father. As children of God, we have inherited something of God's divine character, which gives us power to overcome our earthly trials. True happiness comes from knowing we are divine children of a Father who loves us, watches over us tenderly, and does all He can to help us return to Him.

151. Peter M. Johnson, "Power to Overcome the Adversary," *Ensign* or *Liahona*, Nov. 2019, 112.

9
The Power of Gratitude

"Live in thanksgiving daily, for the many mercies and blessings which [God] doth bestow upon you."

—Alma 34:38

Thank God in All Things

Gratitude is a divine principle. In modern-day revelation, we have been told to "thank the Lord thy God in all things" (Doctrine and Covenants 59:7). Expressing gratitude not only opens our eyes to the many blessings God has bestowed upon us, but it also allows us to receive further blessings. In the Book of Mormon, Alma tells his people, "And now I would that ye should be humble, and be . . . diligent in keeping the commandments of God at all times; asking for whatsoever things ye stand in need, both spiritual and temporal; always returning thanks unto God for whatsoever things ye do receive" (Alma 7:23).

There are many blessings to be thankful for, but none are more glorious than the magnanimous generosity of God in creating this earth so that we might gain a physical body and have mortal experiences that allow us to progress and become more like Him. Another magnificent blessing is Heavenly Father's gift of love in sending His Beloved Son to earth to be our Exemplar and Savior. Through His Atonement, Jesus Christ suffered for our sins and laid down His life to bring about the Resurrection and save us from certain death (see 1 Corinthians 15:22). Another marvelous blessing is the Restoration of the gospel through Joseph Smith, which brings untold blessings.

Too often we let ourselves get caught up in life and our problems instead of taking time to appreciate the host of blessings we receive daily. We can develop a grateful heart by taking a moment to consider the many tender mercies God bestows upon us. Elder Bednar said, "I testify that the tender mercies of the Lord are real and that they do not occur randomly or merely by coincidence. Often, the Lord's timing of His tender mercies helps us to both discern and acknowledge them."[152]

Pondering our blessings helps us develop a spirit of gratitude. President Nelson said, "Practicing gratitude may not prevent us from experiencing sorrow, anger, or pain, but it can help us look forward with hope. We can give thanks for our loved ones, for our bodies and minds, for music and literature, for the beauty of the natural world. By counting our blessings, we can more fully appreciate and enjoy our lives as we work toward greater unity, kindness, honesty, and tolerance."[153]

Even During Hard Times, We Can Be Grateful

In November 2020, while in the midst of a worldwide pandemic, President Nelson issued a global call for people to express gratitude for their blessings on social media. Twitter, Facebook, and Instagram were flooded with millions of posts as people shared personal messages of gratitude. One KSL reader expressed thanks for her cancer:

> I want to express my gratitude for the cervical cancer that I have had these past 3 1/2 years! It has taught compassion; it has taught me that I can handle more than I thought possible; it has taught me to

152. David A. Bednar, "The Tender Mercies of the Lord," *Ensign* or *Liahona,* May 2005, 99.

153. "President Nelson Recommends the Healing Power of Gratitude," The Tabernacle Choir Blog, last modified Nov. 10, 2022, https://www.thetabernaclechoir.org/articles/president-nelson-recommends-the-power-of-gratitude.html.

> reach for God even more than after my husband died from cancer almost 18 years ago, leaving me to raise our 3 young children.
>
> The Lord sent the missionaries to my door in Springfield, Oregon, after he died, and I heard truth in the messages they faithfully brought! I am truly grateful for the many tender mercies and kindnesses that I have received from the Lord.[154]

While the scriptures relate the spiritual value of being grateful, scientists have also found physical benefits. One health study reported, "When we express gratitude, our brain releases dopamine and serotonin, the two crucial neurotransmitters responsible for our emotions, and they make us feel 'good.' They enhance our mood immediately, making us feel happy from the inside. By consciously practicing gratitude every day, we can help these neural pathways to strengthen and ultimately create a permanent grateful and positive nature within ourselves which builds our inner strength to combat stress."[155] Another research study reported that spending just five minutes a day writing about the blessings you are grateful for can increase your long-term well-being by more than ten percent. This study noted, "Gratitude makes us nicer, more trusting, more social, and more appreciative. As a result, it helps us make more friends, deepens our existing relationships, and improves our marriages."[156]

No matter what problems we face, there are blessings for which we can be thankful. When mourning the loss of a loved one, we can be thankful for the Atonement of Jesus Christ, which allows us to be reunited in the next life. When sorrowful over a rebellious child who cuts off all contact, parents can be comforted to know that their pleas

---

154. Lauren Bennett, "Latter-day Saint leaders share Christmas message, express gratitude for #GiveThanks participation," KSL, Nov. 30, 2020, https://www.ksl.com/article/50058524/latter-day-saint-leaders-share-christmas-message-express-gratitude-for-givethanks-participation.

155. "Gratitude: A Tool To Reduce Stress," North Dakota Behavioral Health, accessed Nov. 10, 2023, https://www.hhs.nd.gov/sites/www/files/documents/BH/Gratitude.pdf.

156. Gene P., "Benefits of Gratitude: 31 Powerful Reasons to be More Grateful," Happier Human, Mar. 17, 2023, https://www.happierhuman.com/benefits-of-gratitude/.

to God on their child's behalf will be answered and that God will be with their child even if they cannot. When experiencing chronic physical pain, we can be thankful that one day we will have a perfect, immortal body.

One of the authors, Joshua Sullivan, relates the following personal experience:

> When I was a missionary in the south of France, I became ill with a stomach virus that would not go away. My stomach hurt all the time and then I started throwing up. This went on for days. After I went three days without food, my mission president said he needed to send me to a doctor. He told me that if something was wrong, I would probably be sent home.
>
> I prayed to Heavenly Father for help, asking Him to help me feel better so I could stay in the mission field. I remember waking up on day four and thinking that I had never gone that long without food before. Typically, even fasting for a day makes me very hungry.
>
> That morning, I felt very weak, and when I went to the kitchen table, I saw a box of cornflakes. Since we were poor missionaries, they were the cheapest off-brand, cardboard-tasting cornflakes available in the store. I grabbed a few from the box and ate them. Surprisingly, they tasted better than anything I had ever eaten in my life. I ate a few more and, amazingly, my stomach didn't hurt anymore. When I didn't throw up, I knew I had turned a corner.
>
> I started crying, feeling so grateful for those corn flakes, even though they were the worst-tasting cornflakes in the world. Gratitude filled me, and I felt thankful I had hands to eat with. I looked out the window and felt thankful that our apartment had windows. Waves of gratitude kept washing over me for so many mundane, ordinary things, filling me with thankfulness to God and His blessings. This incident was one of the greatest experiences I had on my mission.

When buffeted by trials, practicing gratitude increases our sense of happiness. President Uchtdorf said:

> Sooner or later, I believe that all of us experience times when the very fabric of our world tears at the seams, leaving us feeling alone, frustrated, and adrift.

> It can happen to anyone. No one is immune.
>
> Everyone's situation is different, and the details of each life are unique. Nevertheless, I have learned that there is something that would take away the bitterness that may come into our lives. There is one thing we can do to make life sweeter, more joyful, even glorious.
>
> We can be grateful!
>
> It might sound contrary to the wisdom of the world to suggest that one who is burdened with sorrow should give thanks to God. But those who set aside the bottle of bitterness and lift instead the goblet of gratitude can find a purifying drink of healing, peace, and understanding.[157]

It's not easy to feel grateful when awash in problems, but it becomes easier if we look at gratitude as a way of living that remains independent of strife and trials. It helps to see tribulations as something that is happening *to* us but which do not define who we are. This makes it easier to stop focusing on our woes and allows us to more clearly see blessings we might otherwise take for granted.

Elder Scott counsels:

> The challenges you face, the growth experiences you encounter, are intended to be temporary scenes played out on the stage of a life of continuing peace and happiness. Sadness, heartache, and disappointment are events in life. It is not intended that *they be the substance of life*. I do not minimize how hard some of these events can be . . . but they should not be allowed to become the confining focus of everything you do. Your life can and should be wondrously rewarding. It is your understanding and application of the laws of God that will give your life glorious purpose as you ascend and conquer the difficulties of life. That perspective keeps challenges confined to their proper place—stepping-stones to further growth and attainment.[158]

---

157. Dieter F. Uchtdorf, "Grateful in Any Circumstances," *Ensign* or *Liahona*, May 2014, 70.
158. Richard G. Scott, "The Atonement Can Secure Your Peace and Happiness," *Ensign* or *Liahona*, Nov. 2006, 41; emphasis added.

The Savior and the Ten Lepers

At the time when the Savior lived, leprosy was a loathsome disease. Those afflicted were constrained by law to stay away from people who were "clean." When the Savior traveled through Samaria and Galilee, the scriptures tell us:

> He entered into a certain village, [and] there met him ten men that were lepers, which stood afar off:
>
> And they lifted up their voices, and said, Jesus, Master, have mercy on us.
>
> And when he saw them, he said unto them, Go shew yourselves unto the priests. And it came to pass, that, as they went, they were cleansed.
>
> And one of them, when he saw that he was healed, turned back, and with a loud voice glorified God,
>
> And fell down on his face at his feet, giving him thanks: and he was a Samaritan.
>
> And Jesus answering said, Were there not ten cleansed? but where are the nine? (Luke 17:12–17)

Because of Christ's divine intervention, ten lepers were spared a gruesome death. Yet only one expressed gratitude. The scriptures tell us that failing to express gratitude for our blessings offends God: "And in nothing doth man offend God, or against none is his wrath kindled, save those who confess not his hand in all things, and obey not his commandments" (Doctrine and Covenants 59:21).

President Faust declared:

> One of the evils of our time is taking for granted so many of the things we enjoy. This was spoken of by the Lord: "For what doth it profit a man if a gift is bestowed upon him, and he receive not the gift?" (Doctrine and Covenants 88:33). The Apostle Paul described our day to Timothy when he wrote that in the last days "men shall be lovers of their own selves, covetous, boasters, proud, blasphemers, disobedient to parents, unthankful, unholy" (2 Timothy 3:2). These sins are fellow travelers, and ingratitude makes one susceptible to all of them.[159]

159. James E. Faust, "Gratitude as a Saving Principle," *Ensign*, May 1990, 85.

Offering gratitude opens the way to blessings. In John 11, Mary and Martha sent word to Jesus that their brother Lazarus was sick, no doubt hoping He would come and heal him. But by the time Jesus got there, Lazarus had been dead for four days. After His arrival, Jesus went with Mary, Martha, and others to the tomb and bid them to move the stone away. Jesus then prayed, and the first words He uttered were to give thanks to God: "Father, I thank thee that thou hast heard me" (John 11:41). Jesus then cried, "Lazarus, come forth" (verse 43), and the dead man arose, bound with graveclothes.

In the Gospel of Matthew, Jesus again offers thanks *before* a miracle occurs. On this day, a great multitude had followed Jesus, who taught them well into the evening. When the disciples told Jesus to send the people away to buy food, Jesus instead told the disciples to feed the crowd. After checking their supplies, the disciples reported that they only had five loaves and two fish—nowhere near enough to feed the crowd of five thousand men and uncounted women and children. Despite this news, Jesus told the multitude to sit. He then prayed and gave thanks. The disciples must have wondered why Jesus gave thanks for the food when there was so little of it. But Jesus showed them that having faith and gratitude can work miracles.

After praying, Jesus broke the bread into pieces and the disciples distributed it. Jesus then asked His disciples to gather the leftovers. Again, the disciples must have wondered why—but not for long. Not only had there been enough food to feed every single person, but the disciples gathered an astounding *twelve baskets* of leftover food! (See Matthew 14:14–21.) One of the many lessons we can learn from this miracle is that we are richly blessed when we offer gratitude to God.

A Grateful Person Sees Much to Be Thankful For

At times, we may be rocked by adversity so intense that it reaches into the depths of our soul, but being grateful for what we *do* have has the power to lift us up and comfort our souls. Sister Linda K. Burton, former Relief Society President, gives an example of this: "A certain woman who has blessed my life for decades has battled for the past 15 years the debilitating, difficult, and progressive disease called inclusion body myositis. Though confined to her wheelchair, she strives to be grateful and keeps up her 'Can Can List:' a running list of things she *can* do, such as I can breathe, I can swallow, I can pray, and I can feel my Savior's love. She bears her Christ-centered *certain* witness almost daily to family and friends."[160]

Being grateful in times of distress does *not* mean we are pleased with our problems—only that we can see beyond them and recognize other blessings we have been given. Developing an attitude of gratitude is an act of faith and requires that we trust God even in adverse circumstances. One of the authors, Marlene Bateman Sullivan, shares a personal experience:

> I've had a profound hearing loss for most of my life. Despite wearing hearing aids and being able to read lips to a degree, I could only understand about 10 percent of what was said during church meetings. At times, I felt disheartened and alone. I wanted to hear *all* of the speaker's messages, not just a fraction. At times, I wondered why I even went to church when I could understand so little of what was said. Wouldn't my time be better spent at home reading the lessons or the scriptures? Certainly it would be much easier to stay home and not feel frustrated at my inability to hear. Still, I wanted to be obedient and partake of the sacrament, so I continued to attend.
>
> One Sunday, the speaker in sacrament meeting had a clear, projecting voice that made it easier to understand. He talked about the woman who suffered from an issue of blood. Because of her faith, this woman believed she could be healed if she could reach out and touch Jesus's robe as He walked by. The speaker remarked that because of the woman's condition, she would have been considered unclean and most likely would not have been allowed to attend church.
>
> For twelve years.
>
> The Spirit touched my heart as I pondered. Although ill, this woman probably was not so unwell that she couldn't attend church, at least occasionally, but because of the social mores of the times, she was not allowed to attend. What a dreadful trial for a faithful woman of God to be banned from attending religious meetings! My heart went out to this woman who was prohibited from worshiping God with her fellow believers because of her physical

160. Linda K. Burton, "Certain Women," *Ensign* or *Liahona*, May 2017, 14.

> condition—something over which she had no control. The Spirit burned within me, and I was filled with gratitude that although I was unable to be a full participant, at least I was allowed the blessing of attending church, joining with other believers, feeling of their spirit, and seeing their smiles! I felt newfound joy that I was able to attend, partake of the sacrament, and renew my covenants with God! Gratitude filled my heart that because of the goodness of God, I could come to His house, commune with Him, and feel His Holy Spirit.
>
> As the Spirit continued to warm me, blinders fell off my eyes as I realized it was far better for me to attend and get the few crumbs I could rather than not gain any at all. I had the choice whether I would attend church or not, whereas the woman who stretched out her arm to Jesus had no choice. My attitude changed that day, and I became determined to focus on what I *could* hear instead of what I *couldn't*. The woman who had touched Jesus's robe had been unable to attend religious services, but I could, and I felt a new and profound sense of thankfulness for whatever crumbs I could gather.

The Prophet Joseph Smith tells us, "The grateful man sees so much in the world to be thankful for, and with him the good outweighs the evil. . . . How much happier we are in the presence of a grateful and loving soul, and how careful we should be to cultivate . . . a thankful attitude toward God and man!"[161]

Live in Thanksgiving Daily

Gratitude is a principle that generates soul-deep happiness. Whenever we express gratitude—not only to God but to families, friends, and strangers—we are filled with the Spirit and forge new connections to those around us. Amulek gave wonderful counsel when he said, "Live in thanksgiving daily for the many mercies and blessings which he doth bestow upon you" (Alma 34:38).

Showing gratitude is a foundation for the development of other virtues, such as faith, humility, and love. Being grateful enlarges our soul and opens our eyes to the multitude of blessings God has given us. President J. Reuben Clark counseled, "Hold fast to the blessings

161. Joseph F. Smith, *Gospel Doctrine*, 5th ed. (1939), 263.

which God has provided for you. Yours is not the task to gain them, they are here; yours is the part of cherishing them."[162]

Our hearts can be filled with gratitude when we look at the starry night sky, consider the vastness of the universe, and know that even though we are very small, Heavenly Father's love for us is very great. We can feel a great sense of gratitude when we understand that God does all He can to help us through our trials. The hymn "The Lord Is My Shepherd" gives us these inspiring words;

> In the midst of affliction my table is spread.
> With blessings unmeasured my cup runneth o'er.
> With perfume and oil thou anointest my head.
> Oh, what shall I ask of your providence more?[163]

As we exercise patience in our trials, remain faithful, and express gratitude for all we have been given, Heavenly Father will bestow great blessings on us. The Lord said, "And he who receiveth all things with thankfulness shall be made glorious; and the things of this earth shall be added unto him, even an hundred fold, yea, more" (Doctrine and Covenants 78:19). Being grateful for our blessings gives us the ability to rise above sadness, strength to surmount disappointments, and power to endure. The Lord said, "Verily I say unto you my friends, fear not, let your hearts be comforted; yea, rejoice evermore, and in everything give thanks" (Doctrine and Covenants 98:1).

162. J. Reuben Clark, quoted in James E. Faust, "Gratitude As a Saving Principle," *Ensign*, May 1990, 87.

163. "The Lord is My Shepherd," *Hymns*, no. 108.

10

Yet Will I Trust in Him

"I do know that whosoever shall put their trust in God shall be supported in their trials, and their troubles, and their afflictions, and shall be lifted up at the last day."

—Alma 36:3

The Lord Is My Strength and My Shield

At times we are engulfed with family difficulties, personal trials, physical problems, or mental challenges. In addition, many people report increased anxiety in our world stemming from economic uncertainty, political discord, societal problems, global warming, dictatorial regimes with nuclear capabilities, and so on. Despite these very real problems, we can find hope by following the Savior: "The Lord is my strength and my shield; my heart trusted in him and I am helped: therefore my heart greatly rejoiceth; and with my song will I praise him" (Psalm 28:7).

The power of God gives us strength to get through the challenges of life. When we truly believe God and trust Him, we can be comforted after losing a loved one, find peace after being diagnosed with an incurable disease, and find strength to forgive after being betrayed by a close friend. Having trust in the Lord Jesus Christ also helps us move forward despite our fears. President Nelson said, "One of the realities of mortal life is that our faith will be tested and challenged," adding that "faith is the antidote for fear."[164]

Sometimes when caught up in tribulation, our trust in the Lord may diminish at the very time we need it the most. President Eyring counseled, "You will need to be sure of your faith in the moment of crisis, which may come at any time, day or night, when you plead for the influence of the Spirit. You must then be unshaken in your confidence that God lives, that He hears your cry for help, and that the resurrected Savior will do for you what He promised to do for His servants in His mortal ministry."[165]

As we go through turbulent times where we are buffeted on every side, we take solace in God's promise that "whoso putteth his trust in the Lord shall be safe" (Proverbs 29:25). Trusting God allows us to keep moving along the covenant path, push aside feelings of discouragement, endure our pain, and face the future with confidence. God will always help us in times of adversity: "Ye may know of a surety that I, the Lord God, do visit my people in their afflictions" (Mosiah 24:14).

Comfort comes in knowing that God does not require perfect faith for us to have access to His perfect power. This principle was demonstrated in an unforgettable way when a distraught father begged Christ to heal his child. When Jesus told the father, "All things are possible to him that believeth," the man humbly replied, surely with tears in his eyes, "Lord, I believe; help thou mine unbelief" (Mark 9:23–24).

When we experience hardships, how do we react? It's easy to trust God when life is going smoothly, but it can be harder when we experience personal struggles. When faced with adversity, do we continue to trust the Lord, or do we doubt? Do we continue to have hope that God will bless us to have everything work out, or are we filled with fear? Do we trust that Heavenly Father loves us and will help us navigate the trials of mortality? At moments of fear and uncertainty, we

---

164. Russell M. Nelson, "Let Your Faith Show," *Ensign* or *Liahona*, May 2014, 29.

165. Henry B. Eyring, "Gifts of the Spirit for Hard Times," *Ensign,* June 2007, 21.

may ask ourselves the question so poignantly phrased in a Primary song: "Heavenly Father, are you really there?"[166]

The good news is that He *is* here for us, just as He has been with all of His children throughout the ages. In the Old Testament, Job faced trials no other man had ever faced. Not only did he lose all ten of his children, but he also lost all of his herds, flocks, wealth, and, finally, his health. Despite these staggering losses, Job declared, "Though [God] slay me, yet will I trust in him. . . . He also shall be my salvation. . . . For I know that my redeemer liveth, and that he shall stand at the latter day upon the earth" (Job 13:15–16; 19:25).

One of the keys to *trusting* God is to *love* Him. In Matthew, we read, "Thou shalt love the Lord thy God with all thy heart, and with all thy soul, and with all thy mind" (Matthew 22:37). We should not take this commandment lightly, for it is no trifling sentiment. If we love God completely, we will trust Him completely and we will do His will.

Heavenly Father helps those who are humble and who put their trust in Him. Mosiah testified of this when explaining why God delivered the Nephites out of bondage: "But behold, he did deliver them because they did humble themselves before him; and because they cried mightily unto him he did deliver them out of bondage; and thus doth the Lord work with his power in all cases among the children of men, extending the arm of mercy towards them that put their trust in him" (Mosiah 29:20).

Trust Helps Us Navigate the Storms of Life

If we trust that Jesus is our Savior and Advocate with the Father, we can handle contrary winds when they blow. Trusting God allows us to stand strong, whether we're encountering a dangerous tempest on Galilee as did the disciples (see Matthew 8:24–27) or a fierce storm on the high seas, such as the one Lehi and his family were faced with (see 1 Nephi 18:13–15). While there are hundreds of trials that can befall us, there is only one source of true hope—God the Eternal Father and His Son, Jesus Christ.

166. "A Child's Prayer," *Children's Songbook,* 12–13.

Helaman told his sons how they could handle the storms of life: "And now, my sons, remember, remember, that it is upon the rock of our Redeemer, who is Christ, the Son of God, that ye must build your foundation; that when the devil shall send forth his mighty winds, yea, his shafts in the whirlwind, yea, when all his hail and his mighty storm shall beat upon you, it shall have no power over you to drag you down to the gulf of misery and endless wo, because of the rock upon which ye are built, which is a sure foundation, a foundation whereon if men build they cannot fall" (Helaman 5:12). Whether the tempests we encounter are severe or mild, the Lord assures us that He will help us navigate our way through them. Consider the following words of comfort that we find in the scriptures:

- "Fear not, little children, for you are mine, and I have overcome the world, and you are of them that my Father hath given me" (Doctrine and Covenants 50:41).
- God will "give [you] answer to [your] prayers" (Doctrine and Covenants 112:10).
- "I myself will go with [you] and be in [your] midst. . . . Nothing shall prevail against [you]" (Doctrine and Covenants 32:3).
- "The Lord in his great infinite goodness doth bless and prosper those who put their trust in him" (Helaman 12:1).
- "Be of good cheer, for I will lead you along. The kingdom is yours and the blessings thereof are yours, and the riches of eternity are yours" (Doctrine and Covenants 78:18).
- "God is powerful to the fulfilling of all his words" (Alma 37:16).
- "Behold, God is my salvation; I will trust, and not be afraid" (2 Nephi 22:2).
- "I will not fail thee, nor forsake thee" (Joshua 1:5).
- "Be not afraid nor dismayed by reason of this great multitude; for the battle is not yours, but God's" (2 Chronicles 20:15).
- "I will strengthen thee; . . . yea, I will uphold thee" (Isaiah 41:10).
- "I am with thee to deliver thee" (Jeremiah 1:8).

In the Book of Mormon, the Jaredites were commanded to cross the ocean to a new land, but they could not do it without God preparing a way for them to be protected against the waves and the winds (see Ether 2:25). Having faith that the Lord would protect them, the Jaredites built the barges as instructed, then "set forth into the sea, *commending* themselves unto the Lord their God" (Ether 6:4; emphasis added). *Commend* is a good choice of word because it means to entrust or to surrender. The Jaredites had to offer up their very lives to God, for they had absolutely no control over the movement of the barges.

Because they trusted the Lord to deliver them, they put aside their fears and commended their lives to God. To move them along, God caused a furious wind to blow. At times, the barges were buried in the depths of the ocean. Although the Jaredites were tossed about on the sea for 344 days, not only did they remain faithful, but they sang praises and thanked the Lord all day and into the night (see Ether 6:5, 9).

We often face our own storms as we make our way through life. At times we may feel bruised and broken from waves tossing us about. We may chafe at the lack of control we have over our lives. This is when we must exercise faith and trust that God is aware of us, knows our struggles, and is using the winds of adversity to propel us to our heavenly home. Elder L. Todd Budge said:

> We live in a world where the monster waves of death, physical and mental illness, and trials and afflictions of every kind break upon us. Yet, through faith in Jesus Christ and choosing to trust in Him, we too can have light continually, whether above the water or under the water. . . .
>
> I testify that as we commend ourselves unto the Lord and consistently and resiliently trust in Jesus Christ and His divine purposes in our lives, He will visit us with assurances, speak peace to our souls . . .
>
> He will not let us perish."[167]

---

167. L. Todd Budge, "Consistent and Resilient Trust," *Ensign* or *Liahona*, Nov. 2019, 48–49.

The Lord Blesses Those Who Put Their Trust in Him

In Proverbs we are counseled, "Trust in the Lord with all thine heart; and lean not unto thine own understanding. In all thy ways acknowledge him, and he shall direct thy paths" (Proverbs 3:5–6). This scripture can be broken down into three parts.

First, we are counseled to "trust in the Lord with all thine heart" and "in all thy ways acknowledge him." In other words, we are to have faith in God, recognize the blessings He gives us, and thank Him for those blessings.

Second, we are warned *not* to "lean unto thine own understanding." This means we should not presume we know more than God, but we should understand that His wisdom and intelligence far surpass our own. With our finite minds, we cannot begin to comprehend the things God does.

Third comes the promised blessing that "he shall direct thy paths." God promises personal revelation to guide us while in mortality. Because Heavenly Father loves us, He will not suffer us to struggle blindly but will *personally* direct our paths if we inquire of Him.

Nephi, that great Book of Mormon prophet, trusted the Lord completely. When Nephi's brothers felt it was impossible to get the plates from the powerful Laban, Nephi declared, "I will go and do the things which the Lord hath commanded, for I know that the Lord giveth no commandments unto the children of men, save he shall prepare a way for them that they may accomplish the thing which he commandeth them" (1 Nephi 3:7).

When they initially failed to get the plates, his brothers were quick to give up, but Nephi did not. Without any clear plan in place as to how to get the plates, Nephi trusted God enough to set out to Jerusalem on his own (see 1 Nephi 4:6). The Lord directed Nephi step by step, and Nephi succeeded in obtaining the plates. During mortality, hope comes when we trust God to guide us step by step through our difficulties. We may not be spared mortal challenges—Nephi certainly wasn't—but God will strengthen and bless us. Let us strive to be like Nephi who poignantly declared, "O Lord, I have trusted in thee, and I will trust in thee forever" (2 Nephi 4:34).

If we fortify our trust in God *before* storms arise, we will be better prepared to meet them. One key to strengthening trust is being humble enough to submit our will to God's. We also increase trust by obeying the commandments, serving others, forgiving those who have offended us, and repenting daily. We increase faith by studying the life and teachings of Jesus Christ in the scriptures, the *Come, Follow Me* manual, and other good books.

As we actively trust God, He will send down heaven's blessings upon us. "The Lord in his great infinite goodness doth bless and prosper those who put their trust in him" (Helaman 12:1). We are promised that the Lord will bless us abundantly: "It shall be given unto you in good measure, pressed down, and shaken together, and running over" (Luke 6:38).

Trust Means Submitting to God's Will

When our heartstrings are stretched with sorrow, we plead for God to help us. But what if the expected assistance doesn't come in the timetable we expect? Do we feel dismayed and wonder if God heard our prayers? Those who trust God know He always hears our prayers, and if the blessing they desire doesn't come, they accept His will and submit their will to the Father's. We must guard against believing in the Almighty *only* when He answers our prayers *when* we want and in the *way* we expect.

God *can* deliver us from adversity, but often He does not. There are virtues Heavenly Father wants us to cultivate, and while He *could* erase our suffering, doing so might eliminate valuable learning experiences. It may be the work of a lifetime and beyond to reach the point where we are patient enough to "submit cheerfully and with patience to all the will of the Lord" (Mosiah 24:15). However, having faith also means having patience enough to trust in the Lord's timing. Blessings will come according to God's will and His timetable. We can trust our all-wise Father enough to know that He has a wise purpose for not removing our trial, even if we do not know the reason. At such times, we can be content to know that God will help us bear our burdens. "Lift up your heads and be of good comfort, for I . . . will also ease the burdens which are upon your shoulders that even you cannot feel them upon your backs" (Mosiah 24:13–14).

Abraham faced one of the most agonizing trials imaginable when God asked Him to offer his only son, Isaac, as a sacrifice. And yet Abraham did not argue, nor did he plead with God to reconsider. Abraham could have listed many reasons why he should *not* kill his only beloved son. But instead, he committed himself to submit his will to God's and traveled with Isaac to Mount Moriah. Only at the last possible moment—when Abraham stood at the altar ready to fulfill God's command—did Heavenly Father stay his hand.

Shadrach, Meshach, and Abed-nego demonstrated unwavering trust in God when they refused the king's command to worship a golden image. When King Nebuchadnezzar ordered them cast into a fiery furnace, they responded with great faith even though they did not know God's will concerning them. Nevertheless, they were determined to submit their will to God's—even if it led to their death. In one accord, Shadrach, Meshach, and Abed-nego said, "Our God whom we serve is able to deliver us from the burning fiery furnace, and he will deliver us out of thine hand, O king. *But if not,* be it known unto thee, O King, that we will not serve thy gods, nor worship the golden image which thou hast set up" (Daniel 3:17–18; emphasis added).

Even Jesus Christ, the Only Begotten Son of the Father, submitted His will to God's. In the Garden of Gethsemane, Christ suffered such agonizing pain that it caused Him—a God—to tremble because of pain, bleed at every pore, and suffer intense agony in both body and spirit (see Doctrine and Covenants 19:18). In His anguish, Jesus asked His Father to remove the cup from Him but submitted His will to the Father's by saying, "Nevertheless not my will but thine, be done" (Luke 22:42).

Having faith in God gives us the strength we need to accept God's will when it differs from our own. In time, instead of praying "Please bless me and make me whole," we can say, "Please bless me with the strength to accept whatever Thou hast planned for me." As we work to develop an unwavering trust in God, we can stand firm and faithful, even if our path leads to Mount Moriah, a fiery furnace, or our own personal Gethsemane.

Partaking of the Bitter Cup without Becoming Bitter

It's easy to have faith in God when He blesses us to overcome our trials, but it's a little harder when He does *not* remove our afflictions. Elder Maxwell said that submitting to God's will allows us to "be able to partake of a bitter cup without becoming bitter; . . . to let our wills increasingly be swallowed up in the will of the Father: to acknowledge . . . that, indeed, 'All these things shall give thee experience, and shall be for thy good,' (Doctrine and Covenants 122:7); and to plow enduringly to the end of the furrow—all the while glorifying Him and using the matchless gifts He has given us."[168]

While in the crucible of mortality, we may not be able to fully understand the virtues we gain from adversity, simply because the end result is not easily visible because of our finite, mortal minds. It may not be until the next life that we truly understand how our difficulties helped polish our characters. Because of that, we might do well to think of trials as "growth experiences" and trust Heavenly Father enough to know that our progress is of paramount importance to Him. We can be sure that our growth can be accelerated when we allow God to guide us through our hardships.

A few months after Jarem Hallows received a cancer diagnosis, he decided to submit to Heavenly Father's will, retain his faith, and remain positive. Even though Jarem's goal was, like everyone else so diagnosed, to become cancer-free, he added a caveat: "My quest is to do as [Elder] Neal Maxwell described by partaking of a bitter cup without becoming bitter."

A few of Jarem's trials included major mouth surgery, radiation of his mouth and throat, and chemotherapy. All of these treatments resulted in excruciating pain, sleepless nights, and endless hospital visits. For nourishment, Jarem had to rely on feeding tubes since at times he was unable to swallow liquids. Once Jarem had recovered enough to attend church, he stood at the pulpit and bore a strong testimony of

---

168. Neal A. Maxwell, "Plow in Hope," *Church News*, Apr. 1, 2001, https://www.thechurchnews.com/2001/4/1/23244569/elder-maxwell-plow-in-hope.

Jesus Christ and how the Savior had chosen to suffer pains and afflictions of every kind so that He would know how to succor his people" (see Alma 7:11–12).

To help others suffering from cancer, Jarem started a blog in which he wrote, "For those of you going through something like this for the first time, those types of [despairing] feelings can be expected. Don't feel guilty for how you feel or where your mind goes. Don't feel guilty. But don't let those emotions take root. They aren't from you and they aren't going to be you. 'For God hath not given us the spirit of fear; but of power, and of love, and of a sound mind' (see 2 Timothy 1:7)."[169]

Elder Scott taught:

> We are like infants in our understanding of eternal matters and their impact on us here in mortality. Yet at times we act as if we knew it all. When you pass through trials for His purposes, as you trust Him, exercise faith in Him, He will help you. That support will generally come step by step, a portion at a time. . . .
>
> To recognize the hand of the Lord in your life and to accept His will without complaint is a beginning. That decision does not immediately eliminate the struggles that will come for your growth. But I witness that it is the best way there is for you to find strength and understanding. It will free you from the dead ends of your own reasoning. It will allow your life to become a productive, meaningful experience, when otherwise you may not know how to go on.[170]

When Answers Are Slow in Coming

When a loved one becomes ill, we pray they will be healed. If a daughter runs away without letting us know where she is, we pray that one day she'll make contact again. If we lose our job and face eviction, we plead for the financial means to remain in our home. And then, after praying, if our loved one remains sick, our daughter does not

169. Carmen Rasmusen, "3 stories of conquering despair, fear from battling cancer through faith in Jesus Christ," *Deseret News*, Apr. 15, 2017, https://www.deseret.com/2017/4/15/20610436/3-stories-of-conquering-despair-fear-from-battling-cancer-through-faith-in-jesus-christ.

170. Richard G. Scott, "Trust in the Lord," *Ensign*, Nov. 1995, 17–18.

call, and we are forced to leave our home, we may wonder why God did not answer our prayers. Was our faith not strong enough? Were we unworthy of meriting God's intervention?

It may help to realize there are times when the Savior focuses on spiritual rather than physical healings. We can be healed if it is expedient in Christ, but His aim might be to heal us spiritually, and usually that takes time. Elder Scott said, "Be thankful that sometimes God lets you struggle for a long time before that answer comes. That causes your faith to increase and your character to grow."[171]

As we submit our will to God, we must also give up our schedule and accept God's timetable. He will provide comfort as we wait and endure. Blessings may not come the way we hoped, but they *will* come in a way that will help us. Elder David A. Bednar explains:

> Righteousness and faith certainly are instrumental in moving mountains—if moving mountains accomplishes God's purposes and is in accordance with His will. Righteousness and faith certainly are instrumental in healing the sick, deaf, or lame—if such healing accomplishes God's purposes and is in accordance with His will. Thus, even with strong faith, many mountains will not be moved. And not all of the sick and infirm will be healed. If all opposition were curtailed, if all maladies were removed, then the primary purposes of the Father's plan would be frustrated.[172]

It is difficult to pray for an extended period for a longed-for blessing and not have our request granted, especially when our desire is righteous and would bring us great joy. Some examples of this are finding an eternal companion, having a child, or having our loved one healed. However, when the answer is no, we must trust God and understand that His wisdom and intelligence are far greater than our own. When the answers we seek do not come right away, we can remember that the Lord's timing is different than our own and that if we continue pressing forward in faith and righteousness, He will help us.

---

171. Richard G. Scott, "The Transforming Power of Faith and Character," *Ensign* or *Liahona*, Nov. 2010, 44.

172. David A. Bednar, "Accepting the Lord's Will and Timing," *Ensign* or *Liahona,* Aug., 2016, 31–32.

As we develop more trust in God, we can rejoice in the blessings we do have as we wait to see the hand of God revealed. Faith is not just believing—it's also trusting enough to continue on, knowing that awaited blessings *will* come. They may not come immediately or even in our lifetime, but for those who remain true disciples of Christ, *they will come.* President Nelson said:

> On occasion, some of our most fervent prayers may seem to go unanswered. We wonder, "Why?" I know that feeling! I know the fears and tears of such moments. But I also know that our prayers are never ignored. Our faith is never unappreciated. I know that an all-wise Heavenly Father's perspective is much broader than is ours. While we know of our mortal problems and pain, He knows of our immortal progress and potential. If we pray to know His will and submit ourselves to it with patience and courage, heavenly healing can take place in His own way and time.[173]

The scriptures make reference to the "process of time" (Moses 7:21), which simply means that certain things take time. If we truly trust in God, we will trust in His timing. We do not pout or become bitter. When we pray for relief from our afflictions, we naturally hope that rescue will come quickly, but covenant-keeping discipleship often requires a willingness to patiently wait for asked-for blessings.

Elder Holland spoke of this, saying the following:

> There will be times in our lives when even our best spiritual effort and earnest, pleading prayers do not yield the victories for which we have yearned, whether that be regarding the large global matters or the small personal ones. So while we work and wait together for the answers to some of our prayers, I offer you my apostolic promise that they are heard and they are answered, though perhaps not at the time or in the way we wanted. But they are *always* answered at the time and in the way an omniscient and eternally compassionate parent should answer them. My beloved brothers and sisters, please understand that He who never sleeps nor slumbers cares for the happiness and ultimate exaltation of His children above all else that

173. Russell M. Nelson, "Jesus Christ—the Master Healer," *Ensign* or *Liahona*, Nov. 2005, 86.

> a divine being has to do. He is pure love, gloriously personified, and Merciful Father is His name.[174]

Trust Prevents Trials from Taking Over Your Life

It's easy to get caught up in personal trials when they significantly impact our lives. Sometimes it can feel like hardships are holding us hostage. But peace can come when we place our trust in the Lord. Perhaps you know someone who has a debilitating physical condition and yet exudes a feeling of peacefulness, which allows them to move forward, accepting what they *can* do and what they *can't*. That is faith. That is enduring. That is also the story of Barbara Jayne Richards, who faced great trials but refused to let her disability take over her life.

Sister Barbara W. Winder, former General Relief Society President, related the story of her friend Barbara Jayne Richards, who was attending Brigham Young University when she was in a car accident that left her paralyzed from the waist down. Barbara Jayne Richards said, "Once I might have thought of paralysis only as a terrible tragedy, but after it became a part of my life, I discovered it could also bring blessings. My paralysis introduced me to a whole new way of living, to many wonderful people, to a new assemblage of problems, adjustments, frustrations, tears, laughter, and joy. [It has taught me] an appreciation for myself as a person and as a child of God, appreciation for other people, and especially a love and appreciation for my Father in heaven."[175]

Barbara Richards went on:

> I used to be embarrassed if I did a clumsy, awkward thing in public; and now clumsy was my middle name. . . . I had to learn to laugh so that others would feel at ease around me and I wouldn't feel so self-conscious. . . . I used to take so many things for granted, things like showering, kneeling to say prayers, dressing in a minute,

---

174. Jeffrey R. Holland, "Waiting on the Lord," *Ensign* or *Liahona*, Nov. 2020, 115–16.

175. Barbara Jayne Richards, "A Joyful Life (In A Wheelchair)," *The Instructor,* July 1970, 244–45, https://archive.org/details/instructor1057dese/page/n13/mode/2up.

> getting places quickly. Now it is a challenge to do these once-simple things. . . . It took losing the use of my legs to make me start appreciating the physical body that I have. Now I became very grateful for a clear mind with which to think, ears to hear, eyes to see God's beautiful world, hands that could do so many things. Although I can't dance, hike, play volleyball or basketball anymore, I have found there are still many things I can do from a wheelchair. I can drive a car, swim better than before, play doubles in tennis, bowl, play catch in softball (nobody dares try to slide home), cook, sew . . . and do many other enjoyable things.
>
> Perhaps the greatest blessing which came from my "tragedy" was the love and appreciation I developed for my Father in Heaven. . . . After my accident I had to depend completely on the Lord for the first time in my life. He became a real person with whom I could talk and who would help me solve the problems and make the adjustments that were to come. Without my understanding of God as my spiritual, loving, concerned Father, I would be in the same rut that I have seen so many others in—that of blaming God for my misfortune.[176]

As we trust and give ourselves into the Lord's capable hands, we can feel the peace that comes from knowing we are loved and supported no matter what emotional, financial, or physical trial we face. "These things I have spoken unto you, that in me ye might have peace. In the world ye shall have tribulation: but be of good cheer; I have overcome the world" (John 16:33).

Hope Comes from Trusting the Lord

It has been said that the sting of suffering can be eased if you find meaning in it. We can find that meaning when we understand that tribulation is a process designed to allow us to rise to the next level in our development. Our souls are soothed to know that afflictions aid us to become humbler, stronger, wiser, more patient, and more compassionate. In fact, trials can be thought of as spiritual rehabilitation—a procedure Heavenly Father prescribes for our benefit. When we trust in the skill of our divine Physician, we will thank Him for His prescription.

176. Barbara Jayne Richards, "A Joyful Life (In A Wheelchair)."

Even when buffeted by life, we can trust in God's love, timing, and purposes, for "he doeth not anything save it be for the benefit of the world; for he loveth the world" (2 Nephi 26:24). Accepting the will of the Father qualifies us for blessings not only in this life but in the life to come. When we have faith, God will give us strength to endure. "Brothers and sisters, I invite you to place all of your trust in God and in the teachings of His prophets," said Elder Soares. "I invite you to renew your covenants with God, to serve Him with all your heart, regardless of the complex situations of life. I testify that by the power of your unwavering faith in Christ, you will become free of the captivity of sin, of doubt, of unbelief, of unhappiness, of suffering; and you will receive all of the promised blessings from our loving Heavenly Father."[177]

When Ammon found King Limhi and his people, the king felt sure that Ammon had been sent by God to help them escape from bondage. King Limhi told his people, "Therefore, lift up your heads, and rejoice, and put your trust in God. . . . If ye will turn to the Lord with full purpose of heart . . . and serve him with all diligence of mind, . . . he will, according to his own will and pleasure, deliver you out of bondage" (Mosiah 7:19, 33).

Although Alma suffered much adversity, he trusted God and testified to his people, "I have been supported under trials and troubles of every kind, yea, and in all manner of afflictions; yea, God has delivered me from prison, and from bonds, and from death; yea, and I do put my trust in him, and he will still deliver me. And I know that he will raise me up at the last day, to dwell with him in glory" (Alma 36:27–28).

Sometimes life's problems keep us awake at night, but we can deal with them if we pray to receive God's strengthening power. Philippians 4:13 assures us, "I can do all things through Christ which strengtheneth me." Elder Holland counsels, "Cling to your faith, hold on to your hope. 'Pray always, and be believing' (Doctrine and Covenants 90:24). Even if you cannot always see that silver lining on your clouds, God can, for He is the very source of the light you seek. He does love

177. Ulisses Soares, "Confide in God Unwaveringly," *Ensign* or *Liahona*, May 2017, 35.

you, and He knows your fears. He hears your prayers. He is your Heavenly Father, and surely He matches with His own the tears His children shed."[178]

When our burdens are heavy, we can drop them at the Savior's feet. "Cast thy burdens upon the Lord, and he shall sustain thee: he shall never suffer the righteous to be moved" (Psalms 55:22). Comfort comes when we truly understand that the Lord knows us better and loves us more than we do ourselves. When we trust in God, we need not fear. "Behold, God is my salvation; I will trust, and not be afraid; for the Lord Jehovah is my strength and my song; he also has become my salvation" (2 Nephi 22:2).

178. Jeffrey R. Holland, "An High Priest of Good Things to Come," *Ensign,* Nov. 1999, 36.

11

Hope Comes from Hearing His Voice

"I will tell you in your mind and in your heart, by the Holy Ghost, which shall come upon you. . . . Now, behold, this is the spirit of revelation."

—Doctrine and Covenants 8:2–3

Personal Revelation: Our Divine Compass

When we came to earth, Heavenly Father knew we would struggle with adversity and temptations but promised to provide us with divine direction. Because of His promise, we need not fumble through life guided only by our limited understanding but can receive personal revelation to enlighten our minds and direct our paths. To receive direction from the Lord in these troubled times, we must prepare ourselves spiritually. President Nelson cautions, "In coming days, it will not be possible to survive spiritually without the guiding, directing, comforting, and constant influence of the Holy Ghost."[179]

When Lehi, Sariah, and their family left Jerusalem and journeyed in the wilderness, they were given the Liahona, a divine compass. This unique instrument worked by faith and provided direction for their

179. Russell M. Nelson, "Revelation for the Church, Revelation for Our Lives," *Ensign* or *Liahona,* May 2018, 96.

travels. Like Lehi, we can receive divine direction to navigate our way through mortality. Personal revelation is one of God's choicest blessings. President Kimball stated, "Of all things, that . . . we should be most grateful [for] is that the heavens are indeed open and that the restored church of Jesus Christ is founded upon the rock of revelation. Continuous revelation is indeed the very lifeblood of the gospel of the living Lord and Savior, Jesus Christ."[180]

If we want to receive personal revelation, one of the first things we can do is obey the teachings of the Savior and try to be diligent at keeping the commandments. As long as we are sincerely trying to follow Christ, the Holy Ghost can reveal God's will to us. Second, we must have faith that God will help us. Our faith will often be tested and, at times, the Lord may require us to walk in the darkness for a few steps before He rewards our faith and shines His light upon our path. Third, we must put forth effort to receive divine guidance. President Nelson reminds us, "To do anything well requires effort."[181] In addition, we can try to pray more sincerely, attend the temple more regularly, be more conscientious at serving others, study the scriptures more diligently, become more engaged in family history work, and be more mindful while partaking of the sacrament.

Fourth, we can be conscientious in obeying the Spirit when He speaks to us. We can't expect God to continue providing us with personal inspiration if we do not follow through on what He has *already* told us. "When you demonstrate your willingness to obey," President Eyring says, "the Spirit will send you more impressions of what God would have you do for Him. As you obey, the impressions from the Spirit will come more frequently, becoming closer and closer to constant companionship. Your power to choose the right will increase."[182]

180. *Teachings of Presidents of the Church: Spencer W. Kimball* (2006), 243. See also Matthew 16:13–19.

181. Russell M. Nelson, "Christ Is Risen; Faith in Him Will Move Mountains," *Liahona*, May 2021, 103.

182. Henry B. Eyring, "The Holy Ghost as Your Companion," *Ensign* or *Liahona*, Nov. 2015, 105.

Strengthen Your Relationship with Heavenly Father and Jesus Christ

We can hear the whisperings of the Spirit much more easily if we have established a deep personal relationship with Heavenly Father and Jesus Christ. Following are some suggestions on how to improve this most important relationship.

- **Increase quality time with Heavenly Father and Jesus Christ.** Just as we create time to be with our family and friends, we can spend time connecting with Heavenly Father and Jesus on more than a superficial level. We can spend time with Them by making Them the focal point of our daily lives. We can also improve the quality of our prayers, which will help us feel the love They have for us.
- **Learn more about Heavenly Father and Jesus Christ.** We learn more as we study the scriptures and other good books, which will give us a deeper appreciation of Christ and of our Father in Heaven. As we read, we will learn more about their divine attributes and better understand the great love Heavenly Father and Jesus have for us. We can also learn more by watching videos of Christ, which can be found on the Church's website.
- **Ponder on the blessings Heavenly Father and Jesus Christ have given you.** Think back to moments when God has answered your prayers, strengthened you during dark times, blessed you with inspiration, or sent you feelings of love and comfort. Remember when God showed His love by touching your heart, opening your mind, and blessing you with divine inspiration.

Recognizing the Spirit

The scriptures often use the word *voice* to describe the promptings that come from the Holy Ghost. And yet a voice does not always adequately describe these delicate spiritual communications because they are rarely heard with our ears. Instead, the Holy Spirit's "voice" most often comes as an impression to our mind and as a feeling to our heart.

It is not always easy to understand the Spirit's voice. When God first spoke to the people of Nephi, the people did not understand, even though His words pierced them to the center, causing their bodies to shake and their hearts to burn. When Heavenly Father spoke a second time, they were still unable to understand. It was not until the third time that the people understood the Father's voice and heard Him introduce His Beloved Son (see 3 Nephi 11:3–7). They felt, then heard. And finally, they understood.

In order to "hear" or recognize the Spirit, we must be paying attention because the Spirit typically speaks so gently that if we are preoccupied or distracted, we may not hear it at all. If we pay attention, God will speak to us, but He will not raise His voice to get our attention. God will not speak over the music we're listening to, and He will not try to get our attention if we are busy texting, emailing, or looking at social media. Neither will He repeat Himself over and over.

As we pay attention and become more acquainted with how God speaks, we grow in our ability to hear Him. We should not expect inspiration to come as loudly and brightly as fireworks—that only happens on rare occasions. The Lord will not use a floodlight when a flashlight will do.

When we pray for confirmation about a decision we have made, the Spirit most often replies by giving us a calm, comforting feeling (see Doctrine and Covenants 36:2; 42:61; 111:8). In February 1847, Joseph Smith appeared to Brigham Young in a dream and said, "Tell the people to be humble and faithful, and be sure to keep the Spirit of the Lord, and it will lead them right. . . . They can tell the Spirit of the Lord from all other spirits; it will whisper peace and joy to their souls."[183]

The Spirit can also manifest itself as an intense, burning feeling. The Lord said that when the Spirit testifies, it would "cause that your bosom shall burn within you" (Doctrine and Covenants 9:8).

183. "Praise to the Man: The Prophet's Legacy," Church History, accessed Nov. 10, 2023, https://history.churchofjesuschrist.org/content/praise-to-the-man.

Mormon described this feeling, saying that it "did cause their hearts to burn" (3 Nephi 11:3). The Spirit may also be characterized by a sense of urgency, insistence, or necessity (see 1 Nephi 4:10–18). If we feel prompted to do something and feel warm and peaceful, we can know this feeling is from God. There may be times when we have decided on something that is *not* in our best interest. In this case, God will speak to us and warn us by blessing us with feelings of anxiety, confusion, and worry that cause us to feel unsure and uncertain. The Doctrine and Covenants tell us, "If it be not right . . . you shall have a stupor of thought" (Doctrine and Covenants 9:9).

At times, we may wonder if what we feel is truly inspiration, or if it's simply a product of our own thoughts. Generally, it is not good to second-guess spiritual promptings because to do so is to dismiss the Spirit of God. The Prophet Joseph Smith taught "that if you will listen to the first promptings, you will get it right nine times out of ten."[184] The Spirit can prompt us to action by gently nudging us to call a friend, speak to a stranger, or check on a family member. As we learn to recognize how the Spirit speaks, we can be more and more confident that such promptings come from God.

One of the authors, Joshua Sullivan, tells about when he was directed by the Spirit:

> When I was twenty-four, I lived in Bountiful, Utah. My grandma lived in southern Utah near St. George. One weekend, my parents decided to visit my grandma and asked if I wanted to go. I declined. Later, a group of friends told me they had rented a condo in St. George and asked me to go. Again, I declined. But late Friday afternoon, I changed my mind and drove to St. George where I played volleyball and soccer with my friends until 11:30 p.m. We then headed to the condo to watch a movie, but my friends got lost and didn't start the movie until 1:00 a.m. Tired, I decided to head to my grandma's house and go to bed.
>
> Once in my car, I discovered my phone had died. It was dark and, not being familiar with the city, I got turned around and lost.

184. Joseph Smith, quoted in Ronald A. Rasband, "Let the Holy Spirit Guide," *Ensign* or *Liahona*, May 2017, 96. See also Truman G. Madsen, *Joseph Smith, the Prophet* (Salt Lake City, UT: Deseret Book, 1989), 103.

I was driving on a side street when I saw someone outside a car parked on the side of the road. Figuring he must have gotten a flat tire, I stopped to help, only to discover that the person was trying to do CPR on a young man lying on the ground.

I ran over to where a panicked sixteen-year-old kid was screaming, "No, Omar! Don't die!" while trying to do CPR with one hand and call 911 with the other. I pushed him off and told him to direct the ambulance to our location because I had no idea where we were. I felt for a pulse and if the kid was breathing. Nothing. I started doing CPR, and I'll never forget the sound it made when I pushed on his chest. Soon an ambulance pulled up. The EMTs took over. They pulled out an AED and shocked him. I thought I saw the young man coming to as they carried him to the ambulance, but I wasn't sure. Even now, I don't know if he lived or not. Feeling shaky, I sat on the ground while the other kid told the cops he thought his friend had overdosed on heroin. One of the cops talked with me, and I explained I had just been driving by.

It wasn't until the next day that it hit me. It was no coincidence that I showed up on that particular back road in the early hours of the morning. I hadn't even planned on going to St. George. I wasn't going to stay so late with my friends. And most certainly, I did not plan on getting "lost." The fact is that I was *supposed* to be there. On that street. Performing CPR on an unresponsive teenager. Although I have never audibly heard the voice of God, there is no doubt He directed me to take off the preceding afternoon and drive four and a half hours to St. George, Utah. Heavenly Father guided me and directed me to drive along a deserted side road so I could be there at the exact moment I was needed.

Joseph Smith's Pattern for Receiving Revelation

Joseph Smith was fourteen years old when he walked out of a grove of trees in Palmyra, New York, after receiving a stunning revelation from God the Father and His Son, Jesus Christ. Joseph now knew of a surety that God communicates with His children in our day and age. President Nelson said of this, "If Joseph Smith's transcendent experience in the Sacred Grove teaches us anything, it is that the heavens are open and that God speaks to His children."[185]

What was the catalyst for this incredible vision? It came because Joseph believed the words written in the Bible: "If any of you lack wisdom, let him ask of God, that giveth to all men liberally, and upbraideth not; and it shall be given him. But let him ask in faith, nothing wavering. For he that wavereth is like a wave of the sea driven with the wind and tossed" (James 1:5–6). Joseph also had a pure faith in Jesus Christ and a humble heart. With those twin virtues, he was prepared to receive revelation that restored the gospel of Jesus Christ to the earth and opened the last dispensation. Like Joseph, we can qualify ourselves to receive divine direction.

It is imperative during these latter days to know how to access the powers of heaven. Receiving personal revelation takes effort, but great blessings come as we hear God's voice and receive personal guidance. Joseph Smith's experience in the Sacred Grove gives us a valuable pattern to follow:

- Joseph kept the commandments and lived an upright, virtuous life. Our efforts to receive personal revelation must include a willingness to live according to the standards God has revealed in the scriptures. We don't have to be perfect to receive revelation, but we need to do our best to keep the commandments.
- By studying and pondering the scriptures often, Joseph gained a steadfast faith in God. Joseph had enough faith to have confidence that when he asked for help, God would answer. As we have faith, God will bless us with revelation. We increase faith by studying the scriptures and spending time seriously reflecting on them. Reading the scriptures opens the door to revelation because it is through them that the Spirit of God bears witness of the truth.
- Joseph humbly acknowledged that he lacked wisdom and asked God which church to join. By this, we learn that it requires a humble heart to ask God for knowledge we lack

185. Russell M. Nelson, "Revelation for the Church, Revelation for Our Lives," 95.

and for wisdom we do not possess. Joseph had pondered on his problem, and then—aware he needed divine guidance—asked God for the wisdom he lacked.

- When Joseph received an answer to his prayer, he did everything God commanded. The principle of obedience should not be overlooked. We cannot expect God to give us direction if we are not willing to do what He asks. When God whispers to us, we must obey His holy promptings, even if we do not fully understand why He is asking us to do what He has asked. Revelation profits us nothing unless we follow through with what God tells us to do.
- Joseph continued to study the scriptures, have faith, and pray for additional guidance. Even after receiving a vision, Joseph continued to study, build his faith, and pray. By staying close to God, he was blessed with additional truth and light. As we obey God's commandments, follow the prophet, read the scriptures, and pray with a sincere heart, we can—like Joseph—continually receive revelation to comfort us in our afflictions and guide us during our mortal journey.

Growing into the Principle of Revelation

"The Spirit speaks words that we feel," Elder Rasband taught. "These feelings are gentle, a nudge to act, to do something, to say something, to respond in a certain way. If we are casual or complacent in our worship, drawn off and desensitized by worldly pursuits, we find ourselves diminished in our ability to feel. . . . If we pay attention to the promptings that come to us, we will grow in the spirit of revelation and receive more and more Spirit-driven insight and direction."[186]

Because Heavenly Father loves us, He wants to help us with our problems. One of the greatest gifts He has given us is the gift of personal revelation, which offers comfort, encouragement, hope, and healing. The voice of the Lord is given unto all people (see Doctrine

186. Ronald A Rasband, "Let the Holy Spirit Guide," 94, 96.

and Covenants 1:2). We can be richly blessed if we do as Joseph Smith taught and "grow into the principle of revelation."[187]

It does take effort to receive communication from God. We cannot ask blithely, expecting God to answer when we put no work into figuring out what we desire to know. The Lord explained, "But, behold, I say unto you, that you must study it out in your mind; then you must ask me if it be right" (Doctrine and Covenants 9:8). Before praying for guidance, we must research the matter, ponder it in our mind, and carefully consider what would be the best action to take.

Our questions may not be answered fully at first. Typically, revelation comes bit by bit over time, with little pieces being added from time to time. Each new piece gives more information and greater understanding and builds upon inspiration which was previously given. The Lord stated, "I will give unto the children of men, line by line, precept upon precept, here a little and there a little; and blessed are they who shall hearken . . . for they shall learn wisdom; for unto him that receiveth I will give more" (2 Nephi 28:30).

Following the pattern of prayer God has given helps us grow into the principle of revelation. When we pray, we should first express gratitude for the blessings God has given us. Then we talk to God the way we would to a good friend, telling Him our worries, fears, and the longings of our hearts. Prayer is not meant to be one-sided, so we should take time listen to what God would like to say to us. When done, we can quietly listen for the Lord's still, small voice and hear the guidance He offers. We might want to write down any thoughts and impressions that come, including what actions we feel prompted to make. Then we act on those promptings.

Personal revelation comes to each of us in an individual and unique manner. Since we are all different and have varying responsibilities, revelation will be designed especially for us. Sister Michelle Craig, of the Young Women General Presidency, spoke about how three great prophets faced similar problems and how each received personalized revelation. She said:

---

187. *Teachings of Presidents of the Church: Joseph Smith* (2007), 132.

> Nephi, the brother of Jared, and even Moses all had a large body of water to cross—and each did it differently. Nephi worked "timbers of curious workmanship" (1 Nephi 18:1). The brother of Jared built barges that were "tight like unto a dish" (Ether 6:5–8). And Moses "walked upon dry land in the midst of the sea" (Exodus 14:29).
>
> They each received personalized direction, tailored to them, and each trusted and acted. The Lord is mindful of those who obey and, in the words of Nephi, will "prepare a way for [us to] accomplish the thing which he commandeth" (1 Nephi 3:7).[188]

Heavenly Father will speak to us as often as we inquire, giving us revelation tailored to our specific circumstances. Some may feel it is only proper to pray about big decisions, such as who to marry, where to attend college, and what job to accept. But it is alright to ask the Lord for guidance about small matters as well, for the Lord has said, "Look unto me in *every* thought" (Doctrine and Covenants 6:36; emphasis added). Because our Father in Heaven loves us, He wants to help us in large *and* small matters.

We Can Rejoice in Personal Revelation

Because Heavenly Father can see the beginning and the end and everything in between, He knows the wisest course of action for us to follow and offers us the opportunity to receive divine direction. Taking time to learn how to recognize God's promptings is just as vital to our emotional and spiritual well-being as proper nutrition is to our physical health. We live in a busy world and often drive ourselves so relentlessly that we hardly have time to think of the Lord and receive His guidance. However, we need the Spirit if we are to safely navigate the pitfalls that arise from living in this day and age.

President Packer taught:

> We live in troubled times—very troubled times. We hope, we pray, for better days. But that is not to be. The prophecies tell us that. We will not as a people, as families, or as individuals be exempt from the trials to come. No one will be spared the trials common to home and family, work, disappointment, grief, health, aging, ultimately death . . .

188. Michelle Craig, "Spiritual Capacity," *Ensign* or *Liahona*, Nov. 2019, 21.

> [But] we need not live in fear of the future. We have every reason to rejoice and little reason to fear. If we follow the promptings of the Spirit, we will be safe, whatever the future holds. We will be shown what to do.[189]

As we live worthily and make a sincere effort to listen, we increase our spiritual capacity to receive personal revelation. Knowing we can receive instruction from the Lord gives us hope—no matter our circumstances. The Lord promises, "If thou shalt ask, thou shalt receive revelation upon revelation, knowledge upon knowledge, that thou mayest know the mysteries and peaceable things—that which bringeth joy, that which bringeth life eternal" (Doctrine and Covenants 42:61).

By making a sincere effort to hear God's still, small voice, we can receive the guiding power He greatly desires to give. "To be sure, there may be times when you feel as though the heavens are closed," President Nelson said. "But I promise that as you continue to be obedient, expressing gratitude for every blessing the Lord gives you, and as you patiently honor the Lord's timetable, you will be given the knowledge and understanding you seek. Every blessing the Lord has for you—even miracles—will follow. That is what personal revelation will do for you."[190]

As we are obedient and listen to the whisperings that come, the heavens will open. We may stumble, but we can rise. We may falter, but with God's help, we can move forward and receive His guidance. Patience may be required, but in God's own way and in His own time, He will answer our prayers and bless us with personal revelation. The Lord has promised, "Verily, verily, I say unto you, I will impart unto you of my Spirit, which shall enlighten your mind, which shall fill your soul with joy" (Doctrine and Covenants 11:13).

---

189. Boyd K. Packer, "The Cloven Tongues of Fire," *Ensign*, May 2000, 8.

190. Russell M. Nelson, "Revelation for the Church, Revelation for Our Lives," 95–96.

12
We Never Walk Alone

"And the Lord, he it is that doth go before thee; he will be with thee, he will not fail thee, neither forsake thee: fear not, neither be dismayed."

—Deuteronomy 31:8

Heavenly Father, Are You Really There?

It can be difficult to feel God's love while floundering in the quagmire of adversity. When flooded with trials of mental or physical illness, natural disasters, poverty, or a hundred other causes, life can seem difficult and frightening. As we struggle to stay afloat, we may ask ourself the question so poignantly phrased in the Primary song: "Heavenly Father, are You really there?" The answer to that is detailed in verse two:

> Pray, he is there;
> Speak, he is listening,
> You are his child;
> His love now surrounds you
> He hears your prayer;
> He loves the children.
> Of such is the kingdom, the kingdom of Heaven.[191]

191. "A Child's Prayer," *Children's Songbook,* 12–13.

We live in a world drowning in fear, pessimism, and animosity. Yet the gospel of Jesus Christ has the power to transcend politics, resentments, and injustice. The most important message mortals have ever been given is that Heavenly Father lives, that He loves us, and that he is personally involved in our lives. Every one of us is a child of a divine God. Heavenly Father is the most powerful being in the universe, and He is the Father of our spirits, making us children of a King. Knowing that we are of noble birth is empowering. As we seek a deeper understanding of God, we are promised, "The Spirit beareth witness with our spirit, that we are the children of God" (Romans 8:16). Because He loves us, Heavenly Father will never leave us alone but walks with us through mortality. We have a bright and glorious future ahead because of who we are and who we can become.

Heavenly Father Loves Us

Elder Holland declared, "The first great *commandment* of all eternity is to love God with all of *our* heart, might, mind, and strength. . . . But the first great *truth* of all eternity is that God loves *us* with all of *His* heart, might, mind, and strength."[192]

All of us want to be loved, *and we are*—by the God of this universe! Knowing that God loves us is transforming. When we accept that great truth, we need never feel alone. We belong to a great eternal family, who are—like us—cherished children of heavenly parents. Each of us has a divine origin, nature, and potential. Heavenly Father loves us perfectly, but it is up to us to decide if we will love Him back. It is also up to us if we will obey God or not. If we do, God will love us. If we don't, God loves us still.

Heavenly Father's love is not found in the condition of our lives but in His *presence* in our lives. Because He loves us, He blesses us with strength when ours runs low, gives us peace when we are fearful, and provides comfort when we are distressed. Nothing we do can ever separate us from the love of our Father and Jesus Christ. "Our Savior, the Good Shepherd, knows and loves us," declared President Uchtdorf. "He knows and loves you. He knows when you are lost, and

192. Jeffrey R. Holland, "Tomorrow the Lord Will Do Wonders Among You," *Ensign* or *Liahona*, May 2016, 127.

He knows where you are. He knows your grief. Your silent pleadings. Your fears. Your tears. It matters not how you became lost—whether because of your own poor choices or because of circumstances beyond your control. What matters is that you are His child. And He loves you. He loves His children."[193]

While we're on earth, Satan will try to separate us from the power that comes from knowing Heavenly Father loves us. Since his aim is to make us miserable like himself, we must jettison any false and destructive thoughts he attempts to plant in our minds, such as the following:

- Satan attempts to make us feel lonely and abandoned by whispering that God is either unaware of or unconcerned about our suffering. The truth is that God loves us dearly, knows everything about our lives, and always tries to help us.
- Satan tries to convince us that Heavenly Father does not love us. The truth is that we are His children, and God loves us with a pure and never-ending love.
- Satan wants us to believe there is no escape from our problems. The truth is that God can strengthen us and give us personal revelation to help us overcome our trials.
- Satan encourages us to believe we are weak and lack the ability to become a better person. The truth is that we are capable, divine children of divine parents. We are more intelligent than we realize and stronger than we think.
- Satan wants us to believe that when we sin, we become worthless in the eyes of God, who stops loving us. The truth is that every child of God is of great worth no matter what we do or what we don't do. His love for us is unconditional and never-ending.

Earth was created as a place where we can learn and reach our full divine potential. Because Heavenly Father and Jesus love us and want us to succeed, they provide us with many resources to learn about the gospel, such as the scriptures, prayer, revelation, and prophets. We are

193. Dieter F. Uchtdorf, "He Will Place You on His Shoulders and Carry You Home," *Ensign* or *Liahona*, May 2016, 102.

never left to struggle on our own but are given instruction so we can learn what we must do to return to our eternal home.

Although Heavenly Father and Jesus Christ love us freely, they *do* have hopes and expectations. They want us to follow the commandments, and when we sin and make mistakes, they want us to repent. Heavenly Father knows what we are capable of becoming and will help us overcome *all* of our trials. We matter to Him. As we believe in Heavenly Father's love and align our lives with His, we come to understand our true worth and divine potential.

Jesus Christ Is Our Advocate with the Father

Because of Christ's sacrifice for us and His great love, Jesus became our Advocate and personally pleads to Heavenly Father on our behalf: "I am he who was slain; I am your advocate with the Father" (Doctrine and Covenants 110:4). The Latin roots of the word *advocate* mean "one who pleads for another." Jesus tells us to rejoice, for He will plead our cause: "Lift up your hearts and be glad, for I am in your midst, and am your advocate with the Father; and it is his good will to give you the kingdom" (Doctrine and Covenants 29:5). We are never left to walk alone, for Jesus is always by our side. "Behold, this is the promise of the Lord unto you, O ye my servants. Wherefore, be of good cheer, and do not fear, for I the Lord am with you, and will stand by you" (Doctrine and Covenants 68:5–6).

As our Advocate, Christ asks Heavenly Father to consider His suffering in the Garden of Gethsemane in order to secure mercy for us: "Listen to him who is the advocate with the Father, who is pleading your cause before him—Saying: Father, behold the sufferings and death of him who did no sin, in whom thou wast well pleased; behold the blood of thy Son which was shed, the blood of him whom thou gavest that thyself might be glorified; Wherefore, Father, spare these my brethren that believe on my name, that they may come unto me and have everlasting life" (Doctrine and Covenants 45:3–5). Could we ever have a better friend than Jesus, who personally pleads to the Father on our behalf? The hymn "Reverently and Meekly Now" speaks movingly of how Christ acts as our friend and Advocate:

At the throne I intercede;
For thee ever do I plead.
I have loved thee as thy friend,
With a love that cannot end.[194]

Knowing that the Savior is our Advocate assures us that when we pray, Heavenly Father will grant our petitions. When Melissa Taylor learned that her breast cancer had returned, she felt an overwhelming sense of gratitude to know that Jesus Christ was her personal Advocate with the Father. Although Melissa faced many dark moments after her second diagnosis, she said an image of the Savior came vividly into her mind, and she stated, "I realized the Savior had the power to release those bonds of fear. He is always on our side, pleading to the Father for us, just as sincerely as we are. He feels what we are feeling. He is our advocate. And he is always there."[195]

As our Savior, Christ comforts us during our trials and stands by us in our time of need. The Apostle Paul experienced many intense ordeals and knew what it was like to be downtrodden. He also knew who could help him in times of need. He declared:

> It is Christ that died, yea, rather, that is risen again, who is even at the right hand of God, who also maketh intercession for us.
>
> Who shall separate us from the love of Christ? shall tribulation, or distress, or persecution, or famine, or nakedness, or peril, or sword? . . .
>
> I am persuaded, that neither death, nor life, nor angels, nor principalities, nor powers, nor things present, nor things to come,
>
> Nor height, nor depth, nor any other creature, shall be able to separate us from the love of God, which is in Christ Jesus our Lord. (Romans 8:34–35, 38–39)

194. "Reverently and Meekly Now," *Hymns*, no. 185.

195. Carmen Rasmusen Herbert, "3 stories of conquering despair, fear from battling cancer through faith in Jesus Christ," *Deseret News*, Apr. 15, 2017, https://www.deseret.com/2017/4/15/20610436/3-stories-of-conquering-despair-fear-from-battling-cancer-through-faith-in-jesus-christ.

God Never Leaves Us Alone

During times of deep suffering, we may feel alone and overwhelmed, wondering where God is and why He does not help us. Jesus Christ understands how we feel, for He faced His own suffering as He fulfilled the demands of the Atonement. One of Christ's most difficult moments could have been when the Father briefly withdrew His presence while Jesus hung on the cross at Golgotha. For some moments, the Savior felt completely alone and cried out, "My God, my God, why hast thou forsaken me?" (Matthew 27:46). Because of this, Christ knows, with chilling clarity, how it feels to be alone, and so He knows how to comfort us when we feel forsaken. When in need, Jesus lovingly assures us, "I will not leave you comfortless: I will come to you" (John 14:18).

Elder Holland taught:

> One of the great consolations of this Easter season is that because Jesus walked such a long, lonely path utterly alone, *we* do not have to do so. His solitary journey brought great company for our little version of that path—the merciful care of our Father in Heaven, the unfailing companionship of His Beloved Son, the consummate gift of the Holy Ghost, angels in heaven, family members on both sides of the veil, prophets and apostles, teachers, leaders, friends. All of these and more have been given as companions for our mortal journey because of the Atonement of Jesus Christ and the Restoration of His gospel. Trumpeted from the summit of Calvary is the truth that we will never be left alone nor unaided, even if sometimes we may feel that we are.[196]

Because Jesus took upon Himself the full weight of the sins and afflictions of the entire human family, He perfectly understands any pain we feel. Christ's suffering was intense and unimaginable as He paid the price for our sins and was made perfect in understanding. Although we may be called to face our own Gethsemanes, we will never face them alone, for God is always there. He "shall neither slumber nor sleep" (Psalm 121:4). Jesus Christ promises us His constant

196. Jeffrey R. Holland, "None Were with Him," *Ensign* or *Liahona*, May 2009, 88.

companionship: "I will go before your face. I will be on your right hand and on your left, and my Spirit shall be in your hearts, and mine angels round about you, to bear you up" (Doctrine and Covenants 84:88).

Even when we feel abandoned, God is beside us, holding our hand, although unseen by our mortal eyes. President George Q. Cannon said:

> No matter how serious the trial, how deep the distress, how great the affliction, [God] will never desert us. He never has, and He never will. He cannot do it. It is not His character. He is an unchangeable being; the same yesterday, the same today, and He will be the same throughout the eternal ages to come. We have found that God. We have made Him our friend, by obeying His Gospel; and He will stand by us. We may pass through the fiery furnace; we may pass through deep waters; but we shall not be consumed nor overwhelmed. We shall emerge from all these trials and difficulties the better and purer for them, if we only trust in our God and keep His commandments.[197]

When caught up in suffering, we may feel like we are walking alone, but in truth, God never leaves our side. Heavenly Father knows each of us personally and loves and watches over us. We can receive the comfort of God's presence when we invite Him into our lives. There is a well-known picture that shows Jesus Christ standing in front of a wooden door, waiting for the home owner to open the door and receive Him. This picture illustrates the doctrine of agency and that we can choose whether to invite Heavenly Father and Jesus to enter and be part of our lives. God loves us and wants to help, but to receive His guidance and help, we must open the door.

There may be moments when we are unable to feel His presence, yet God is there. All we have to do is open the door and let Him in. Christ assures us, "For the mountains shall depart and the hills be removed, but my kindness shall not depart from thee, neither shall the covenant of my peace be removed [from thee]" (3 Nephi 22:10).

---

197. George Q. Cannon, "Remarks," *Deseret Evening News*, Mar. 7, 1891, 4.

God Is Aware of Each of Us Individually

We all struggle because of trials. Even Joseph Smith felt discouraged at times. One of those moments came when he was imprisoned at Liberty Jail in horrific conditions. In anguish, Joseph cried, "O God, where art thou? . . . How long shall thy hand be stayed?" (Doctrine and Covenants 121:1). Gently and with utmost kindness, God responded, reassuring Joseph and all who suffer, "My son, peace be unto thy soul; thine adversity and thine afflictions shall be but a small moment; And then, if thou endure it well, God shall exalt thee on high" (Doctrine and Covenants 121:7–8). Note the loving tenderness of God referring to Joseph as His son. God *knew* Joseph's suffering. He also knows of our afflictions.

During times of trouble and trials, some may feel that God doesn't care or that He is unaware of their struggles. But God knows us personally. Not only does He know our name but He knows our circumstances and our thoughts. Speaking at a commencement at Brigham Young University, President Hugh B. Brown said:

> Now some of you as you go forward are going to meet with disappointment—perhaps many disappointments, some of them crucial. Sometimes you will wonder if God has forgotten you. Sometimes you may even wonder if He lives and where He has gone. But in these times when so many are saying God is dead and when so many are denying His existence, I think I could not leave with you a better message than this: God is aware of you individually. He knows who you are and what you are, and, furthermore, He knows what you are capable of becoming. Be not discouraged. . . . Have the courage to go on.[198]

It brings comfort and strength to our souls to know that Heavenly Father and Jesus Christ love us and are aware of us individually. He knows our sorrows, our joys, and every part of our life—so much that we are told even the very hairs of our head are numbered (see Matthew 10:30). President Monson taught:

198. Hugh B. Brown, "God Is the Gardener" (Brigham Young University commencement address, May 31, 1968), 5, speeches.byu.edu.

> The entire message of the New Testament breathes a spirit of awakening to the human soul. Shadows of despair are dispelled by rays of hope, sorrow yields to joy, and the feeling of being lost in the crowd of life vanishes with the certain knowledge that our Heavenly Father is mindful of each of us. The Savior provided assurance of this truth when He taught that even a sparrow shall not fall to the ground unnoticed by our Father. He then concluded the beautiful thought by saying, "Fear ye not therefore, ye are of more value than many sparrows" (Matthew 10: 29–31).[199]

President Eyring also testified, "I bear you my witness that the Savior knows and loves you. He knows your name as you know His. He knows your troubles. He has experienced them. By His Atonement, He has overcome the world."[200]

God Will Neither Fail nor Forsake Us

When our afflictions seem overwhelming, and there does not appear to be any light at the end of our tunnel, we may be tempted to wonder if God is aware of our struggles. When we feel lost and discouraged, we may wonder why God does not rescue us. God *does* know of our struggles. Indeed, He is the most constant and loyal friend we can have. He will *never* leave us alone. His very name, Emmanuel, means "God with us" (Matthew 1:23).

When faced with adversity, we must hold on to our faith and take comfort in God's divine promise that "I will be with thee; I will not fail thee, nor forsake thee" (Joshua 1:5). Elder Holland powerfully taught:

> Whenever [the] moments of our extremity come, we must not succumb to the fear that God has abandoned us or that He does not hear our prayers. He *does* hear us. He *does* see us. He *does* love us. When we are in dire circumstances and want to cry "Where art Thou?" it is imperative that we remember He is right there with us—where He has always been! We must continue to believe, continue to have faith, continue to pray and plead with heaven, even if we feel for a time our prayers are not heard and that God has

---

199. Thomas S. Monson, "The Spirit Giveth Life," *Ensign*, May 1985, 68.

200. Henry B. Eyring, "Try, Try, Try," *Ensign* or *Liahona*, Nov. 2018, 93.

> somehow gone away. He *is* there. Our prayers *are* heard. And when we weep, He and the angels of heaven weep with us.[201]

Our paramount task in mortality is to obey our Father's commandments and strive to become more godly. Since mortality is a time of testing, we can expect hard times, but we also know that as we stay close to God, He will stay close to us. As we seek Him diligently, we will find Him, and if we knock, the doors to the kingdom of heaven will be opened unto us (see Doctrine and Covenants 88:63). When we pray for help and reassurance while hiking the rocky path of mortality, we can know that God is there. "Put your trust in God, and move forward with faith and confidence in the future," President Hinckley counsels. "The Lord will not forsake us. . . . If we will put our trust in Him, if we will pray to Him, if we will live worthy of His blessings, He will hear our prayers."[202]

During times of woe and suffering, it is good to know that what we are presently experiencing is not what forever will be. We are not doomed to feel loneliness, sorrow, or pain forever. Hold on to hope and have faith in God's promise that He will always remember and abide with us. President Uchtdorf offers this counsel: "Learn to love your Heavenly Father and become His disciple in word and in deed. Be assured that if you but hold on, believe in Him, and remain faithful in keeping the commandments, one day you will experience for yourselves the promises revealed to the Apostle Paul: 'Eye hath not seen, nor ear heard, neither have entered into the heart of man, the things which God hath prepared for them that love him' (1 Corinthians 2:9)."[203]

In verse seven of "How Firm a Foundation," we find comfort that God will never forsake us:

---

201. Jeffrey R. Holland, "Lessons from Liberty Jail" (Brigham Young University devotional, Sept. 7, 2008), 5, speeches.byu.edu.

202. "Latter-day Counsel: Excerpts from Addresses of Gordon B. Hinckley," *Ensign*, Oct. 2000, 73.

203. Dieter F. Uchtdorf, "You Matter to Him," *Ensign* or *Liahona*, Nov. 2011, 22.

The soul that on Jesus hath leaned for repose
I will not, I cannot, desert to his foes;
That soul, though all hell should endeavor to shake,
I'll never, no never, I'll never, no never,
I'll never, no never, no never forsake![204]

Heavenly Father is there for us—ever faithful and loving, even when we stumble and fall. Elder Hans T. Boom of the Seventy said, "Heavenly Father will never leave us when we reach for Him. We can fall and get up, and He will help us brush off the dirt from our knees. Some of us are wounded, but the first-aid kit of the Lord has bandages big enough to cover all of our wounds."[205]

Nothing we do will ever cause Christ to turn away from us. God watches over us tenderly and makes sure we never walk alone. The Book of Mormon testifies of the pure and unfailing love God has for us in a clear and unequivocal way: "Can a woman forget her sucking child, that she should not have compassion on the son of her womb? Yea, they may forget, yet will I not forget thee, O house of Israel. Behold, I have graven thee upon the palms of my hands; thy walls are continually before me" (1 Nephi 21:15–16).

204. "How Firm a Foundation," *Hymns*, no. 85.

205. Hans T. Boom, "Knowing, Loving, and Growing," *Ensign* or *Liahona*, Nov. 2019, 105.

13
There Are Angels among Us

"Have angels ceased to appear unto the children of men? Or has he withheld the power of the Holy Ghost from them? Or will he, so long as time shall last, or the earth shall stand, or there shall be one man upon the face thereof to be saved?"

—Moroni 7:36

Angels Round About

These are challenging times, but in this day of weariness, we cannot lose hope in Heavenly Father and Jesus Christ. One thing we can be sure of is that God loves us completely and never leaves us alone. He is aware of us and what is going on in our life. We may not always feel His presence, but He is always there. We have every reason to rejoice, knowing that God loves us and will help us.

God watches over us with all the tenderness of a loving parent. There are special moments when He sends angels to help in time of need. Most often, He inspires earthly angels to come to our aid. These angels come in the form of family members, Church members, teachers, missionaries, friends, and neighbors. Occasionally, God may see fit to send heavenly angels to strengthen and bless us.

Heavenly angels are a blessed expression of God's love. Ever since an angel first visited Adam and Eve (see Moses 5:6), angels have been sent as authorized ministers from God to aid mortals. The scriptures are full of angelic experiences, and since God is the same yesterday, today, and forever, we can be sure He is still sending angels in our day. "I testify that angels are *still* sent to help *us,*" Elder Holland declared, "even as they were sent to help Adam and Eve, to help the prophets, and indeed to help the Savior of the world Himself (see Matthew 4:11)."[206]

Quite often, angelic visits remain undetected because of the veil that covers our mind. The Lord has said, "Behold, verily, verily, I say unto you that mine eyes are upon you. I am in your midst and ye cannot see me" (Doctrine and Covenants 38:7). Even though we may not *see* an angel, we may sense their presence. Feeling the presence of an angel is perhaps one of the most common interactions between mortals and heavenly angels. On very rare occasions, mortals may be allowed to hear an angel. And rarer still is when a person sees an angel.

Why are mortals limited in their communication with heavenly beings? We do not have all the answers, but one reason could be because angelic visits could thwart the purpose of mortality, which is to see if we will remain faithful even when we are not in the presence of God. Another reason may be that our bodies are not constructed in a way that allows us to see angels, who are of a finer and purer matter. Regardless of the reason, if we keep our spiritual eyes and ears open, we may discern moments when Heavenly Father sends an angel to give hope in times of distress and comfort in times of adversity.

Elder Melvin J. Ballard taught:

> I am sure that our departed loved ones are near us, and belong to this sphere; yet they have difficulty in talking to us. We sometimes wish we could meet them, shake their hands, and counsel with them . . . but I suppose there is a good reason why we cannot. There must be some law which prevents the law-abiding spirit from talking with man in the flesh. . . . law-abiding spirits abide the law under which they dwell and do not come unless there is some very

206. Jeffrey R. Holland, "The Ministry of Angels," *Ensign* or *Liahona,* Nov. 2008, 29.

> good reason, and special permission given; and occasionally that permission is granted.[207]

Angels Are Often Our Departed Loved Ones

Hope comes from knowing that there are angels among us, and it can touch us deeply to know that when angels come to offer love and support, they are often our own departed ancestors. As President Joseph F. Smith taught:

> When messengers are sent to minister to the inhabitants of this earth, they are not strangers, but from the ranks of our kindred [and] friends. In like manner, our fathers and mothers, brothers, sisters and friends who have passed away from this earth, having been faithful, and worthy to enjoy these rights and privileges, may have a mission given to them to visit their relatives and friends upon the earth again bringing from the divine Presence messages of love, or warning, or reproof and instruction, to those whom they had learned to love in the flesh.[208]

Bruce Hunt, his wife, and their two sons, Tyler and Bryson, were on their way to the Salt Lake City airport where Tyler planned to board a plane for the Missionary Training Center in Brazil. They were traveling on slick roads when their car spun out of control and was struck by an oncoming car. All four of them were killed. President Packer spoke at the funeral service and told the youngest surviving family member, fourteen-year-old Trevor, that despite his loss, he could still stay close to his family. President Packer said, "The spirits of those who have departed are among us, and if we are spiritually minded we can hear them. In your own private way, in a way you will not be able to explain, you will not be alone."[209]

---

207. Melvin J. Ballard, *Crusader for Righteousness* (Salt Lake City, UT: Bookcraft, 1966), 271.

208. Joseph F. Smith, *Gospel Doctrine*, 5th ed. (1939), 435–36.

209. "Family That Died in Crash Eulogized," *The Salt Lake Tribune*, Dec. 22, 2002, B5, https://newspapers.lib.utah.edu/details?id=27884649.

"I Will Still Watch Over You"

Lydia Knight—along with her husband, Newel, and their seven children—left their home intending to join the Saints in Winter Quarters. However, because of delays, they were forced to spend the winter in a small encampment. In January 1847, Newel fell ill with a fever and pain in his right side. After a few days, it became apparent that Newel was dying. He told Lydia, "It is necessary for me to go. . . . Don't grieve too much, for you will be protected." Heartbroken, Lydia told him, "Don't give up. . . . Think of me, Newel, here . . . alone, with my seven little children. . . . I cannot let you go."

Despite her plea, Newel passed away. Without him, Lydia felt it would be impossible to take her seven children to Winter Quarters, much less the subsequent journey of a thousand miles to the Salt Lake Valley. Lonely and discouraged, Lydia found a quiet place to pray and cried out, "O Newel, why has thou left me?"

The account then states the following:

> As she spoke, he [Newel] stood by her side, with a lovely smile on his face, and said: "Be calm, let not sorrow overcome you. It was necessary that I should go. I was needed behind the vail to represent the true condition of this camp and people. You cannot fully comprehend it now; but the time will come when you shall know why I left you and our little ones. Therefore, dry up your tears. Be patient, I will go before you and protect you in your journeyings. And you and your little ones shall never perish for lack of food. Although the ravens of the valley should feed you and your little ones you shall not perish for the want of bread."

After Newel's death, Lydia learned she was pregnant. Knowing Newel was watching over her gave Lydia the courage to travel with a group of Saints to Winter Quarters in April. Lydia's thirteen-year-old son, Samuel, drove one wagon and James, who was nine, drove the other. They arrived safely but lacked the supplies to make the journey to the Salt Lake Valley that year and remained behind with nine other families. That August, Lydia's baby boy was born.

When the infant was a week old, there was a violent rainstorm. Lydia lay in bed with the baby and the other children as rain came through the roof. She covered the newborn with blankets and removed them when they became soaked, but soon there were no more dry blankets. Lydia told her daughter, "Sally, go to bed, it's no use doing any more unless some power beyond that which we possess is exercised. . . . We will trust in God, He has never failed to hear our prayers."

However, later that night, Lydia became discouraged and cried aloud, "Oh Newel, why could you not have stayed with and protected me through our journeyings?"

A beloved voice answered her from out of the darkness: "Lydia, be patient and fear not. I will still watch over you, and protect you in your present situation. You shall receive no harm. It was needful that I should go and you will understand why in due time." Even though she was still wet to the skin, Lydia began to feel warmer and drifted off to sleep.

It took three years for Lydia to gather enough provisions to make the westward trek, but she and her family arrived in the Salt Lake Valley in October 1850.[210]

"Your Father Is Here, Assisting Me in Sealing This Anointing"

Charles R. Woodbury and his wife were attending the Hinckley Ward when the bishop, Jonathan Pratt, passed away. In 1957, Jonathan Pratt's son, William, became gravely ill, and Charles Woodbury was asked to give William a blessing.

Elder Woodbury wrote, "The doctors had very little hope for [William's] recovery. I was called in to administer to him. There was no other Elder there to accompany me. As I anointed him and sealed the anointing, I said, 'Brother Pratt, though there's no mortal man on this earth to assist me in sealing this anointing, your wonderful father, who filled such a great mission on this earth, is here standing by my side with his hands on your head, assisting me in sealing this anointing.'"

---

210. Susa Gates, *Lydia Knight's History: The First Book of the Nobel Women's Lives Series* (Salt Lake City, UT: Juvenile Instructor Office, 1883), 69–70. Also found in Marlene Bateman Sullivan, *And There were Angels Among Them* (Bountiful, UT: Horizon Publishers, 2001), 34–37.

Charles later explained why William's father, Jonathan, had been allowed to return to earth and assist in giving his son a blessing: "Though [Jonathan's] body was laid in mother earth, the Priesthood he honored on earth went with the spirit . . . and he is here today with me in sealing this anointing." In the blessing, Woodbury then promised William, "You have a great mission to perform on this earth, and because of your great faith and that of your wife, you shall be healed perfectly and become a great leader in the Church and Kingdom of God and fill a mission on this earth. If you should become discouraged at times, if you will offer a prayer to your Father in Heaven, you shall feel the presence of your father come to you and give you strength to perform any duty that you shall be called on to perform in the Church and Kingdom of God."

Later, Charles Woodbury declared:

> I bear testimony that I know those of our loved ones are aware of what we're doing. . . . Brother Pratt is not the only one that I have felt the presence of as the departed loved ones assisted me. One woman I administered to told me her husband was there. She said, "I could have put my hand out and touched him. I know he was standing there by my side." So I bear testimony that these things are true, that our loved ones who have departed this life know what we are doing, and we'll get strength from it if we'll pray for it as needed.[211]

"I Saw My Father and Mother Clearly"

Urvin Gee related an experience when he saw his departed parents:

> I was ordained a Patriarch by Elder George Albert Smith of the Quorum of the Twelve on August 30, 1936. Both of my parents were dead, but I often thought that they would be interested in knowing of my special calling in the priesthood. I did not worry

211. Charles R. Woodbury, *Faith Promoting Experiences of Patriarch Charles R. Woodbury,* unpublished manuscript (Salt Lake City, UT: LDS Church History Library), 29–30. Also found in Marlene Bateman Sullivan, *Visits from Beyond the Veil* (Bountiful, UT: Horizon Publishers, 2002), 60–62.

about it because I felt that if it were important that they know, that it would be possible for them to find out.

A few months after my ordination I was attending a funeral in the Fountain Green [Utah] chapel. The speaker was President James L. Nielsen of the Moroni Stake. While he was speaking, he quoted from a book which he had recently acquired. While he was reading the quotation I lost consciousness. I know that I was not asleep, nor was it possible for me to see the people and interior of the chapel, but I did see my Father and Mother as clearly as I ever saw them in my life. They approached me and smiled and nodded to let me know that they recognized me and were well pleased. They did not speak to me or I to them. They were with me probably about one minute. The reason I specify the time was that President Nielsen was still reading the quotation when I again realized where I was and what was going on. I afterward borrowed the book and was able to pick out the part of the quotation which I missed, and it would have taken President Nielsen about one minute to read the missing part. After that I never had any doubt in my mind whether my parents knew of my activities. I always felt certain since then that they did know and were well pleased.[212]

Angels Can Console Us When a Loved One Dies

One of the times we stand in need of consoling the most is after losing a loved one. Hope comes from knowing that although death temporarily separates us, family bonds can remain intact through the covenants we have made. God's loving kindness is never more apparent than when He allows our departed loved ones to return briefly and console us. President Benson said, "I promise you, dear children, that angels will minister unto you also. You may not see them, but they will be there to help you, and you will feel of their presence."[213]

212. Urvin Gee, *Urvin Gee, autobiography, 1969*, unpublished manuscript (Provo, UT: L. Tom Perry Special Collections, Harold B. Lee Library, Brigham Young University, 1969), 19–20. Also found in Sullivan, *Visits from Beyond the Veil,* 127–128.

213. Ezra Taft Benson, "To The Children of the Church," in Conference Report, Apr. 1989, 105.

He Saw Both of His Departed Daughters

When a successful businessman, whose name is not given, lost his first-born daughter in 1878, he was unable to reconcile himself to her loss. Although not a member of The Church of Jesus Christ of Latter-day Saints, he began to pray and fast for consolation. Every evening, he went to a nearby orchard to kneel and ask God to guide him. Prompted by the Spirit, the businessman began reading the Bible and the Book of Mormon. Six months later, he was baptized. He was then called on a mission and traveled thousands of miles to preach the gospel in another country.

One month after his departure, his wife had another daughter. Shortly after the man returned home from his mission, the baby became ill and died. He relates the following experience, which occurred as he and his wife were riding to the cemetery to bury their departed child:

> At her burial my wife and I rode in a carriage with the coffin between us. After lamentation by the mother over her child's fate . . . and my own vain effort to comfort and console her, my spiritual vision was opened by God's grace, and I saw the spirit of the little one whose corpse we were taking to the cemetery for the last earthly rite; and along with her, holding her hand and walking in a most beautiful place like a garden, was the sister who died several years before.
>
> The two looked perfectly happy and contented, and both of them were running up to and taking hold of a woman's skirt like children in playful mood will do. The woman who, to all appearance was acting as mother or nurse, was a dearly beloved girl who died in her girlhood days in the old country, and never had been acquainted with these girls of mine in the flesh. But they apparently showed an acquaintance and knowledge of each other anterior to mortal life. To finish I may say that . . . the main point is that the children are taken care of and feel happy after death, though parents mourn and sigh.[214]

214. "Comfort in Bereavement," *Liahona, The Elder's Journal* 7 (July 3, 1909): 31–32. https://books.google.com/books?id=Px-aLHRzGLIC&pg=PA32&lpg=PA32.

"I Dwell in a Beautiful Place"

When Elder Lorenzo Snow went to serve a mission in Italy, he left behind two of his wives, Sarah Ann and Charlotte. In 1850, while Elder Snow was in Italy, Charlotte died. Bereft at Charlotte's passing, Sarah Ann commented that she could not even think of sleeping in the same room she had shared with Charlotte. Then Charlotte appeared to comfort her. Sarah Ann related her experience to Eliza R. Snow, who wrote the following account:

> The family were all seated in their dining room, when a very bright light, above the brightness of the sun, burst into the apartment, and in the midst of that light Charlotte entered, sat down and took her little daughter, Roxey Charlotte, on her lap, and the extra light in which she came disappeared. She said she was happy, which her calm, settled expression verified.
>
> [Charlotte] said, "I dwell in a beautiful place." The brilliant light returned after a short time, and Charlotte went as she came, in the midst of the light. At this time, Sarah Ann was fully awake, and although no moon was shining at the time, her room was sufficiently lighted that (as she describes it) "one could see to pick up a pin."

Seeing Charlotte happy and serene was a great comfort to Sarah Ann, and she was able to again sleep in the bedroom she had once shared with Charlotte.[215]

Visited by His Departed Wife

George G. Bywater related the following incident that occurred in Wales:

> The wife of one of our brethren in a Welsh parish was nigh unto death with typhoid fever. Before she died, her husband begged her to come back to him from her heavenly home [when she arrived there] and tell him how things were there. She did so. One morning,

215. Eliza R. Snow Smith, *Biography and Family Record of Lorenzo Snow*, (Salt Lake City, UT: Deseret News Company, 1884), 232–234, https://catalog.churchofjesuschrist.org/record/4a300fe8-856d-4e4e-9f3b-6b5c0e224c13/0?view=summary.

> a few weeks afterwards, the husband was sitting in his bedchamber when his dead wife walked naturally into the room. As she came towards him, his mind was filled with a hundred questions which he desired to ask; but she, divining his thoughts, raised a restraining hand and said: "It is no use asking me those questions for I am not permitted to answer them. But I can tell you some things. We have our organizations and our meetings, just as you do here. We have our work and our duties to attend to just as you have on earth. We hold council meetings and talk over matters."[216]

Angels Bless, Strengthen, and Comfort

When the trials of mortality cause distress and grief, Heavenly Father can send angels to console us. President George Q. Cannon stated:

> Now, this is the truth. There is not one of us but what God's love has been expended upon. There is not one of us that He has not cared for and caressed. There is not one of us that He has not desired to save, and that He has not devised means to save. There is not one of us that He has not given His angels charge concerning. . . . The truth remains that we are the children of God, and that He has actually given His angels—invisible beings of power and might—charge concerning us, and they watch over us and have us in their keeping.[217]

"Daddy, Who Is That Standing beside You?"

Sherrie Grigg was nine years old in the fall of 1991 when she began feeling weak and started losing weight. When medication failed to improve her condition, Sherrie's doctor arranged for tests to be done at Primary Children's Medical Center in Salt Lake City, Utah. After extensive testing, doctors discovered a rare tumor, called an astrocytoma, growing along Sherrie's spinal cord. The tumor started at the base

---

216. "Interesting Incidents," *The Young Woman's Journal* 9 (1898): 503. https://contentdm.lib.byu.edu/digital/collection/YWJ/id/24222/rec/9.

217. George Q. Cannon, quoted in Marvin J. Ashton, "On Being Worthy," *Ensign*, May 1989, 21.

of her brain stem and stretched nearly nineteen inches down her spine. Even a few short years before, surgery would have been impossible, but with recent improvements in medical technology, doctors decided to operate.

Sherrie underwent a fourteen-hour operation. Following the surgery, her parents, Clayne and Debbie Grigg, took turns keeping vigil at Sherrie's bedside in the intensive care unit. Her father was delighted when Sherrie woke the next morning, but her words puzzled him. "Daddy, Aunt Cheryl is here," Sherrie said, "and . . . Grandpa Norman . . . and Grandma Brown . . . are here. And Daddy, who is that standing beside you? . . . He looks like you, only taller. . . . He says he's your brother, Jimmy."

Clayne Grigg was three years old when his brother Jimmy died. "I doubt that during Sherrie's life Jimmy's name had ever been mentioned," Clayne said. "She had never even seen a picture of him."

Terrified this meant Sherrie was going to die, Clayne hurried to get his wife who was sleeping nearby. He told Debbie, "There are visitors. I can't see them . . . but I can feel them."

For almost an hour, Sherrie described her deceased family members then fell asleep. Later she told her father, "Daddy, all of the children here in the intensive care unit have angels helping them."

Sherrie needed to have more surgeries along with painful tests and procedures. She said, "When I was really in pain, they [her departed family members] would come and help me calm down. They told me that I would be okay and that I would make it through."[218]

"She Was Sent to Commune with Me"

Parley P. Pratt described his wife, Thankful, as tall and slender with large dark eyes and glossy black hair. The couple longed for children, but Thankful had poor health and was unable to conceive. After Heber C. Kimball gave her a priesthood blessing, Thankful became pregnant. But she died a few hours after giving birth to a son on March 25, 1837. Parley mourned his wife's death but took comfort in knowing that one day they would be reunited.

---

218. Michael R. Morris, "Sherrie's Shield of Faith," *Ensign,* June 1995, 46.

At this time, the Saints were greatly persecuted, and leaders of the Church often found themselves falsely accused and imprisoned. Two years after Thankful's death, Parley, along with several other brethren, were arrested in Richmond, Missouri, and put in prison on bogus charges. Parley became despondent as days, weeks, and months passed without any progress made toward their release. The guards joked about how some prisoners had languished for years in those cells. Parley wrote:

> After some days of prayer and fasting and seeking the Lord on the subject, I one evening retired to my bed in my lonely chamber. . . . I lay in silence, seeking and expecting an answer to my prayer, when suddenly I seemed carried away in the spirit and no longer sensible to outward objects with which I was surrounded. A heaven of peace and calmness pervaded my bosom; a personage from the world of spirits stood before me with a smile of compassion in every look, and pity mingled with the tenderest love and sympathy in every expression of the countenance. A soft hand seemed placed within my own, and a glowing cheek was laid in tenderness and warmth upon mine.
>
> A well-known voice saluted me, which I readily recognized as that of the wife of my youth, who had then for nearly two years been sweetly sleeping where the wicked cease from troubling and the weary are at rest. I was made to realize that she was sent to commune with me, and to answer my question. Knowing this, I said to her, in a most earnest and inquiring tone: "Shall I ever be at liberty again in this life, and enjoy the society of my family and the saints, and preach the gospel, as I have done?"
>
> She answered definitely and unhesitatingly: "Yes!"
>
> "Can you tell me how, or by what means, or when, I shall escape?"
>
> She replied: "That thing is not made known to me yet."
>
> Her gentle spirit then saluted me and withdrew. I came to myself. The noise of the guards again grated on my ears, but heaven and hope were in my soul.

The next morning, Parley related his experience to his two fellow prisoners, who rejoiced to know that at some point they would be freed. Thankful's assurance that her husband would be freed came true. With the help of fellow Saints who orchestrated a daring breakout, Parley and his brethren were able to escape.[219]

Visitations of Heavenly Hosts

While speaking in general conference, Elder Robert D. Hales briefly mentioned his serious health challenges. He then commented wryly, "On a few occasions, I told the Lord that I had surely learned the lessons to be taught and that it wouldn't be necessary for me to endure any more suffering. Such entreaties seemed to be of no avail, for it was made clear to me that this purifying process of testing was to be endured in the Lord's time and in the Lord's own way."

Elder Hales then related how he'd been comforted by angels during his latest recovery: "I . . . learned that I would not be left alone to meet these trials and tribulations but that guardian angels would attend me. There were some that were near angels in the form of doctors, nurses, and most of all my sweet companion, Mary. And on occasion, when the Lord so desired, I was to be comforted with visitations of heavenly hosts that brought comfort and eternal reassurances in my time of need."[220]

Angels Provide Guidance

Angels can be sent to earth to give instruction and guidance to bless our lives and the lives of those around us. President Brigham Young stated that angels are sent to act in God's name and to help us in mortality: "The Lord is not everywhere in person; but he has his agents speaking and acting for him. His angels, his messengers, his apostles and servants are appointed and authorized to act in his name. And his servants are authorized to counsel and dictate in the greatest and what might be deemed the most trifling matters, to instruct, direct and guide his Saints."[221]

---

219. Marlene Bateman Sullivan, *And There Were Angels Among Them,* 37–38.

220. Robert D. Hales, "The Covenant of Baptism: To Be in the Kingdom and of the Kingdom," *Ensign,* Nov. 2000, 6.

221. Brigham Young, in *Journal of Discourses*, 12:245.

Get Up and Go Baptize Niels Larsen!

Elder Christoffer Jensen Kempe was serving as a missionary when a storm arose on the evening of October 31, 1862. Elder Kempe took shelter from the driving rain in a nearby barn. While there, he felt the hand of an angel on his shoulder and heard a distinct voice giving him specific instructions. The account states:

> Some time after retiring to rest he [Elder Kempe] was aroused by feeling a hand laid upon his shoulder and hearing a voice tell him to get up and go to Aalborg and baptize . . . [Niels] Larsen, whom he had seen at the Saints' meetings—that if he ever joined the church he would have to be baptized the next evening. Obedient to the voice of the spirit, he arose and set out afoot in the storm. He walked the entire distance (forty-two miles) and on his arrival in Aalborg, he called upon Niels at his lodgings and informed him that he had come to baptize him.

Astonished to see the exhausted and soaked missionary, Niels asked what had prompted him to come out in such weather. Elder Kempe explained that an angel had directed him to come. Niels confessed that although he was a Lutheran, he had been secretly investigating the Church but had never told anyone. Niels then said that while he had gained a testimony of the truthfulness of The Church of Jesus Christ of Latter-day Saints, he hadn't quite been able to bring himself to be baptized. Elder Kempe's astonishing and unexpected appearance proved to be the spiritual nudge Niels needed, and he agreed to be baptized.

Afterward, Elder Kempe discovered that a group of Lutherans in the area had begun to organize a group of people in the area to bring extreme pressure on Niels *not* to join the church. If this group had been fully organized, they would have caused Niels to lose his job, leaving him unable to support himself.[222]

222. George C. Lambert, *Treasures in Heaven: Fifteenth Book of the Faith Promoting Series* (Salt Lake City, UT: by the author, 1914), 13–14. Also found in Sullivan, *And There Were Angels Among Them*, 81–82.

Sent by Her Departed Father

Elizabeth Drake Davis, an only child, was born in Devonshire, England. Her father died when Elizabeth was ten, and never being close to her mother, Elizabeth often felt alone growing up. One day, she decided to pray about her loneliness. During her prayer, Elizabeth was shown a vision that eventually led her to join The Church of Jesus Christ of Latter-day Saints.

In time, Elizabeth married and had two little girls. When her husband died unexpectedly, Elizabeth went to America and settled in Philadelphia. When she'd saved enough money to travel to Salt Lake City, Elizabeth and her children traveled to Florence to join a group of Saints who were preparing to cross the plains. Elizabeth relates:

> We reached Florence late one evening; it was quite dark and raining; we were helped from the wagons and put in one of the vacant houses—myself, my two little daughters and Sister Sarah White. Early next morning we were aroused by someone knocking at the door; on opening it we found a little girl with a cup of milk in her hand; she asked if there was "a little woman there with two little children."
>
> "Yes," said Sister White. "Come in."
>
> She entered, saying to me, "If you please my ma wants to see you; she has sent this milk to your little girls."
>
> Her mother's name was strange to me, but I went, thinking to find someone that I had known. She met me at the door with both hands extended in welcome.
>
> "Good morning, Sister Elizabeth," said she. I told her she had the advantage of me, as I did not remember ever seeing her before.
>
> "No," said she, "and I never saw you before. I am Hyrum Smith's daughter (Lovina Walker); and my father appeared to me three times last night, and told me that you were a child of God, that you was without money, provisions or friends, and that I must help you."

Grateful for Lovina's help, Elizabeth declared, "It is needless to add that this excellent lady and myself were ever thereafter firm friends."

Over time, the two women lost track of each other. Then, thirteen years later, Elizabeth had the opportunity to bless her friend's life as Lovina had once blessed hers. Elizabeth relates, "I will add that previous to her [Lovina's] last illness I had not seen her in thirteen years; then one night her father [Hyrum Smith] appeared to me, and making himself known, said his daughter was in sore need; I found the message was too true." When Elizabeth went to see Lovina, she found her in dire circumstances and was able to help her old friend. Elizabeth concluded, "Yet it will ever be a source of gratitude to think I was at least able to return her generous kindness to me when we were strangers."[223]

"There She Is Now!"

The love of a parent for their child is one of the strongest bonds there is, and it once led a mother to appear to her son in around 1880. Elderly and in poor health, Sister H. was living near Salt Lake City when she realized her remaining time on earth was short. Her son, who is known in this account only by the initials A.D.H., was around thirty years old at this time. Brother E. Stevenson, a good friend of the family, wrote the following account as it was told to him by A.D.H.:

> Two days before her demise, the mother—being aware of approaching death—called her children around her, and, addressing herself to them, exhorted them to diligence and faithfulness. She had previously arranged for her burial clothes and coffin; and [that] the Elder who had been captain of the company in which she had crossed the plains twenty years before should preach the funeral sermon.
>
> One son, A.D.H., who was rather skeptical, said, "Mother, you very well know my sentiments regarding God and the future. If there is a reality in future life, will you come back and let me know about it?"
>
> After a pause, the reply was, "I will if I can."
>
> On the following Saturday, I [E. Stevenson] was called upon to preach the funeral sermon. About forty vehicles followed the remains to the grave where the body was deposited, that the dust might "return to earth as it was and the spirit return to God who gave it."

223. Sullivan, *And There Were Angels Among Them*, 116–118.

The following Monday after the funeral, Sister H. kept the promise she had given to her son. The account relates:

> Sister H., his mother, appeared by [A.D.H.'s] side, about eight or ten feet from him. She told him she had come to redeem her pledge; and she desired that he should go, on the following Thursday, and be baptized by his Bishop, taking with him two witnesses, who she named. She further desired [A.D.H.] to be faithful and eventually receive his endowments and help to do the work for her dead friends, which she had failed to accomplish. She said it had cost her grief and sorrowful feelings to come and visit him, but if he failed to carry out her instructions, she would come again. Several questions were asked by the son, but no reply to them was given by the mother.
>
> Not long after this, the son [A.D.H.] was returning from the store in company with one of the persons whom his mother had desired to be a witness of the baptism. This man was not a member of the Church, but a friend of the family. The two were conversing about the vision, and when they came near an opening in a field, where the son had previously parted with his mother, he pointed to the southward, and said, "There she is now!"
>
> The friend looked, but could see nothing, though as he afterwards stated, he felt a peculiar influence, and did not doubt that the son actually saw the spirit of his mother. The young man saw her distinctly, and can describe her appearance. He stated that her movements were graceful, and that she passed over the ground without any apparent effort. She was clothed in white robes, and appeared far more beautiful than when in the flesh. Her voice, also, as he heard it in the first vision, was very natural.

His mother's appearance had a great impact on her son, who did everything she asked. Stevenson continued, "Her son has been baptized and, in a meeting that I attended, bore a faithful testimony of the existence of God and the future. He asked God and the brethren to forgive him for his unbelief and lack of faith, and promised that, by the help of the Lord, he would be faithful henceforth."[224]

---

224. E. Stevenson, "A Spirit's Return," *The Juvenile Instructor* 16 (Feb. 1, 1881): 29. Also found in Sullivan, *Visits from Beyond the Veil*, 124–25.

Angels Can Protect Us from Harm

We are taught to pray for God's protection and have faith that if such protection is in accordance with God's will, He will safeguard us and even send angels if necessary. When the prophet Elisha became surrounded by a large army, his servant lost all hope and cried out in fear, for he could see no way to escape. But hope was reborn when Elisha prayed on his behalf: "The Lord opened the eyes of the young man; and he saw: and, behold, the mountain was full of horses and chariots of fire round about Elisha" (2 Kings 6:17). In the latter days, President Heber C. Kimball declared, "Perhaps there are some who do not believe much in spirits, but I know that they exist and visit the earth. . . . We do not see them, but they are here watching us, and are anxious for our salvation. . . . The Lord has hosts of angels who are qualified to defend us."[225]

The Apostle Marriner Wood Merrill, who was once saved from certain death by an unseen power, declared, "I can truthfully testify in all soberness, that some power which I did not see assisted me from the position which would speedily have cost me my life. As I was preserved for some purpose known to my Heavenly Father, so do I also believe that God will bless and preserve the lives of His faithful children . . . and He will, if necessary, send angelic visitors to sustain and preserve those who put their trust in Him."[226]

His Father Appeared and Dragged Him from the Track

When Christopher Elias Jensen and his brother Lorenzo were hired as brakemen on the Oregon Short Line railroad, they knew it was dangerous work. Although Christopher had not been in the habit of praying, he decided it was a good time to start. Christopher promised God that he would live righteously, abstain from tobacco and liquor, and never take God's name in vain. He and his brother were working in Utah in 1898 when they had the following experience:

---

225. Heber C. Kimball, in *Journal of Discourses*, 3:229–30.

226. Marriner Wood Merrill, "Lives of Our Leaders—The Apostles," *Juvenile Instructor* 35, no. 20 (Oct. 15, 1892): 630.

While going north on one of our trips, we stopped at the station of Collinston, about twenty miles north of Brigham City. We were doing some switching of the cars. I was on top of a large furniture car giving signals to the engineer while my brother, Lorenzo, and another brakeman by the name of Hill, were cutting the cars. My brother was attending the switch and Mr. Hill was between two of the cars making an effort to uncouple the cars. He failed to get the cars uncoupled, and, thinking that something had happened to him, I ran across the top of the car to see what was the matter. The cars were still traveling at a fast rate of speed and as I approached the end of the car where Mr. Hill was working, the engineer suddenly reversed the engine brakes, which caused it to stop very suddenly. It uncoupled the cars and sent me headlong from the top of the car to the ground where I fell on my back across the rails.

The train immediately proceeded again in the direction it was going and was within a very few feet of where I lay. I cannot say how I ever got off the track, for I was unconscious, but my brother, who was standing at the switch a short distance from where I lay, testifies that he saw our father suddenly appear and take me by the shoulders, drag me from the track and lay me down on the ground a few feet from where my brother stood—the cars by this time having passed over the spot where I had lain. It will be remembered that my father had died in the preceding July and this incident happened during the month of December of the same year.[227]

An Audible Voice Said, "Get Up"

After returning home from a mission in 1868, Orson Smith, who years later was called as president of the Cache Stake in northern Utah, began learning how to operate a sawmill. In autumn, when temperatures began to fall, precautions needed to be taken at the end of each day's work. Because the water would freeze and expand at night, Orson was taught to close the gate at the head of the race and open the gate of the Leffel water wheel before leaving the mill at night

227. *Mads Christian Jensen—Ancestors and Descendants, 1600–1960* (Salt Lake City, UT: LDS Church Archives, 1960), 393–94. Also found in Sullivan, *And There Were Angels Among Them,* 118–19.

so that the water could drain and not freeze, an action that prevented the mill race from bursting.

One frosty fall morning, Orson went to the mill and moved the gate lever to close the wheel gate. Then he went outside to the head gate to let the water in. Upon returning to the mill, Orson began filing the circular saw to sharpen it. It was his customary practice to put his left leg over the saw frame as he filed, bringing his left thigh close to the saw. Orson recounts what happened next:

> I had proceeded with my task but a few moments when an audible voice said to me, "Get up." I knew no other person was in the mill. Still, I hesitated and looked around as if to see who was speaking to me. I made another stroke with my file, when I was aroused by the same voice in a louder tone and such a perceptible shaking of my body, as if some power had hold of me, that I was compelled to rise. I had no sooner become disentangled from the saw teeth than it started at full speed. The wheel gates had frozen to the rim of the wheel, and had not closed as they should have done, thus causing the entire current to rush through the wheel; not until the water had thawed the ice from the gates would they close, but just as soon as they were released the wheel started at full speed.
>
> Had not the warning come to me as it did, my body would have been sawed asunder, as I was totally ignorant of the danger to which I was exposed. It was some time before I could return to my work, so great was the shock upon me, when I saw how miraculously I had been delivered from a shocking death.[228]

"Whenever You Are in Danger, I Will Come"

Elder Tom Shreeve was serving a mission in New Zealand when, on February 27, 1879, he decided to go to North Island hoping to find someone to teach, even though he had never had any luck in his previous attempts. He was unable to find anyone to teach and began having dark, uneasy feelings. As Elder Shreeve prepared for bed, the dismal feelings increased to the point that he wondered if he was in danger. He relates the following:

228. Orson Smith, "How Others Have Risen," *Juvenile Instructor* 31 (1896): 18.

> While I lay, wide awake, in my bed I suddenly saw a hand . . . holding a torch in its hand. . . . Gradually the flame grew greater and the light stronger, until it filled the whole room; and then from out the darkness . . . stepped the figure of a little girl. I recognized it instantly as that of my young sister Sophia, who had died six years before in England, while I was in Utah. At the time of her death she was eight and a half years old, and had but recently been baptized into the Church. She came toward the bed, and I saw that she was dressed in beautiful white raiment. From her whole person a pleasing light seemed to emanate. She approached the bed and leaned over it, placing her arms around my neck and kissing me. . . . Then, still with her hands clasped, she leaned back and looked intently into my face, saying at the same time: "Tom, don't be afraid! Whenever you are in danger I will come to warn you."
>
> She bent forward and kissed me again; afterward leaning back to take another look at my face. Repeating the same words as before, once more she kissed me; and then slowly withdrew her arms and moved back from the bed. . . . She waved her hand three times with a farewell gesture toward me. . . . The light of the torch grew for a moment brighter; then suddenly it vanished and I found myself leaning upon my elbow in the bed and gazing fixedly at the blank darkness where the glorious presence and the light torch had disappeared. So real and certain had been the presence of my sister that after she was gone, I still felt the pressure of her warm arms around my neck.[229]

The Ministry of Angels

The ministering of angels is one of the most wondrous forms of interaction between heaven and earth. Not only do these visits demonstrate God's love, but they also give tangible reassurance and comfort. Elder Holland declared:

> My beloved brothers and sisters, I testify of angels, both the heavenly and the mortal kind. In doing so I am testifying that God never leaves us alone, never leaves us unaided in the challenges that we face. [Nor] will he, so long as time shall last, or the earth shall stand, or there shall be one man [or woman or child] upon the

229. Sullivan, *And There Were Angels Among Them*, 128–29.

> face thereof to be saved. On occasions, global or personal, we may feel we are distanced from God, shut out from heaven, lost, alone in dark and dreary places. Often enough that distress can be of our own making, but even then the Father of us all is watching and assisting. And always there are those angels who come and go all around us, seen and unseen, known and unknown, mortal and immortal.[230]

Knowing that God is aware of our needs and sends angels to minister to us serves as a testimony that God lives and loves us. In a conference talk, President Heber C. Kimball said, "Do you suppose that there are any angels here to-day? I would not wonder if there were ten times more angels here than people. We do not see them, but they are here watching us, and are anxious for our salvation. . . . The Lord has hosts of angels who are qualified to defend us."[231]

Besides heavenly angels, there are many earthly angels who provide hope and help to us. The Savior often depends on mortals to serve as His hands and bless the lives of others. President Brigham Young testified, "The Lord is here with us, not in person, but his angels are around us, and he takes cognizance of every act of the children of men, as individuals and as nations. He is here ready by his agents, the angels, and by the power of his Holy spirit and priesthood, which he has restored in these last days, to bring most perfect and absolute deliverance unto all who put their trust in Him."[232]

---

230. Jeffrey R. Holland, "The Ministry of Angels," 31.

231. Heber C. Kimball, in *Journal of Discourses*, 3:230.

232. Brigham Young, in *Journal of Discourses,* 11:14.

14

Hope Allows Us to Endure to the End

"Nevertheless, he that endureth in faith and doeth my will, the same shall overcome, and shall receive an inheritance upon the earth when the day of transfiguration shall come."

—Doctrine and Covenants 63:20

Hope Helps Us Endure

To return to our Heavenly Father's presence, we must prove ourselves worthy *and* endure to the end. All of us have dark days—moments when we are tested to the very limit—but hope helps us hang on. "Enduring is one of the cardinal attributes," declared Elder Maxwell. "It simply cannot be developed without the laboratory time in this second estate. Even the best lectures about the theory of enduring are not enough. All the other cardinal virtues—love, patience, humility, mercy, purity, submissiveness, justice—they all require endurance for their full development."[233]

We learn in Moroni 8:26 that if we are meek and lowly in heart, the Holy Ghost can fill us with hope and perfect love. The Lord promises eternal salvation as we retain our hope and endure our trials: "As

233. Neal A. Maxwell, "Endure It Well," *Ensign*, May 1990, 34.

many as would believe and be baptized in his holy name, and endure in faith to the end, should be saved" (Doctrine and Covenants 20:25). No matter what adversity we face, as we cultivate Christlike attributes of hope in and trust in God, He will strengthen us and enable us to bear our burdens.

A Story of Hope and Endurance

Stillman Pond, an early-day member of the Church, continued to have hope throughout his lifetime, and it was that hope which helped him endure to the end. Stillman and Almyra, his wife, had five children before Almyra passed away. In 1834 Stillman married Maria Davis, and seven years later, he and Maria learned about the gospel. They were baptized as members of The Church of Jesus Christ of Latter-day Saints and, two years later, moved to Nauvoo. While there, the Pond family fell ill, as did many of the Saints, to malaria, cholera, and consumption. Then, in September of 1846, Stillman, Maria, and their family were driven out of Nauvoo along with other members of the Church. While traveling to Winter Quarters, three of their children fell ill and died. During their journey, Maria—still suffering from malaria—gave birth to a baby, but the infant died a few days later.

Stillman, Maria, and the surviving children arrived at Winter Quarters on the October 16, 1846, only to discover there weren't enough houses for everyone. The Pond family, along with other unfortunates, were forced to live in tents during much of the bitterly cold winter.

Horace K. and Helen Morr Whitney kept a journal and wrote the following about the Pond family: "On Wednesday, December 2, 1846, Laura Jane Pond, age 14 years . . . died with chills and fevers. . . . Friday, December 4, 1846: Harriet M. Pond, age 11 years . . . died with chills. . . . Monday, December 7, 1846: Abigail A. Pond, aged 18 years . . . died with chills. . . . Friday, January 15, 1847: Lyman Pond, aged 6 years . . . died with chills and fever. On May 17, 1847, Maria Davis Pond died." The record added, "The sorrow and the grief that Stillman went through . . . was a test supreme. He never faltered but remained true and steadfast."

After arriving in Utah, Stillman helped colonize Utah and became the senior president of the thirty-fifth Quorum of Seventy. Despite losing his wife and nine children and experiencing many ordeals, Stillman Pond retained his hope in Christ. His faithfulness and devotion to the gospel never wavered.[234]

Jesus Christ Will Help Us Bear Our Burdens

Although we may not face the intense suffering Stillman Pond endured, we do live in a time of escalating world and societal challenges and face an increasing number of hardships that test our faith and prove our hearts. Yet through it all, the Savior stands ready to help us bear our burdens. President Eyring said, "When you wonder how much pain you can endure well, remember Him. He suffered what you suffer so that He would know how to lift you up. He may not remove the burden, but He will give you strength, comfort, and hope. He knows the way. He drank the bitter cup. He endured the suffering of all."[235]

Although hardship is difficult to bear, we can learn from it if we place it in perspective and look beyond the pain of the moment. President Kimball said:

> If we looked at mortality as the whole of existence, then pain, sorrow, failure, and short life would be calamity. But if we look upon life as an eternal thing stretching far into the premortal past and on into the eternal post-death future, then all happenings may be put in proper perspective. Is there not wisdom in his giving us trials that we might rise above them, responsibilities that we might achieve . . . sorrows to try our souls? Are we not exposed to temptations to test our strength, sickness that we might learn patience, death that we might be immortalized and glorified?[236]

234. Leon Y. Pond, "Stillman Pond: 1847 Utah Pioneer and his Family, Biographical Sketch," https://content.byui.edu/file/743cc524-6d90-4e96-8bdc-e8691ca3cdb5/1/FileMS018_StillmanPondBiography.pdf.

235. Henry B. Eyring, "Tested, Proved, and Polished," *Ensign* or *Liahona*, Nov. 2020, 97.

236. *Teachings of Presidents of the Church: Spencer W. Kimball* (2006), 15.

Although hardships can make us feel anxious and fearful, as we exercise faith and retain hope in the future, we can receive the sanctifying power of God to help us bear our afflictions. Hope allows us to know that one day, our suffering will end. "Let us not be weighed down by our mortal trials," President Uchtdorf counseled. "Please understand that what you see and experience now is not what forever will be. You will not feel loneliness, sorrow, pain, or discouragement forever. We have the faithful promise of God, who said, 'I will never leave thee, nor forsake thee' (Hebrews 13:5). Have hope and faith in that promise. Learn to love your Heavenly Father and become His disciple in word and in deed."[237]

Stand Firm and Endure

Life is hard, but it's doubly so if we waver like grass before the wind of adversity. Having a determination to endure, and having our feet planted firmly in the gospel of Jesus Christ, allows us to remain steady. Although *standing* firm implies staying in one spot, the Lord wants us to actively *work* and *do* those things that help us stay close to God. When we're buffeted by adversity, it is only when we take action that we can remain anchored by faith and endure. Following are a few suggestions that will help us stand firm.

Make the Decision to Let God Prevail

When we decide to stand with Heavenly Father and Jesus Christ, we choose to let God prevail in our lives. Evil abounds, but if we let God take precedence over all else, the heavens will be opened and pour out personal revelation, which we need in order to stand against evil in these latter days. Receiving inspired guidance will help us understand eternal truths, guide our footsteps, and lighten our burdens. As we demonstrate a willingness to let God prevail in our lives, we allow God's will to be the determining factor in everything we do. As we follow God, we will be blessed to withstand the challenges of mortality.

---

237. Dieter F. Uchtdorf, "You Matter to Him," *Ensign* or *Liahona,* Nov. 2011, 22.

President Nelson asks, "Are *you* willing to let God prevail in your life? Are *you* willing to let God be the most important influence in your life? Will you allow His words, His commandments, and His covenants to influence what you do each day? Will you allow His voice to take priority over any other?" He then declared, "The only way to survive spiritually is to be determined to let God prevail in our lives, to learn to hear His voice, and to use our energy to help gather Israel."[238] Instead of swaying to and fro with the ever-changing standards of the world, we can stand firm in our allegiance to God, who has the power to bless us with the strength to rise above our day-to-day challenges.

Stand in Holy Places

Although we live in troubled times, the Lord provides us with a safety net and counsels, "Stand ye in holy places, and be not moved, until the day of the Lord come" (Doctrine and Covenants 87:8). Standing in holy places is a powerful spiritual blessing that protects us from the world, provides us with divine inspiration, and helps us stand firm.

What *is* a holy place? It is a place where the Spirit of God can come without reservation. It is a place where we can receive the blessed companionship of the Holy Ghost, which fills our souls with peace. The temple is one of the holiest places on earth. Churches are also holy places. Our homes are also holy places as long as we are doing our best to follow Jesus Christ. By living the standards of the gospel, we invite the Light of Christ into our lives, no matter where we are.

Although the latter days are rife with fear and turmoil, we can have hope. "Take heart, brothers and sisters," Elder Rasband declared. "Yes, we live in perilous times, but as we stay on the covenant path, we need not fear. I bless you that as you do so, you will not be troubled by the times in which we live or the troubles that come your way. I bless you to choose to stand in holy places and be not moved. I bless you to believe in the promises of Jesus Christ, that He lives and that He is

238. Russell M. Nelson, "Let God Prevail," *Ensign* or *Liahona*, Nov. 2020, 94–95.

watching over us, caring for us and standing by us."[239] As we focus our minds and hearts on the Savior, we will stand in holy places and have the Lord with us as He guides us back to our heavenly home—the holiest place of all.

Read the Book of Mormon

The Book of Mormon was written for our time and brought forth by the power of God. In its pages, we learn the plain and precious truths of the gospel and the reality of Jesus Christ and His atoning sacrifice. As we read, we are inspired by faithful people who endured despite their heavy trials. We learn of the perils of pride, procrastination, immorality, and hypocrisy. This inspired book teaches divine principles and provides solutions for problems we face in everyday life.

One of the most important doctrinal truths the Book of Mormon illustrates is that when we walk in obedience to the commandments of God, we will prosper. Reading this book helps us develop a stronger testimony of Heavenly Father and Jesus Christ and enables us to feel the Spirit more powerfully. By conscientiously reading this powerful book, we are blessed with greater spiritual discernment and increased strength to resist temptations. We also come to understand the rewards of seeking the Spirit, knowing that if we endure, we will receive great blessings. Reading the Book of Mormon lifts our spirits as it draws us closer to Heavenly Father and Jesus Christ.

Decide to Be Strong

Another factor of enduring is to make a conscious choice to be strong. All of us struggle at times. We feel weak, broken, or damaged by life's adversities. But still, we do the best we can to hold on. This is what strength is—choosing to go forward despite our challenges. Strength comes not by sailing through life without any obstacles but by working hard and doing our best to sail through stormy seas without giving up and without giving in.

The first step to becoming strong is to understand that we already *are* strong! One of the authors, Joshua Sullivan, makes the following observation:

---

239. Ronald A. Rasband, "Be Not Troubled," *Ensign* or *Liahona,* Nov. 2018, 21.

> There is never a one-size-fits-all approach to dealing with challenges. People need to have a toolbox of techniques to draw upon to help themselves. One of those tools is to believe you are stronger than you think. During therapy, I often tell clients who feel weak, inadequate, and incapable of facing up to their problems, "You are stronger than you think you are."
>
> Once, I had a personal opportunity to test this idea. I was snowboarding and there was a lot of fresh powder. I was not an experienced snowboarder, but I wasn't a newbie either. I went on a side trail that was not compacted and lost my momentum, which caused me to fall into several feet of powder. I tried to move, but each time I would sink. I tried again and again to get out but failed. Soon I was exhausted. I wasn't in any real danger, but knew I only had two choices. I could stay there and be really cold until someone came along, or I could keep moving until I had compacted the powder enough to stand up. I chose the latter, reminding myself that I was stronger than I thought. If we tell ourselves during times of trouble that we are stronger than we think, it can help us make the decision to *be* strong.

Although being strong won't take away our tribulations, it *will* help us deal with them. All of us are braver than we think, stronger than we seem, and smarter than we believe. Then we can decide whether to be strong or to be sad and miserable. Both take about the same amount of work.

Hang On

When dealing with problems and discouragement, there will be times when you simply have to hang on. Of course, this counsel doesn't apply to clinical depression, anxiety disorders, and other debilitating challenges or illnesses. Mortal trials, even the common challenges everyone faces, can still test us. At such times, trust in God, have patience, pray for strength, and submit to the trials He sees fit for you to pass through. President Benson said, "There are times when you simply have to righteously hang on and outlast the devil until [he] . . . leaves you. . . . To press on in noble endeavors, even while surrounded by a cloud . . . will eventually bring you out on top into the sunshine."[240]

Everyone who endures trials can be strengthened because of the sacrifice made by our Elder Brother. In Gethsemane and on Calvary's cross, Jesus took upon Himself *all* of our anguish, even the most devastating and unbearable trials a mortal can suffer. He overcame all. By holding on, we amplify those virtues we came to earth to acquire: compassion, faith, understanding, patience, persistence, and, most of all, love. Hold fast to the knowledge that God loves you and wants you to become the best person you can be. He may not take away our trials, but God can help us hang on.

Take the Outstretched Hand of Christ

We can trust the Savior to bless us with the capacity to withstand our trials. When we are battered and bruised, Jesus Christ reaches His mighty arm out to succor us. All we need to do is take hold of His hand and never let go. Too often, we blame ourselves, at least in part, for our difficulties, feeling that if we were stronger, had more faith, or were a better person, we could bear our trials more easily. But we are human and doing the best we can. And we must realize that even our little bursts of fortitude and strength can never match the infinite power that comes from the Savior. Having faith in Jesus Christ means believing not only that He is our Savior but that "through his infinite goodness and grace, [He] will keep you through the endurance of faith on his name to the end" (Moroni 8:3).

As our Redeemer, Christ suffered not only for our sins but also for our hardships. Because of Jesus Christ's Atonement, He knows precisely how to help us bear our afflictions. If we feel lost, we can search out Jesus, who will then claim us as His own. "Fear not, little children, for you are mine, and I have overcome the world, and you are of them that my Father hath given me; And none of them that my Father hath given me shall be lost" (Doctrine and Covenants 50:41–42).

Often in life, we need strength beyond our own, and the source of that strength comes from Christ. Because Christ has risen above all things, He is in the perfect position to lift us up. But we must ask.

240. Ezra Taft Benson, "Do Not Despair," *Ensign*, Nov. 1974, 67.

"Therefore, if you will ask of me you shall receive; if you will knock it shall be opened unto you" (Doctrine and Covenants 6:5). As we follow Jesus and learn more *of* Him, we can become more *like* Him. In doing so, we can be strengthened to endure. Even though our pains are microscopic compared to what Christ endured, we are to patiently endure our afflictions.

Strengthen Your Spiritual Foundation

Without a strong foundation, we will find it difficult to withstand the storms of life. President Nelson counseled, "My dear brothers and sisters, these *are* the latter days. If you and I are to withstand the forthcoming perils and pressures, it is imperative that we each have a *firm* spiritual foundation built upon the rock of our Redeemer, Jesus Christ."[241]

One important element in building a strong foundation is to discover for ourselves that Heavenly Father lives and that Jesus is our Savior. We must have a testimony that through Christ's Atonement, He brought about the Resurrection and paid the heavy price for our sins. We strengthen our foundation by learning more about Heavenly Father and Jesus Christ through studying the scriptures and communing with God in prayer. Prayer is a lifeline to our receiving heavenly assistance. By listening to God's still, small voice, we can receive invaluable inspiration.

The best foundations are deep, and each time we choose to follow Christ, we add another layer to our personal foundation, which improves our ability to stand strong against our trials. As we fortify our spiritual foundation, God will guide us safely through the darkness of our present-day world.

Attend Church Meetings

The Church is the structure God has given us to grow spiritually, and we are to gather together often to strengthen one another. Church attendance helps us stay on the covenant path because it opens our hearts to God and sanctifies our souls. If we rely only on individual

---

241. Russell M. Nelson, "The Temple and Your Spiritual Foundation," *Ensign* or *Liahona*, Nov. 2021, 93; emphasis added.

and solitary spirituality, we are separating ourselves from the fullness of restored doctrine as well as the power and blessings of the priesthood. We attend church to increase our faith, increase in knowledge, and find peace.

Attending church is not just for our benefit but a way to minister to others. We can brighten the lives of other people as we make a point of smiling, saying hello, sitting next to those who sit alone, and welcoming visitors. If we make it a goal to attend with the intent of being active in our worship and gaining strength from others, church attendance can make a positive difference not only in our life but in the lives of others.

Endurance Brings Eternal Blessings

On one of those rare occasions when Heavenly Father spoke to mortals, He gave the comforting assurance that "he that endureth to the end . . . shall be saved" (2 Nephi 31:15). There were many things Heavenly Father could have said to the world, but He stressed endurance. Why was that? God knew that mortality would be difficult, and perhaps He wanted to stress how important it is that we continue faithful to the end.

It takes stamina not to weary from continual adversity. Enduring means we take one more step when we don't think we can and bear one more burden that we would rather not. As we prevail, joy will be ours. "Weeping may endure for a night, but joy cometh in the morning" (Psalms 30:5). As always, our Savior set an example for us to follow. Christ endured the most excruciating suffering possible because He focused on the blessings that He would provide for our sake when He fulfilled His mission. We can be helped through our trials by "looking unto Jesus the author and finisher of our faith; who for the joy that was set before him endured the cross" (Hebrews 12:2). Even though our trials can be painful and at times overwhelming, we can follow Christ's example and do our best to focus on the joy that will come in time. The Lord tells us, "Ye shall be sorrowful, but your sorrow shall be turned into joy" (John 16:20).

The very nature of enduring comprises the expenditure of emotional and physical energy over a long period of time. For this reason, we are also counseled to be patient: "Let us lay aside every weight, and the sin which doth so easily beset us, and let us run with patience the race that is set before us" (Hebrews 12:1). Although this life can seem long, it is but a micro-dot on the timeline of our eternal existence. In the next life, the pain inflicted by earthly hardships will be a bygone memory, and we will consider those trials to be well worth the price paid because of the glorious blessings we will receive.

Despite all we are called to endure, we can trust God to help us overcome our difficulties. In the late 1800s, Niels Eskildz suffered a serious spinal injury when he was a young boy. While recuperating, Niels spent many long hours in bed, and to help pass the time, his mother taught him how to sew. Niels's injury stunted his physical development, and as an adult, his body was short and bent. He received some assistance from others, but he was nearly able to fully support himself with his sewing skills. Although Niels tried to stay busy and remain happy, he became downcast at seeing how repelled people were by his twisted body. Over time, he became depressed and found it hard to see any good in life. Then, a few months before Niels learned about the Church, he had a remarkable vision that had a tremendous impact on him. George C. Lambert wrote the following account:

> During the summer preceding [Niels's] baptism, after a day of extreme melancholy, an incident occurred that produced an entire change in his feelings. While engaged preparing his evening meal a glorious vision burst upon his view. It was not a single scene that he beheld, but a series of them. He compares them to the modern moving pictures, for want of a better illustration. He [Niels] beheld as with his natural sight, but he realized afterwards that it was with the eye of the spirit that he saw what he did. His understanding was appealed to as well as his sight.
>
> What was shown him related to his existence in the spirit world, mortal experience, and future reward. He comprehended, as if by intuition, that he had witnessed a somewhat similar scene in his premortal state, and been given the opportunity of choosing the class of reward he would like to attain to. He knew that he had deliberately made his choice. He realized which of the rewards he had selected, and understood that such a reward was only to be gained by mortal suffering—that, in fact, he must . . . endure severe physical pain, privation and ignominy. He was conscious too that

> he still insisted upon having that reward, and accepted and agreed to the conditions.
>
> He emerged from the vision with a settled conviction that to rebel against or even to repine at his fate was not only a reproach to an Alwise Father whose care had been over him notwithstanding his seeming abandonment, but a base violation of the deliberate promise and agreement he had entered into, and upon the observance of which his future reward depended.

Although Niels realized that others might ridicule the vision and think it a product of his imagination, he knew without a doubt that it came as a gift from a loving, compassionate Father in Heaven. The account continues by saying that Neils had "unshaken faith in [the vision] and . . . has derived comfort, satisfaction, resolution and fortitude from it. He has ever since been resigned to his affliction, and, though never mirthful, is serene and composed and uncomplaining. He has always felt that the vision was granted to him by the Lord for a wise and merciful purpose—that he might, through a better understanding of his duty, be able to remain steadfast thereto."[242]

Approximately a year after his vision, Niels was baptized a member of The Church of Jesus Christ of Latter-day Saints. Through a series of miraculous blessings, Niels managed to immigrate to the United States and join a group of Saints who were preparing to travel to Utah. Although Niels endured tremendous hardships crossing the plains, he bore them and expressed gratitude to God for preserving his life during the arduous journey. The following song, often sung during the pioneer's trek west, held special meaning for Niels:

> Come, come, ye Saints, no toil nor labor fear;
> But with joy wend your way.
> Though hard to you this journey may appear,
> Grace shall be as your day.
> 'Tis better far for us to strive
> Our useless cares from us to drive;

242. George C. Lambert, *Treasures in Heaven: Fifteenth Book in the Faith Promoting Series* (Salt Lake City, UT: George C. Lambert, 1914), 21–22. Also found in Marlene Bateman Sullivan, *By the Ministering of Angels* (Springville UT: Horizon Publishers, 2006), 119–21.

Do this, and joy your hearts will swell—
All is well! All is well!

Why should we mourn or think our lot is hard?
'Tis not so; all is right.
Why should we think to earn a great reward
If we now shun the fight?[243]

We all have times of testing, but we can always turn to the Savior for consolation. Christ tells us, "I am he; yea, I am he that comforteth you" (2 Nephi, 8:12). Experiencing adversity can build faith in God as He helps us through them. Alma charged his son to remember that God would deliver him from trials if he placed his trust in God: "I would that ye should remember, that as much as ye shall put your trust in God even so much ye shall be delivered out of your trials, and your troubles, and your afflictions, and ye shall be lifted up at the last day" (Alma 38:5).

As we rise above our problems, we develop a depth of spirituality that will guide us to our heavenly home. "I counsel you to look to the lighthouse of the Lord," advised President Thomas S. Monson. "I have said it before; I will say it again: there is no fog so dense, no night so dark, no gale so strong, no mariner so lost but what the lighthouse of the Lord can rescue. It beckons through the storms of life. It calls, '*This way to safety. This way to home.*' It sends forth signals of light easily seen and never failing. If followed, those signals will guide you back to your heavenly home."[244]

Having faith allows us to endure and receive the comfort of the Holy Ghost, which strengthens us and fills our souls with peace. "And blessed are they . . . for they shall have the gift and the power of the Holy Ghost; and if they endure unto the end they shall be lifted up at the last day, and shall be saved in the everlasting kingdom of the Lamb" (1 Nephi 13:37).

---

243. "Come, Come, Ye Saints," *Hymns*, no. 30.

244. Thomas S. Monson, "Believe, Obey, and Endure," *Ensign* or *Liahona*, May 2012, 127; emphasis in original.

15
God Will Wipe Away All Tears

"These are they which came out of great tribulation, and have washed their robes, and made them white in the blood of the Lamb. Therefore are they before the throne of God . . . and he that sitteth on the throne shall dwell among them. They shall hunger no more, neither thirst any more; neither shall the sun light on them, nor any heat. For the Lamb which is in the midst of the throne shall feed them, and shall lead them unto living fountains of waters: and God shall wipe away all tears from their eyes."

—Revelation 7:14-17

When Hurt Tears a Hole in Your Heart

No one can forget where they were and what they were doing on September 11, 2001, when terrorists attacked the World Trade Center and the US Pentagon and downed a plane in a field near Shanksville, Pennsylvania. We will never forget the pain and horror that tore a hole in our hearts. From these horrific acts, 2,977 people were killed, more than 6,000 were injured, and the world mourned.

On a much smaller scale, all of us experience our own personal 9/11 moments. There are some sorrows that sear our souls to a degree that we realize life will never be the same. Some trials are so immense that they change our lives in ways we never expected—shaking our very foundation like an earthquake shakes a house. In the aftermath of tragedy, we are left to metaphorically clear away the debris of our personal Ground Zero in order to begin the process of healing. Naturally, our souls will need to be repaired, much like a house needs restoration after a massive earthquake.

If we experience a physical earthquake, once the tremors subside, the first thing we might do after checking with our loved ones is to survey the damage to our home. There will be decisions to make regarding which damaged items can be saved and which ones need to be discarded. Likewise, after a "personal" earthquake, we need to survey the damage and decide how to proceed. We may ponder our lifestyle and our beliefs, looking for those that are useful and valuable because they draw us closer to God. As we examine our souls in time of crisis, we might decide to discard some behaviors because they do not lead to Christ.

After an earthquake, there may be structural damage to our house, making it necessary to call in a professional to repair that which was broken. When a personal earthquake strikes, we might decide to talk with our bishop and see a therapist to restore the damage done to our shattered heart and soul. When trials rock our world, we might choose to change our priorities and devote more time to personal growth with scripture study, temple attendance, and other good works and to mend or enhance personal relationships with family and friends.

At such times, we will certainly want to turn to God, the one and only true source of healing. We will plead with Him to restore our souls and provide comfort, strength, and guidance as we come to terms with the altered landscape of our life. Heavenly Father will show us the way. With Him as our constant companion, we will be empowered to emerge from our ordeal stronger than we were before.

When we feel broken, our Savior can restore what we cannot repair ourselves. He can heal the wound we cannot mend and fix that which has been broken and which we cannot fix. When unable to take another step, He can carry us in His arms. When we are left with shattered dreams and there does not appear to be any light at the end of the tunnel and no sunrise at the end of a dark night, only Christ can repair broken dreams, bless us with hope, and give us the ability to see the light of a new day.

Jesus Christ's ministry was about healing, and His work is to lift, strengthen, and guide us through the storms of life. When we're swamped with sorrow, Jesus offers us hope and rest from our sorrows. "Come unto me, all ye that labour and are heavy laden, and I will give you rest. Take my yoke upon you, and learn of me; for I am meek and lowly in heart: and ye shall find rest unto your souls. For my yoke is easy, and my burden is light" (Matthew 11:28–30). When weakened by adversity, we must turn to God and rely on His spiritual power to save us. When worn down by difficulties, we can draw upon the powers of heaven to recharge ourselves spiritually.

In the scriptures, God constantly asks us to come to Him so He can bless us. In fact, there are over ninety times when God invites us to come to Him. As we continue to exercise hope and have faith, we can stand in the kingdom of heaven and receive glorious blessings that will far exceed the suffering we endured on earth.

Trials Help Us Develop Godly Attributes

When walking the challenging path that leads to exaltation, there can be many rocks embedded along the trail. Some of these rocks might be physical challenges or mental illness. Others might be unmet dreams of marriage and children. Still others might include the difficulties that come from abuse, loss of a loved one, financial reverses, aging, relationship issues, or a host of others. Despite the personal pain of our own pathway, we know that opposition is a crucial element in God's divine plan to help us develop godly attributes (see 2 Nephi 2:11). As we put forth effort to build celestial character traits, we are blessed by a loving God who offers spiritual guidance that enables us to keep our feet on the narrow path that leads to exaltation.

Heavenly Father's plan of salvation ensures eternal progress for His children. This plan teaches us the purpose of mortality and provides experiences we need "to progress toward perfection and ultimately realize [our] divine destiny as heirs of eternal life."[245] Adversity sculpts us into better disciples of Christ as we learn to become like a child: meek, patient, full of love, and willing to submit our will to Heavenly Father's in all things (see Mosiah 3:19). Hardships also test us to see

245. "The Family: A Proclamation to the World," Gospel Library.

if we will stay true to God. The Lord tells us, "My people must be tried in all things, that they may be prepared to receive the glory that I have for them, even the glory of Zion . . . for my Spirit is sent forth into the world to enlighten the humble and contrite" (Doctrine and Covenants 136:31–33).

While trials play a role in helping us develop Christlike attributes, we cannot hope to obtain eternal life if we do not put in the work. Adversity may stretch our souls, but we only learn heavenly lessons if we put forth effort into our education. Turning our afflictions into blessings takes work. When the Olympic games are televised, reporters often give background stories on the arduous training that fashions athletes into Olympians. Only those who put in rigorous training can ever hope to become a world-class athlete who's qualified to participate in the Olympics. Likewise, we must put in our own rigorous training and improve ourselves through the obstacles we encounter. Trials—difficult as they may be—are the demanding training method God uses to refine our spirits. The renowned psychiatrist Elizabeth Kübler-Ross explained, "You will not grow if you sit in a beautiful flower garden, but you will grow if you are sick, if you are in pain, if you experience losses, and if you do not put your head in the sand, but take the pain and learn to accept it, not as a curse or punishment, but as a gift to you with a very, very specific purpose."[246]

Adversity helps us see which parts of our soul need improvement. We need trials, for it is only when things are *not* going smoothly that our weaknesses are revealed and we discover exactly what areas we need to work on. The real test of character comes not from how we are when sailing on smooth waters but from how we react when buffeted by the storms of life. Only then will we see what virtues need further polishing. "The path to [exaltation] is rugged and steep. Many stumble and fall," said President Harold B. Lee. "The forces of evil cloud the path with many foggy deterrents, often trying to detour us in misleading trails. But through all this journey, there is the calming assurance that if we choose the right, success will be ours, and the

246. Elizabeth Kübler-Ross, *Death is of Vital Importance* (Barrytown, NY: Station Hill Press, 1995).

achievement of it will have molded and formed and created us into the kind of person qualified to be accepted into the presence of God."[247]

Suffering Will Be Consecrated for Our Good

No suffering is without meaning if it helps us put off our natural self and increase in virtue.

There is godly purpose in pain, for when our hearts are broken, we become humble and more open to the purifying Spirit of God. As we learn the lessons adversity teaches, our souls become sanctified and we develop celestial qualities that qualify us for eternal glory. Elder Orson F. Whitney wrote, "No pain that we suffer, no trial that we experience is wasted. It ministers to our education, to the development of such qualities as patience, faith, fortitude, and humility. . . . It is through sorrow and suffering, toil and tribulation, that we gain the education that we come here to acquire."[248]

The Apostle Paul taught that tribulations purify and perfect us: "For our light affliction, which is but for a moment, worketh for us a far more exceeding and eternal weight of glory" (2 Corinthians 4:17). Note Paul's phrase "our *light* affliction." Such a description seems an unusual way to describe his hardships considering that Paul suffered tremendous tribulations after becoming a disciple of Christ. His life was constantly in peril. He was frequently imprisoned, whipped five separate times, beaten three times, shipwrecked on three occasions, stoned once, and was often cold and hungry (see 2 Corinthians 11:23–28). It is doubtful anyone except Paul himself would characterize such afflictions as "light." But Paul wanted people to realize that even extreme afflictions are a small price to pay for the glorious blessings we receive by remaining true and faithful. The progression we make *because* of our trials is of far greater magnitude than any suffering we endure *during* our trials.

Even when tormented by trials, we exhibit faith by holding on to our testimony that Heavenly Father lives and loves us and that Jesus Christ is the Savior of the world. Then we can say, as did Paul, "We are

---

247. *Teachings of Presidents of the Church: Harold B. Lee* (2000), 206–207.

248. Orson F. Whitney, in Spencer W. Kimball, *Faith Precedes the Miracle* (Salt Lake City, UT: Deseret Book, 1972), 98.

troubled on every side, yet not distressed; we are perplexed, but not in despair; persecuted, but not forsaken; cast down, but not destroyed" (2 Corinthians 4:8–9). As we trust in God and overcome adversity, we gain hope, which replaces pain with peace and soothes our sorrows with the balm of Gilead (see Jeremiah 8:22). Trust in God brings heaven's grace, by which He can convert our trials into blessings and can "give . . . beauty for ashes" (Isaiah 61:3).

It is a blessing to know that the lessons we learn from personal hardships will be consecrated for our good and that we reap great rewards when we remain faithful. President Brigham Young assures us that the glorious blessings we receive in the next life will more than compensate for any earthly suffering:

> We talk about our trials and troubles here in this life, but suppose that you could see yourselves thousands and millions of years after you have proved faithful to your religion during the few short years in this time, and have obtained eternal salvation and a crown of glory in the presence of God? Then look back upon your lives here, and see the losses, crosses, and disappointments, the sorrows . . . you would be constrained to exclaim, "But what of all that? Those things were but for a moment, and we are now here. We have been faithful during a few moments in our mortality, and now we enjoy eternal life and glory . . . enjoying the smiles and approbation of our Father and God, and of Jesus Christ our elder brother."[249]

After completing our mortal probation and graduating from earthly life, we enter the eternal realms above, and the veil will be removed from our minds. Memories of the premortal world will be restored, enabling us to comprehend that the hardships we suffered on earth were necessary to refine our souls and prepare us to receive the blessings God desired to bestow on us. Once our eyes have been fully opened, we will see that the difficulties we once faced and the night that was once so dark has given way to a bright and joyful new dawn.

249. Brigham Young, "Remarks," *Deseret News*, Nov. 9, 1859, 1, https://contentdm.lib.byu.edu/digital/collection/desnews2/id/6499/rec/45. Also found in *Journal of Discourses*, 7:275.

All Injustices Will Be Resolved

When Jesus Christ fulfilled His divine mission and overcame the world, He completed the great atoning sacrifice that would allow us to have peace in this world and in the eternities. Although we don't completely understand the process, we do know that as part of Christ's Atonement, He somehow "absorbed" all the injustices that come to us in mortality. In the wilderness, Lehi told his son Jacob that God would recompense him for all of the unjust sufferings he had endured, and that God would "consecrate thine afflictions for thy gain" (2 Nephi 2:2).

God will do the same for us.

But that is not all. God will bless us with a multiplicity of blessings—far beyond any sufferings we endure! When Job endured extraordinary losses through no fault of his own, God restored unto Job *twice* what he had lost (see Job 42:10, 12–13).

Unjust suffering occurs when someone cruelly abuses another, when a parent loses their child in a school shooting, when you lose your savings to financial fraudsters, when a drunk driver slams into your car and leaves you with lifelong physical disabilities, or from a host of other causes. We are told that the wicked will be held accountable for the atrocities they perpetrate (see Luke 17:1).

Elder Joseph B. Wirthlin assures us, "The Lord compensates the faithful for every loss. That which is taken away from those who love the Lord will be added unto them in His own way. While it may not come at the time we desire, the faithful will know that every tear today will eventually be returned a hundredfold with tears of rejoicing and gratitude. . . . A principle of compensation prevails."[250]

Because Christ met the strict demands of justice, all those who have been misused, maligned, or downtrodden by others, who have been treated unfairly, or who have been mentally or physically injured will have their wrongs mitigated and made right through the Atonement of Jesus Christ. In the Book of Mormon, Jacob tells his people, "Look unto God with firmness of mind, and pray unto him

---

250. Joseph B. Wirthlin, "Come What May, and Love It," *Ensign* or *Liahona*, Nov. 2008, 28.

with exceeding faith, and he will console you in your afflictions, and he will plead your cause, and send down justice upon those who seek your destruction" (Jacob 3:1). Whatever unfair pain and suffering we receive at the hands of others will be resolved, and we will be compensated to our full satisfaction. Sometimes this means being patient and trusting in God's timing. Justice is often not meted out in mortality but comes in the next life.

This principle of restitution also applies if we did not receive certain blessings in mortality, such as marriage or being able to have children. Some may worry about their child who dies young and did not have the opportunity to find a spouse, have children, or receive temple covenants. However, hope comes from knowing that all blessings not received in this life will be ours in the next. President M. Russell Ballard offers the following assurance: "If we are faithful and endure to the end, no righteous desire will be denied, and *all blessings* ultimately will be received. Each of you must come to know what the Lord wants for you, given the choices before you. Once you know the Lord's will, you can move forward in faith to fulfill your individual purpose."[251]

We can have hope in our heart because of the Atonement of Jesus Christ, which reclaims us from death, pays for our sins when we repent, resolves all injustices, and blesses us with strength to endure our tribulations. In the next life, our personal trials—which now seem so arduous—will be resolved, and our heart will know peace. "Wherefore, if ye shall press forward, feasting upon the word of Christ, and endure to the end, behold, thus saith the Father: Ye shall have eternal life" (2 Nephi 31:20).

Power to Overcome All Things

We live in a world full of turmoil. At times, we may become discouraged and wonder if we can endure the trials we are called to bear. When downtrodden, some may question if God is even aware of their struggles and if there is any lasting meaning or purpose for them. However, when we look through the wide and clear lens of the gospel

251. M. Russell Ballard, "The Essential Role of Women," *Liahona*, Mar. 2021, 10; emphasis in original.

instead of the limited lens of our mortal eyes, we can see more clearly how adversity provides us with accelerated growth toward godhood.

President George Q. Cannon wrote:

> There are and have been times when men and women too, have felt downcast, and have wondered if God had forgotten them, but I say to all such, Fear not, the clouds will pass away, the light will shine, and your joy and courage will return. If you preserve your integrity and wait for the salvation of your God, it will surely come and seek you out. He always has delivered and comforted His people, and he will not forsake us now; His arm is not shortened, He is not asleep nor gone on a journey. He will succor us in the deepest distress and deliver us in the direst extremities, if we will live so that we may have the fellowship of the Holy Ghost, which is the minister of God, and whose presence is the presence of God.[252]

During dark and difficult moments, we can remember that the Savior overcame *all* things. Because He endured excruciating suffering in Gethsemane and on the cross, He has the power to bless us to overcome our afflictions. We have great cause to hope, knowing that Heavenly Father and Jesus Christ can guide us through our difficulties. Although peace will be taken from the earth in the latter days, peace does not have to be taken from our hearts.

Knowing we are never left to struggle on our own gives us hope. God yearns to provide inspiration to guide us as we learn our lessons while in this school of life. Although we must be proved in all things, God can bless us with the ability to overcome our challenges. "For he will give unto the faithful line upon line, precept upon precept; and I will try you and prove you herewith" (Doctrine and Covenants 98:12).

In these turbulent days, we must strive to remain committed to the Lord, for the gospel of Jesus Christ is designed to help us achieve our righteous desires and rise above our hardships. As we hold on and strive to develop divine attributes, we will be blessed. God declared, "Ye cannot behold with your natural eyes, for the present time, the

252. George Q. Cannon, "Discourse," *The Deseret Weekly*, Mar. 7, 1891, 322, https://contentdm.lib.byu.edu/digital/collection/desnews9/id/21567/rec/20.

design of your God concerning those things which shall come hereafter, and the glory which shall follow after much tribulation" (Doctrine and Covenants 58:3).

Heavenly Father loves us and never wearies of watching over and blessing us. As we make our way through the thorns and thistles of mortality, God will strengthen us. "And the Lord provided for them that they should hunger not, neither should they thirst; yea, and he also gave them strength, that they should suffer no manner of afflictions, save it were swallowed up in the joy of Christ" (Alma 31:38). Even though we feel weak, God's grace will allow us to accomplish great things and prevail above those afflictions that currently may seem above our ability to endure. "By giving heed and doing these things which ye have received, and which ye shall hereafter receive . . . the kingdom is given you . . . and *power to overcome all things*" (Doctrine and Covenants 50:35; emphasis added).

When we're swamped in the storms of life, Jesus Christ offers hope to each of us: "Come unto me, all ye that labour and are heavy laden, and I will give you rest" (Matthew 11:28). There are no conditions to that magnificent promise. All can receive the bounteous blessings of God if they will but come to Christ. The Savior's healing power can cover any sin, wound, or trial, no matter how grievous. His grace is sufficient for all. And with that knowledge, we can move forward with faith, knowing that when difficult times come—and they surely will—the Savior stands "with healing in his wings" (see Malachi 4:2).

We have hope in Christ, for He offers us rest from sorrow, fear, and pain, replacing our suffering with peace and tranquility. We can stand firm in this life of strife by knowing that a better world awaits. The Lord has promised to redeem those who follow Him and will bless us beyond anything we can imagine. "Eye hath not seen, nor ear heard, neither have entered into the heart of man, the things which God hath prepared for them that love him" (1 Corinthians 2:9). Whatever we are called to endure while following the path back to our heavenly home will one day seem like no sacrifice at all. For when we return to His presence, we will "be received into the kingdom of the Father to go no more out, but to dwell with God eternally in the heavens" (3 Nephi 28:40).

As we patiently endure the travails of mortality and remain faithful, God will bestow blessings upon us. We can trust in the Savior's promise that "they that wait upon the Lord shall renew their strength; they shall mount up with wings as eagles; they shall run, and not be weary; and they shall walk, and not faint" (Isaiah 40:31).

As we strive to be true disciples, we will be blessed with the heartfelt assurance that God knows and loves us with an eternal love. Our Savior supports us while we are on our mortal mission and will never let us down. It is the pure love of Christ that helps us bear all things, believe all things, hope all things, and endure all things (see Moroni 7:45). No matter where we are currently standing on the ladder stretching to our heavenly home, we can trust the Lord to help us climb the next rung.

With each rising of the sun comes the inherent hope of a new day. Hope is not crossing our fingers or holding our breath that things will work out the way we want. Hope is also more than just hanging on as we wait to see light at the end of our particular tunnel of affliction. Hope is a lantern we hold high as we endure our trials. Hope helps us move forward and lets us know we are not alone and that God is beside us every step of the way.

In time, our tears of earthly sorrow will be changed to tears of joy when we return to our heavenly home and see Jesus Christ, who laid down His life for us and healed our wounds with His stripes. There will be no more darkness, for Jesus, the light of the world, will reign. "Thy sun shall no more go down; . . . for the Lord shall be thine everlasting light, and the days of thy mourning shall be ended" (Isaiah 60:20). At that time, Heavenly Father will provide comfort for the crosses we were called to bear and dry the tears we have shed. "And God shall wipe away all tears from their eyes; and there shall be no more death, neither sorrow, nor crying, neither shall there be any more pain: for the former things are passed away" (Revelation 21:4).

About the Authors

Marlene Bateman Sullivan was born in Salt Lake City, Utah. She graduated from the University of Utah, and she and her husband currently live in North Salt Lake, Utah. Marlene has been published extensively in magazines and newspapers and has written a number of nonfiction books for members of The Church of Jesus Christ of Latter-day Saints, including *Latter-day Saint Heroes and Heroines*; *And There Were Angels Among Them*; *Visits from Beyond the Veil*; *By the Ministering of Angels*; *Brigham's Boys*; *Heroes of Faith*; *Gaze Into Heaven: Near-Death Experiences in Early Church History*; and *The Magnificent World of Spirits: Eyewitness Accounts of Where We Go When We Die*.

In addition, Marlene has written two best-selling romance/suspense novels, *Light on Fire Island* and *Searching for Irene*. She has written three other mysteries—*Motive for Murder*, *A Death in the Family*, and *Crooked House*—as well as a romance, *For Sale by Owner*. She and her son Joshua are coauthors of *Finding Your Way After Losing a Loved One*.

Joshua M. Sullivan was born in Salt Lake City, Utah. He and his wife live in Riverton, Utah. Joshua received a master's degree in social work from the University of Utah and a second master's degree in education administration from Southern Utah University. He has worked for years as a school counselor, with a specialty in childhood and adolescent mental health. Joshua has provided counseling to clients of all ages and has worked with those seeking assistance in dealing with grief, depression, and trauma. Joshua and Marlene are coauthors of *Finding Your Way After Losing a Loved One.*

Scan to visit

www.marlenebateman.info.com